ZISK *Presents*

Fan Interference

A Collection of Baseball Rants and Reflections

Edited by
Mike Faloon and Steve Reynolds

Fan Interference: A Collection of
Baseball Rants and Reflections

© 2013 by Blue Cubicle Press, LLC. All rights reserved.
Printed in the United States of America.

Published by
Blue Cubicle Press, LLC
Post Office Box 250382
Plano, Texas 75025-0382

ISBN 978-1-938583-04-9
Library of Congress Control Number 2013933270

First Edition

No part of this book may be reproduced or transmitted in any form or by any means, electronic or mechanical, including photocopying and recording, or by any information storage and retrieval system without the prior written permission of the copyright owner unless such copying is expressly permitted by federal copyright law. Blue Cubicle Press is not authorized to grant permission for further uses of copyrighted selections reprinted in this book without the permission of their owners. Permission must be obtained from individual copyright owners as identified herein. Address requests for permission to make copies of Blue Cubicle Press material to Permissions, Blue Cubicle Press, P.O. Box 250382, Plano, TX 75025-0382.

Cover Art © 2013 by Jason Willis
Foreword © 2013 by Josh Wilker

Contents

Foreword   v

Introduction   vii

Part I: Close Encounters of a Different Kind – Brushes with Fame

PEACE IN THE NL EAST BY MIKE FALOON	1
JUNIOR FLIPPED ME THE BIRD BY MATT BRAUN	4
WHO IS DICK ALLEN? – AN INTERVIEW WITH ZIFF SISTRUNK BY JAKE AUSTEN	6
PETE ROSE'S BLOODY STEAK NAPKIN BY FRANK D'URSO	10
THE KING AND I – REMEMBERING AND WRITING ABOUT DAVE KINGMAN BY CHARLIE VASCELLARO	14

Part II: Because We Hate You – Fury Has Many Faces

MIKE FALOON VS. BARRY BONDS BY MIKE FALOON	23
YES, I'VE HEARD, THEY SUCK BY DR. NANCY GOLDEN	25
THE LAST DAYS AT FULTON COUNTY STADIUM BY SEAN CARSWELL	28
DUCKIE NATION: TWO WRITERS AND FRIENDS, ONE A YANKEE FAN AND THE OTHER A RED SOX DIEHARD, DISCUSS THE VERY NATURE OF THEIR DISAGREEMENTS THROUGH THE LENS OF POP CULTURE BY DAN DUNFORD AND ARI VOUKYDIS	35

Part III: Personality Trumps Performance – How > How Well

THE HACK MAN BY KEN DERR	40
JOSE VALENTIN'S MOUSTACHE BY JAKE AUSTEN	43
BATMAN: MAKING THE CASE FOR THE AKRON AEROS MEP BY MIKE FALOON	45

Part III (Cont.)

THE WHAM OF SAM BY JAKE AUSTEN	47
BASEBALL IS JUST BASEBALL – AN INTERVIEW WITH DAVID SHIELDS BY MIKE FALOON	52

Part IV: Those Who Study History Want to Repeat It – Looking Back Agog and Aghast

MITCH BY KEN DERR	59
ADRIÁN BELTRÉ'S RIGHT NUT BY TODD TAYLOR	62
KY JELLY AND MORAL RESPONSIBILITY BY KEN DERR	66
A HISTORY OF CHEATING IN BASEBALL BY JOHN SHIFFERT	68
WINNING IS EVERYTHING, YOU ASSHOLE BY KEN DERR	74
DISCO DEMOLITION NIGHT BY TODD TAYLOR	81
STATUTORY RATE: ZISK LOOKS AT BASEBALL STATUES BOMBARDING CHICAGO BY JAKE AUSTEN	91
NOW THESE WERE THE REAL IDIOTS BY JEFF BODA	97
THANKS, KIRBY BY STEVE REYNOLDS	100
YA GOTTA BEREAVE BY JOHN WEBER	102
RUSTY STAUB: HEROISM FROM LEFT TO RIGHT FIELD BY BRIAN COGAN	104

Part V: F Is For Fake Not Phony – Fiction and Humor

DON'T YOU KNOW HE'S A 3,000 MAN: MILWAUKEE'S PROUD FAKE BASEBALL TRADITION LIVES ON BY REV. NORB	109
HEY, TALK TO THE SOCK! BY STEVE REYNOLDS	114
ZISK VS. ESPN BY MIKE FALOON	116
A RAY OF HOPE: THE DEVIL SPEAKS OUT BY STEVE REYNOLDS	119
DARRYL, OFF BROADWAY – AN INTERVIEW WITH CHRIS GETHARD BY MIKE FALOON	121

Part VI: Chin Music – Musicians Talk Baseball

TOM SAWYER TO TOM GLAVINE – AN INTERVIEW WITH RUSH'S GEDDY LEE BY STEVE REYNOLDS	127
GROOVING TO GORMAN THOMAS – AN INTERVIEW WITH THE MINUS 5'S SCOTT MCCAUGHEY BY STEVE REYNOLDS AND MIKE FALOON	135
A GOLDEN VOICE FOR THE BRAVES – AN INTERVIEW WITH EMMYLOU HARRIS BY STEVE REYNOLDS	141
TAKE ME OUT...TO BASEBALL SONGS – AN INTERVIEW WITH BILLY BRAGG BY STEVE REYNOLDS	143
MY LIFE AS A ~~BIG LEAGUE MINOR LEAGUE COLLEGE BALL~~ COLLEGE SUMMER BALL ANNOUNCER BY REV. NORB	145

Part VII: Buy Me Some Peanuts and Cracker Jack – Ballpark Visits Good, Bad, and Psychedelic

TOP 10 GAMES I'VE ATTENDED BY KEVIN CHANEL	153
MY 5 MOST MISERABLE EXPERIENCES AT THE BALLPARK BY JAKE AUSTEN	157
TEN CULTURAL OBSERVATIONS WHILE SITTING IN THE RIGHT FIELD CORNER OF THE TOKYO DOME DURING A YOMIYURI GIANTS GAME THIS PAST JULY, OR WHY BILLY BEANE WILL NEVER HIRE A MANAGER FROM THE JAPANESE LEAGUE BY JEFF BODA	161
BURNING DOWN THE HOUSE: WHY CAMDEN YARDS STINKS BY BOB MASON	166
GOODBYE TO STADIUMS	171
SHEA STADIUM BY MIKE FALOON	171
SHEA STADIUM BY STEVE REYNOLDS	172
CANDLESTICK PARK BY KEN DERR	172
CONNIE MACK STADIUM BY JOHN SHIFFERT	173
MEMORIAL STADIUM, SHEA STADIUM, CANDLESTICK PARK BY FRANK D'URSO	174
MACARTHUR STADIUM BY MARK HUGHSON	175
ARLINGTON STADIUM BY KIP YATES	176

Part VII (Cont.)
COMISKEY PARK BY JAKE AUSTEN — 178

Part VIII: Rest Thy Quill, Pick Up A Glove – Playing Fans

IN THE PINK BY DR. NANCY GOLDEN — 180
MY BIG LEAGUE TRYOUT BY MATT BRAUN — 183
1876 BARNSTORMING TOUR BY KIP YATES — 185

Part IX: Baseball Warps the Mind – Oddities of the Game

I'M PETER PAN, I'M THE KING OF ENGLAND, I HAVE HIGH CHEEKBONES: THE WIT, WISDOM, AND FACIAL HAIR OF KEITH HERNANDEZ BY STEVE REYNOLDS — 190
FOUR FANS, ONE SHIRT – AN INTERVIEW WITH MARCO REOSTI BY MIKE FALOON — 194
BASEBALL TRULY IS A RELIGION BY JOHN SHIFFERT — 197

Part X: Those Who Can't Talk with Those Who Can – Interviews with Players

SEMI-AMAZING DEEDS BY MINOR LEGENDS OF AMATEUR BASEBALL – AN INTERVIEW WITH OLIVER HUGHSON BY MARK HUGHSON — 203
THEY SHOT THE WRONG MCKINLEY – AN INTERVIEW WITH BILL MONBOUQUETTE BY MIKE FALOON — 206
DON'T STEP IN THE BUCKET – AN INTERVIEW WITH RICHIE ZISK BY MIKE FALOON — 211

Part XI: Credits

ABOUT THE CONTRIBUTORS — 222
ACKNOWLEDGEMENTS — 226

Foreword

My brother called me recently on my birthday and said he doesn't follow American sports anymore. I hadn't talked to him in months.

"Futbol," he said, spiking a European enunciation with ironic, self-lacerating air quotes that someone else may or may not have picked up on. But we're brothers.

"That's about it for me," he said. "That and fishing."

"Yeah? Still fishing a lot?" I said. For his birthday a few months earlier, I'd sent him a book on fishing in North Carolina, where he lives. I hadn't heard if he uses it, or even if it got there.

"All I want to do these days," he said.

I imagine him in a rowboat in the middle of some lake, casting his line out into the water, each cast a beat in a slow pulse across the afternoon: *Zisk.*

***

When we were kids, we were allowed to pick one day a year to stay up as late as we wanted. We always picked the same day, the Major League Baseball All-Star game. The funny thing is, I don't remember the conclusions of any of the games. I don't even remember any particular thrill in being up past our bedtime. I remember the beginnings, the introductions. Each player got a moment, his name announced, a cheer rising. I loved the gradations of fan reaction, the greatest players getting louder cheers, topped only by the cheers for the hometown players. I loved the names, one after another, loved seeing my most-valued baseball cards come to life and wave to the sound that I imagined I was contributing to.

Richie Zisk appeared in two of these games right in the sweetest spot of my childhood, batting in the heart of the order both times for the team I was rooting for. The first name was key, the hint in it that childhood could endure—he was not Richard or Rich or Rick or Dick but Richie, a grown man who was also somehow still a kid. But it was the second name that hooked me, that hooked a lot of us, I guess.

***

I never got the hang of fishing, but I like the idea of it, of sitting there, waiting, reeling in, finding nothing, casting out again. *Zisk.* Nothing. *Zisk.* Nothing.

***

I followed my brother into baseball, wanting to follow him everywhere, be wherever he was all the time. Now I don't even talk to him but three or four times a year. But I still follow baseball. It's challenging to do so because it's not challenging to do so. Every game is available. You can fall out of a tree and hit a televised baseball game. The coverage now would have sounded to me when I was a kid growing up in the country, separated from games by oceans of static, like a dream come true, but it's like the difference between dreaming as a kid of wolfing an entire box of Cap'n Crunch and as an adult on some useless afternoon while watching reruns of *Charles in Charge* nauseatingly attaining that dream. The sugar shock of it all: every dugout miked, every participant rendered unbearably mundane by in-game interviews and twitter blathering, statistics once restricted to precious Sunday newspaper batting average lists now as readily available as a glass of water and about as tasteless except when churned into acid for use in online confrontations. The game comes at you like noise. And it's worse at the stadium, every speaker blotting out the sounds on the field by blaring rutted arena rock and mechanized orders to cheer. It pounds your brains to mush. It's like going to a lake hoping to row out into it and fish and finding the place a whining frenzy of jet-skis and speedboats, everyone racing ferociously past any moment that might matter. Small wonder my brother said fuck it.

***

You have to cast your line out and wait. You have to imagine the game. That's what's missing. That's why I'm grateful to find the sanctuary of *Zisk*-murmurers in these pages. They imagine a game much rougher and wider and wilder and sillier and, finally, more meaningful than the constant eructation of data and flash that threatens to pulverize baseball, along with pretty much everything else, to sound and fury signifying nothing. The endangered game still lives in *Zisk*. It still lives in the crappy seats and in drunken last days at abandoned ballparks and in the hope of a fan in a four-man T-shirt, rooting with absurd passion, along with the other guys crowding into the same shirt, for a last place team and in celebrations of Dick Allen and Jeff Leonard and Kong Kingman and Adrián Beltré's pummeled nuts and Curt Schilling's bloody sock come to life and in an aging Rusty Staub, bordering on obesity, chasing down a fly ball on rickety legs for all our sins. To find a game means nothing anymore. But to hook a game, to live it and love it, you have to cast your line out into wide water and wait and wait and like a fool keep waiting until something hooks you for real.

Josh Wilker

Introduction

A Brief Look at the History of Zisk by Mike Faloon

Toronto. Summer, 1981. Ask my parents or my brothers, and they'll paint the same picture. It was a miserable family vacation. The five of us were camping just outside the Toronto city limits. By day, we saw the sights—the CN Tower, the zoo. By night, we got sick. Someone was up vomiting every hour of the night, stepping out of the pop-up camper and hurling their guts out. Loud, awful dry heaves that left achy stomach muscles in their wake. It was horrible.

I barely recall any of it. I remember vividly, however, seeing my first major league ballgame that weekend. It was wonderful. White Sox versus Blue Jays. Exhibition Stadium. Our seats were halfway down the first base line. I filled out my scorecard early. I snapped blurry photos with a Kodak Instamatic. I wondered how much my family relished attending the game. They weren't baseball fans. Plus, they were wiped out by stomach bugs and sleep deprivation. I wanted them to enjoy the game as much as I did. I told my brothers which Blue Jays used to play for the Triple A affiliate in Syracuse, our hometown. I tugged on my parents' shirtsleeves, told them that three of the White Sox were bound for the Hall of Fame.

Carlton Fisk was an easy call. He had over a decade behind the dish. He had Game 6 of the '75 World Series. I'd just turned twelve, but even I knew he was destined for a plaque in Cooperstown.

Greg Luzinski? Ron LeFlore? My crystal ball was cloudy. I wanted them to be Hall of Famers. I wanted the game to be significant for all of us. I wanted my family to be as giddy as I was.

Baseball has that effect on me. The game warps things, distorts perceptions, leads to impulsive reactions, with the facts to follow, if at all. *Zisk* was inevitable.

In one sense, *Zisk* started on my mom's back deck. My high school friends and I spent hours hanging out there. Baseball wasn't a big part of our lives at that point. We seldom watched or listened to or read about the game—*SCTV* and progressive rock were more likely topics—but baseball references were a given. Whether it was great names (Joe Zdeb, Chet Lemon) or distinctive hair (Rollie Fingers, Oscar Gamble) or the combination of both (Bake McBride), we were constantly mining the baseball minutiae we'd absorbed as kids.

In another sense, *Zisk* began on the lower east side of Manhattan. I'd moved to New York by the mid-1990s. I was playing in bands. Matt Braun and Ethan Cohen were, too. The three of us would hang out after shows at the Continental on 3rd Avenue talking about obscure players from the '70s. The setting had changed but the conversations were similar to those in Syracuse.

Matt, Ethan, and I all wrote in some capacity, and one of us proposed starting a baseball zine. It seemed like a strange idea, starting an underground publication to cover mainstream content, but they pointed out that Johnny Ramone was a rabid Yankees fan and *Maximum Rock and Roll* editor Tim Yohannan was rumored to be a Giants fan. More importantly, Matt had access to free photocopying. Naming our zine was easy. I went back to those high school conversations and proposed my go-to: Richie Zisk.

Zisk #1 appeared in the fall of 1999. We sent copies of the debut issue to every sympathetic soul we could think of. The coup was an interview with our namesake. I can still recall being at work one day and hearing my uber-authoritarian boss say in her subzero Czech accent, "Michael, there is someone named Richie Zisk for you." I called in sick the next day and conducted *Zisk*'s first interview.

But *Zisk* didn't really take hold until Steve Reynolds came on board as co-editor. He and I are friends from college. Steve was a contributing writer from the start. A few issues later, he was doing the layouts. By issue #8 he was organizing our production schedule, too. *Zisk* would have run aground long ago without him.

Steve and I meet up once or twice a year to battle photocopiers, gripe about the Mets, and marvel over the writing we've had the good fortune to publish. Few thrills match that of seeing a new essay from the likes of Rev. Norb (Boris the Sprinkler) or Todd Taylor (*Razorcake*) waiting in my inbox. Or John Shiffert (*The Breaks Even Out and Midnight Comes Quickly for Cinderella*). Or Ken Derr (how is it that no one else is publishing this guy?).

What's surprised me the most over the years is how often I hear: "I don't like baseball, but I love *Zisk*." Our writers are wonderful at conveying their passion for baseball, exploring ideas not addressed elsewhere. Need a guide to the best baseball statues in Chicago? It's not likely that you do, but Jake Austen knew that when he embarked on such a guide. It's his enthusiasm that makes the piece compelling, along with the precision of his thinking and his humor. Likewise for Nancy Golden's "In the Pink" or Frank D'Urso's "Pete Rose's Bloody Steak Napkin." In one form or another, they all tug on shirtsleeves and share our love for this silly, beautiful game.

The Baseball Magazine For People Who Hate Baseball Magazines

ZISK

Peace in the NL East

Mike Faloon

A hot stove dinner for a minor league team is a strange affair. You're there—fans, team employees, sportswriters, local high school and college players—to celebrate the idea of a team, in this case the Syracuse Chiefs, more than the team itself, the players. There are no members of the 2008 Chiefs at the dinner. It's February. Pitchers and catchers have yet to report to major league training camp. MLB rosters are still undetermined and no one can say with any certainty which players will be sent to Triple A Syracuse. In truth, no one wants to play for the Chiefs in the coming season. They want to make it to the parent club, the Blue Jays, the Chiefs' major league affiliate. "No one really wants to play here!" is common knowledge, and yet the mood at the Chiefs' 47th annual Hot Stove Dinner, which doubles as a fundraiser for a local charity, is festive. Baseball is on the horizon, and everyone gathered at the Holiday Inn is chomping at the bit for the season to begin.

I have to keep that generous, celebratory spirit in mind because the evening's keynote speaker is Braves manager Bobby Cox. You may shrug with indifference. You may think, "Cool, a future Hall of Famer is in the room." Not me. I'm a Mets fan. Orange and blue course through my veins, and Bobby Cox has inflicted more damage on the Mets than anyone else, Bobby Bonilla included.

When my brother and I arrive at the dinner, we buy a couple of LaBatts—Syracuse drinks more of the stuff than any city outside of Toronto—and cruise the auction items. I distract myself with a Sal Fasano game-used batting helmet. (How best to convince the missus that our mantle needs to be adorned with Sal's sweat-soaked brain bucket?)

My brother, Casey is giddy. He loves being immersed in baseball, the talk, the detritus, the luminaries looming everywhere we look. He is unburdened by Bobby Cox. "Check it out," he says, scanning the program of auction items, "a Mariano Rivera autographed baseball." When Casey, a Red Sox fan at the front of the line of extremists, looks at anything Yankee-related without seeing crosshairs, the flags of diplomacy are surely flapping in the breeze.

Our food is served as the high school and college preseason players of the year are honored. (I love awards given in anticipation of performance: "Dudes, we think you're going to kick ass this year, take a trophy!") Bobby Cox introduces each kid and poses for pictures. He's aloof, at first, uncertain where to turn for the photos, but he seems genuine. He chats with each recipient, his smile broad and his cheeks rosy, none of which fits the profile of a villain.

The evening moves along. The speakers are funny, especially Bill Monbouquette, a former Red Sox pitcher. The Jake Myers Great Guy Award is given, and then there is the final item for auction: the autographed Mariano Rivera ball. The opening bid is too expensive for the room. Heads turn to see who'll take the plunge. Before the lack of participants becomes uncomfortable, a hand raises. It's Bobby Cox. He's bidding. He's sparing us the shame of being unwilling or, more likely, unable to buy the ball. It's a kind gesture and the applause isn't thunderous but its well past polite.

Frank Tepedino, former Chief, former Yankee, is the speaker just before Bobby Cox. They met as teammates, and Tepedino, Teppy to his friends, who later played for Cox, relates how understanding his former manager was when delivering the news that he, Teppy, had been traded.

Bobby Cox laughs as he steps to the podium. "I kind of started liking myself after hearing Teppy talk." Before he breaks into his speech Cox gives away the Rivera ball. It's not surprising that he gives the ball to a kid but then he makes the kid, who's wearing a Yankee jersey, say, on mic, that the 2008 Braves will win the World Series.

Like everyone else attending the dinner, I smile, laugh, and applaud. Any decent human being would do the same. But I'm something less than a decent human being when it comes to the Braves. They've squashed the Mets dreams many times over, and Cox is the man who signs the line-up card every night. He's the skipper responsible for sending Chipper "I Named My Child 'Shea'" Jones onto the field nearly 2,000 times over the past decade. I've cursed Bobby Cox hundreds of times. I've disparaged his skills. I've questioned his manhood and been, in nearly all ways, unfair. And, yet, I'm applauding him. My grudge has washed away, and Cox isn't done.

Cox tells jokes and shares anecdotes. He talks about how he thinks of long-time Chiefs owner Tex Simone every time the Braves experience a rain delay. (Tex always used to say, "Let's get this game in, there's a lot of fans coming.") He even thanks the Ross family. They own the local Twin Trees pizzerias and they used to live in the neighborhood where I grew up. They were on my paper route, and they'd always forget to cancel their subscription when they went south for the winter. The papers would pile up on their porch but they'd make up for it with generous tips. All those years of bringing the *Herald Journal* to Mr. and Mrs. Ross and now I find out that Bobby Cox and I have mutual acquaintances.

Cox's stories all involve him but they're not tainted by ego. He graciously plays the role of baseball celebrity, patiently waiting to hang out with his buddies, talk about the good old days, make fun of the old teammate now wearing Velcro loafers, while tossing back a few beers. I don't lead the standing ovation Cox receives when he finishes his speech but I join in.

Epilogue: My brother and I linger after the dinner is over. Casey wants his picture taken with Tex Simone. And Teppy. And Bill Monbouquette. Casey's still giddy. He nudges me into approaching Bobby Cox for a picture. "C'mon, it'll make a great cover for the zine." I know he's right.

"Hey, Bobby, do you have time for a picture?"

"Sure thing." Cox turns to pose and politely puts his arm around my shoulder.

"I have to tell you, Bobby, that I'm a Mets fan."

My brother snaps the picture.

Cox shakes my hand and flashes a knowing smile. "I love the Mets, especially when we beat them."

Originally appeared in issue #16, Spring 2008.

Junior Flipped Me the Bird

Matt Braun

Living in British Columbia in the late '80s you had three choices. You could root for the Blue Jays, who were perennial contenders but had a roster comprised of thoroughly unlikeable players like Dave Stieb, Tony Fernandez, and the always-sullen Jorge (later George) Bell. On the other hand, there were the Montreal Expos with their clown-like tricolored (or in Canada, tricoloured) chapeaus. Back then, les Expos were an exercise in futility and any Anglophone who cheered for the Buck Rodgers-led squad was viewed with, at the very least, suspicion. And then there were the Mariners.

The year was 1989, and my friends and I were bound for the Kingdome. In those days, one didn't visit a Mariners game to see the Mariners so much as their opponents. There was no Ichiro, no Pay-Rod, just names like Jimmy Presley, Alvin Davis, Pete O'Brien, and a young kid in center. The year prior, I had ventured south of the border to see Nolan Ryan's triumphant return to the American League with the George W. Bush-owned Texas Rangers. On the day prior to that, I came ever so close to seeing Charlie Hough break the record for most walks by a pitcher in a winning effort. Alas, it was not to be. He won but fell a walk or two short. But this time around, on that fateful summer day in 1990, we had gone to see who everyone wanted to see, the greatest home run hitter of the day, Cecil Fielder.

Chortle not, dear reader! At the time, Fielder was well on his way to doing what had, during my adolescence, become seemingly impossible: hitting 50 home runs. Sure, many had come close. Kevin Mitchell had hit 47 the year before and both rookie phenom Mark McGwire and former 'Spo Andre Dawson had reached 49 back in 1987; but in those days, it seemed as though George Foster of the Big Red Machine might well be the last player of the twentieth century to reach such heights. That was until "Big Daddy" came along.

Ah, youth. We were so excited! Surely Fielder would be hitting dinger after dinger against Scott Bankhead or whatever lame excuse for an ace the M's would pit against him. As such, we purchased seats in the outfield so as to best be able to catch a little piece of history. My friend, Vince, who was sporting a Detroit Tigers cap and jersey, even brought his glove.

Well, it never happened. Fielder didn't homer. Neither did Lou Whittaker or anybody else on that all-or-nothing Tigers club. The game was a real yawner. As our boredom turned to frustration (as it so often does with teenage boys) we turned our ire on the M's fans newest darling and, it just so happened, the player positioned closest to our seats: Ken Griffey, Jr.

We weren't impressed with "The Kid." Anyone who had followed the M's at all over the last ten years would be smart enough to realize that he was a so-so player hyped up by a team desperate for a star. We'd heard it before. Alvin Davis, Harold Reynolds, Mark Langston, Phil Bradley, Mickey Brantley—the list went on and on. Surely this Griffey character would be no different. Heck, even his old man wasn't all that great. He was no Cecil Fielder, that's for sure.

Oh my, the witty barbs we threw his way! "You suck, Griffey," one of us would shout.

"Fuck you, Griffey," another would cry.

"Hey, Griffey, you suck."

Well, you get the idea, I suppose. This went for some time. Then there were the obscene gestures. Clearly it was starting to get under the Kid's skin somewhat as he looked back in our direction repeatedly throughout the course of several innings of such nonsense.

And then it happened. Ever slowly, and not so subtly, Kenny turned his head so that his right profile was facing us. He reached up and scratched his temple with his middle finger. *His middle finger!* Ken Griffey, Jr. gave us the head-scratch-bird just as countless thousands of working stiffs before him had to their bosses throughout the course of human endeavors. We were speechless.

It was then that I realized something quite profound. Griffey was different. Ken Phelps would have never done such a thing. This kid *was* special. No longer would the M's be the hapless, lovable losers of the AL West. Griffey simply wouldn't take any crap.

In only a few short years, thanks to "The Kid," the Mariners would win in excess of 81 games in a single major league season!

Originally appeared in issue #4, Summer 2001.

Who Is Dick Allen? – An Interview with Ziff Sistrunk

Jake Austen

Richard Anthony Allen should be remembered as one of the greats: he hit over 350 home runs, had over 1,000 RBIs, and was the decisive AL MVP in 1972 when he led the league in home runs, RBIs, walks, and slugging. Instead, when he is remembered, it is often in a negative light, based on his incendiary chemistry with the fans and press. As Richie Allen, he slugged for the Philadelphia Phillies from 1963-1969, where the notoriously brutal Philadelphia sports fans had it in for him. (These are fans that historically have booed Santa Claus, the Easter Bunny, and Destiny's Child.) When he came to the American League, he found a home with the Chicago White Sox (along with a new name—his experience in Philadelphia was so bad he insisted on being called "Dick" instead of "Richie"). He was a fave with the royal family of Chicago, Mayors Daley I and II, and as one old joke goes, "Who was the first black manager in baseball? Dick Allen. He ran the White Sox from 1972-1974." On the other hand, the press didn't cotton to his unusual habits (he didn't practice with the team, he smoked in the dugout, he didn't give interviews) and the notoriously frank Sox announcer Harry Carey gave him hell, declaring, "Dick Allen has a million dollars worth of talent and ten cents worth of brains."

Well one man is trying to right the injustices Dick Allen suffered, and that man is Ziff Sistrunk, Dick Allen's #1 fan. We had a chance to talk with Ziff, and this is how it went down:

Zisk: Who is Dick Allen?
Ziff Sistrunk: Dick Allen was a famous baseball player from the seventies. He was a person who was an example of the true American spirit of independence and freedom . . . a free spirit. He was a man who had tremendous power. Essentially, the black Babe Ruth.

Zisk: When did you become interested in Dick Allen?
ZS: I was a bat boy for him in the seventies. In those days, they had contests, and I wrote a letter to the Cubs and White Sox, Why I Want to Be a Bat Boy. I won based on my letter and become the White Sox bat boy from 1973-74. I was the first black bat boy in Chicago history.

Zisk: What is your greatest memory of Dick Allen?

ZS: Sparky Lyle on the mound for the Yankees, in front of a gigantic White Sox crowd. It was the second game of a doubleheader, bases loaded, ninth inning. (White Sox manager) Chuck Tanner sent me in to the clubhouse to tell Dick Allen he was pinch hitting. He was sitting out because his contract said he didn't play the second game of a doubleheader. He came out and hit a screaming line drive into the upper deck. Me and the trainer were jumping up and down, screaming and hugging each other! Dick Allen brought excitement to Chicago sports (comparable to) Michael Jordan and Scottie Pippen. Nancy Faust, the White Sox organist, plays a different song for every player, and for him she played, "Jesus Christ Superstar." I asked her why and she said, Because he approached the plate like a king!

Zisk: Do you consider yourself his number one fan?

ZS: Not only do I consider myself his number one fan (other than his wife and his mother who just died a few years ago . . . he was a mama's boy), I am also the official president of the Dick Allen International Fan Club on Race Relations. It is called that because Allen was subjected to a lot of racism, and baseball needs to acknowledge what he went through if the sport is ever to achieve real racial harmony. When he played Triple A for the Little Rock (Arkansas) Travelers he was the first black baseball player in that state. When he first arrived, the governor and two hundred fans met Allen at the airport with a sign reading "Don't Niggerize Our Baseball." When he went to the Philadelphia Phillies, the Phillies had never had a black superstar. On the field, one game, Frank Thomas, a veteran on the team who was near retirement, called Allen a "nigger son of a bitch." Allen knocked him down, and Thomas hit Allen on the shoulder with a bat. This was in front of fans, and the Phillies fans turned on Allen. The next day the attendance shot up, just to boo Dick Allen. They brutally rode him out of Philadelphia. He had to wear a batting helmet in the field because they threw things— nails—at him. His life was in danger. If you threw a nail at a player today you would go to jail. Baseball didn't protect Dick Allen. Can you imagine the mental strain? You can't!

Zisk: What does being his number one fan entail?

ZS: What it does is it has me trying to correct the way that Dick Allen was painted as a bad person or troublemaker. He was an independent person who exercised the United States Constitution's right to free speech. He chose the freedom to not speak to reporters, so of course they wrote bad things about him. I've been working on a documentary about Dick Allen for years, but it doesn't have an end yet. I'm going to take my Dick Allen museum on the road and collect a million signatures and present them to the baseball commissioner so that he will make a special proclamation. I think Dick Allen should be in the Hall of Fame. It's the only way his career could wind up and it's the only way that baseball can achieve racial harmony in the sport. I was talking to (Allen), and he said he wouldn't want to be in the Hall of Fame unless they also put me in as the first black bat boy. That was a nice thing of him to say. You know, this is the 30th anniversary of the season he saved the Sox. They were going to move to Seattle or Florida before Allen doubled the attendance. I am trying to get the White Sox to retire his number and erect a statue. Roland Burris (Illinois gubernatorial candidate) said it best, he said I'm "keeping Allen's legacy alive." No, Channel 7's Bob Petty said it best, "If Dick hadn't been like Dick, then there wouldn't be a Dick Allen!"

Zisk: What's the single act that you've done that best exemplifies your devotion to Mr. Allen?

ZS: I've collected over five hundred pieces of memorabilia for my traveling Dick Allen Museum—his old uniforms, his bat, his glove. I went to the Academy Awards to support Michael Clarke Duncan (nominated for *The Green Mile*) who I went to King High School with, and he told me he had Dick Allen's glove, which I thought was strange. Allen only had two gloves, I didn't know him and Allen were close. Duncan sent the glove to me and now it's in the museum.

Zisk: How would you like history to remember Dick Allen?

ZS: As one of the finest ballplayers to ever play the game. He ran like a deer, hit like Hercules, and dressed like the president. When everyone in the locker room had cotton drawers, he was walking around with silk drawers and a big afro. They say he was a bad guy. He never threw his bat, never argued with the umpire. His mother raised him to be at peace with himself and to believe in God. The hostility he was subjected to was unfair. But he went through these things so others wouldn't have to. Ballplayers are murdering people now, and Dick Allen is supposed to be bad. Yes, he didn't like playing the second game of a doubleheader, he didn't go to spring training or take batting practice. He wasn't perfect; once he had three homers and six RBIs and had given the team an eight-run lead in the seventh inning and asked the manager if he could go. He went to the racetrack, and the team lost the lead and the game, and the reporters saw him at the track, so you can imagine how they let him have it. But ballplayers are murdering people now! He wasn't a bad guy, just a rebel, an independent, free spirit.

Zisk: How would you like history to remember Ziff Sistrunk?

ZS: As a person who stood for what was right in Dick Allen's case, who put this in front of his own career. This isn't about racism, it's about racial harmony. We're still not over Jackie Robinson. As long as baseball looks at Dick Allen as bad, there will never truly be racial harmony in the game.

Originally appeared in issue #5, Spring 2002.

Pete Rose's Bloody Steak Napkin

Frank D'Urso

This is a story about fame, fortune, a very rare steak, two bottles of wine, and a round of toxicity called Blue Hawaiian.

Every summer the guys all get together in Cooperstown. I'm the newest member so they call me the Rook even though it's my second "season."

We call ourselves GALCO, short for Get A Life Company. They made a trophy that we present to ourselves every hot summer on the "Field of Dreams." Each participant gets his name engraved on it. For 364 days a year, the trophy stays in an old cardboard box.

We usually gather on Friday and have a nice meal at an authentic Italian restaurant on Main Street in Cooperstown. A few ballplayers and celebrities will show up and be seen. The whole village is filled with the best living baseball players. This year, old-time pop crooner Jerry Vale was there. He caused quite a stir with the older crowd.

Saturday, we'll usually grab some hot dogs and street sausages while we investigate Main Street's collection of stores and museums, capped off by a quick visit to the mighty Baseball Hall Of Fame itself. Last year, I saw Kirby Puckett up close—he's a lot taller than when I viewed him from the outfield seats of Fenway Park.

Saturday night, we go a little way out of the village to a steak house. I don't know if it's a custom or not, but the "rookie" buys the gang a round of drinks while we wait for everyone to show up and get a table. My first year we all drank whiskey, so this year, I asked the bartender to surprise us. She took the challenge wholeheartedly and made a strong concoction called a Blue Hawaiian. She took a liking to me and even gave me an extra one. I was well on my way to getting lubricated.

My other nickname, besides the Rook, is Da Bare because that's what my last name means in Italian. The other guys are: El Presidente, Commander Kelshmo, Bull-Man, WhoreGay, DougLips, BoBo, Pretzelman, and Morgan (whose real name is Morgan). These guys have been coming to Cooperstown for induction week for over ten years. I'm the youngest at 37 and Bull-Man is the eldest just having turned 60. Bull-Man is a large man with lots of momentum, and as can be expected of a former Marine, he can keep up with each of us and more.

The steakhouse usually gets a few ball players to come out and get away from the crowds. Last year, we saw Stan Musial and Doc Gooden.

Fan Interference

This year, along with his posse, right in the front room was the living, breathing dynamo called Charlie Hustle. Even the waiters were impressed. They whispered gleefully that they hoped he tipped well. Pete Rose has been haunting the festivities, hoping to gain some sympathy for his cause.

I peeked around the corner and there he was, Moe Howard haircut and all, entertaining his group of about ten people. I noticed the two sexy women that were dining with them. From the state of their table I also noticed that they were almost through with dinner. Bull-Man ran out to the car to get something for Pete to sign. WhoreGay staked out the corner of the bar that the Rose ensemble would have to pass when they left. He wasn't a fan of Pete's, but did want to get a good look at the female talent. I stayed at the edge of the bar feeling the happy tonic of the Blue Hawaiian course through my veins. The other guys, El Presidente in particular, stayed on their barstools, angry about Pete's desecration of the game.

Suddenly, I noticed the two women walking toward me. Pete was behind them and, again, I noticed his haircut first. He threw a quick "get away from my bowl" dog scowl at WhoreGay and then turned toward my side of the bar. The moment of truth was suddenly upon me. How would I deal with this brush with greatness?

I thrust out my hand at the aged yet still virile short stack of power. "Hey, Pete," I blurted out between what must have been blue blurred lips. His scowl turned into a quick smile as he took my hand and shook briskly. He patted me with his left hand, and I proudly patted Pete Rose on the back. In the brief second that we had contact I was sure that this man could still play major league baseball. I could feel the tight twirling energy within his diminutive frame. His chest muscles were bursting through his shirt.

When the entourage made its way past us, they were met by Bull-Man, who at 6'4" made Pete Rose look like a little boy. We were seated at the table next to the one Pete and company had vacated. The waitstaff were buzzing, as if they had been holding their breath. They scurried off and did not return for quite some time. Meanwhile, us GALCO guys started in on a bottle of wine. I was so buzzed I couldn't choose from the menu. I was feeling good. I'd just shaken hands with *Pete Rose*. For him or against him, we all were having a good laugh. Pete Rose was a good topic of conversation, especially when baseball fans are drinking.

I decided to go look at the mess of Pete Rose's table. Perhaps I could learn something about him, something that would damn him or provide his salvation. Either that or I was just a semi-drunk, nosey bastard.

I picked up his white linen napkin, it was smeared with all sorts of steak blood—perhaps he likes his steak very rare? Yes, a baseball animal like Pete Rose would certainly eat his meat raw, preferably off the near dead frame of an animal in the wild. His butter knife was smeared with the stuff, surrounded by many breadcrumbs on the table cloth. That's it, Pete, no worries about arteries hardening with you, you're made of steel! The shrimp fork was an oddity; it sat between the seats where Pete and the blonder woman had been sitting. I imagined they shared a shrimp cup, he feeding her like a master would feed its pet. I noticed the one bottle of wine they all shared. Good for Pete, I thought, not drinking too much. He had enough vices. I picked up the cork—hmmm, I sniffed the same wine that Pete Rose drank!

At this point, the guys grabbed me and we made our way to the salad bar; apparently, I had a salad with my meal. While we selected our vegetable portions from the sneeze-guarded buffet, a family of five enjoyed our Rose-related jocularity. I noticed that the daughter had an "I'm With Stupid" T-shirt on, with the arrow pointing at her Dad. I couldn't help but blurt out, "Your shirt says I'm with stupid." I turned to the dad, "Does that make you stupid?" Somewhere in between thinking and saying that I started to realize that it was a pretty dumb thing to say, but to my amazement and gratitude the entire family responded with the best entire family laugh that I have ever experienced. I said something else equally stupid, and they responded uproariously.

I decided to finish with one last laugh. I granted them Pete Rose's butter knife for their good-naturedness. I made my way back to our table. Commander Kelshmo was taking his turn entertaining the family, followed by Bull-Man. Every time I heard this family laugh, I felt so good inside; these people were hearty laughers. A table behind us had asked us what the commotion was, and I explained how they had missed out on Pete Rose. I gave them the cork from the wine bottle and was rewarded with a kiss on the cheek from the thirty-something hootchie mamma.

Things settled down for a while as we ate. Then Bull-Man decided to do a magic trick. He took our empty wine bottle, pushed the cork back in, and using his napkin to create pressure, launched the cork. I was impressed and inspired. I bet that he couldn't do that again with Pete Rose's empty wine bottle. I got the bottle off the still-ignored table, drank the last drops (I drank wine with Pete Rose!), and presented it to Bull-Man. After about five minutes, he earned the $20 bet, but the result was the cork flying out of the bottle and hitting a guy at the table next to us in the head. They were a little upset, of course, but after we explained the Pete Rose scenario, the victim was kind of honored. I gave them the bottle as a keepsake, and Bull-Man did the trick for them one more time.

We left quickly after paying our bill. I still had the bloody steak napkin and shrimp fork, and I didn't want to get nabbed with them. Bull-Man gave me the golf ball that he had Pete Rose sign; it was the only thing he could find. Pete tried to sign it but there was just a blue squiggle. We tried to trace out what the signature said. If it were a baseball it would be worth over one hundred dollars. As a golf ball with a blue squiggle it was worthless, but it didn't matter because I was the owner of Pete Rose's bloody steak napkin!

Originally appeared in issue #5, Spring 2002.

The King and I – Remembering and Writing About Dave Kingman

Charlie Vascellaro

I've recently become reacquainted with my old home run hero Dave Kingman. During the past few Cactus League spring-training seasons in Arizona, I keep seeing the man they call "Kong" on the autograph circuit where he signs balls, bats, and photos with a group of old timers known as "Fergie and Friends." Organized by Hall of Fame pitcher Fergie Jenkins, some of the money goes to charities and some of it goes into Kingman's pocket.

Seeing Kingman always evokes nostalgia for me. Kingman and I go way back; all the way to the dark days of the New York Mets from his arrival with the team at Shea Stadium in 1975, when I was an 11-year-old baseball crazy kid growing up on Long Island. I gravitated to Kingman for the fleeting flashes of glory he provided with his prodigious long-ball blasts.

I didn't pay the $20 they were asking for his autograph last spring, he's already signed plenty of items for me, but I did get him to pose for a nice photo of the two of us standing together.

I haven't been stalking Kingman, we just keep ending up in the same places at the same time. In fact, it feels more like he's been following me around. Like I said, I was already a Mets fan when Kingman joined the team, and I was still living on Long Island when he was traded to San Diego in 1977. It was Kingman who followed me to Arizona in the spring of 1979, after my family had moved there in the summer of 1978.

Kingman and I have had numerous interactions over the years that I've attempted to remind him of the last few times we've met but he either failed to remember or didn't want to acknowledge knowing me.

My interest in Kingman has bordered on obsession ever since he began belting balls over the wall for the Mets and one dream-like moment when I actually retrieved one.

During his first few seasons with the Mets, Kingman established himself as the greatest home run hitter in the team's relatively brief history, knocking a single-season franchise record 36 in 1975, which was also good enough for second place in the National League, just behind Mike Schmidt of Philadelphia.

The Mets also moved up to third place in the NL East posting an 82-80 record following an abysmal 71-91, 1974 season.

Prior to Kingman's arrival, the relatively successful Mets teams from 1969-1973 were built around their pitching staffs, and my favorite player was the team's cantankerous catcher Jerry Grote, who was just about on his way out when Kingman came to town.

Kingman provided a new kind of excitement for me and the rest of us Mets fans who, at best, had grown used to grinding it out offensively while our sturdy starting pitching staff kept opponents at bay. With one swooping swing, Kingman provided the kind of instant offense that could win, or at least keep us in the game.

On the days and nights when I was lucky enough to get my preadolescent ass into a seat at Shea, I'd be whoopin' it up with the rest of Mets faithful in eager anticipation for every one of his at-bats.

Most of the time he struck out, but every now and then he'd knock the kind of moon shots that earned him the nickname "Sky King," and in those joyous moments, we'd all be laughing and smiling all the way down the ramps after the game and all the train ride home.

On the truly horrible Mets teams that Kingman played for in the mid-1970s and again in the early '80s, Kingman was a glimmer of hope and an object of fascination. But as much as we were drawn to him for the excitement he enticed, he did not welcome our embrace and preferred to be left alone by the media unless he thought it suited his purpose during heated contract negotiations with the notoriously thrifty Mets brass.

Kingman's relationship with my other heroes at the time, the New York baseball press, was contentious at best. When I was a kid at Shea Stadium, I used to hitch rides on the stadium elevator and slip out in the press level where I would get the Mets beat writers to sign their mug shots on the back pages of the team's yearbook.

Among my favorites was Jack Lang, who covered the team for the *Long Island Press* since its inception. Lang wrote of an incident with Kingman that pretty much summed up their relationship: after missing a team flight during the spring training season of 1976, Kingman asked Lang if he could hitch a ride with him across Florida from Miami to St. Petersburg. After sharing the ride, including a stop for dinner and exchanging casual and friendly conversation for the duration of the drive, Kingman failed to acknowledge Lang's presence in the clubhouse the next day.

"I said good morning to Kingman. He never looked at me. He walked right past me as if I didn't exist. The day before we had spent five hours together in a car and now he didn't even know me. That was Dave Kingman," wrote Lang.

Kingman's kind of been that way with me, too.

After my family's move from Long Island to Arizona, at the height of my obsessive teenage baseball fandom in June of 1978, I was elated to catch up with Kingman, or have him catch up with me, at a spring training game in Mesa eight months later. I had only recently made the serendipitous discovery of spring training baseball in Arizona through the window of a school bus on the way to my new junior high school. Many hooky-playing days would ensue. Kingman had signed with the Chicago Cubs during the off-season, and I could barely believe he was out in Arizona with me. I'd chase him all around the Cubs Hohokam Park facility, peeling off paparazzi shots on my Kodak Instamatic, a camera that I would take to the one-hour developing photo booths and whose picture I would bring back to the ballpark for him to sign the next day.

The spring training season and the month of March would fast become my favorite time of year in my new home state.

At the end of the school year, I returned to Long Island, and on June 28, 1979, together with a pair of old pals, I rode the Long Island Railroad to Shea Stadium to see Kingman and the Cubs play the Mets. With the sole intention of catching a Kingman home run ball, we purchased $1.50 general admission tickets and chose to sit almost by ourselves in the left-field mezzanine section.

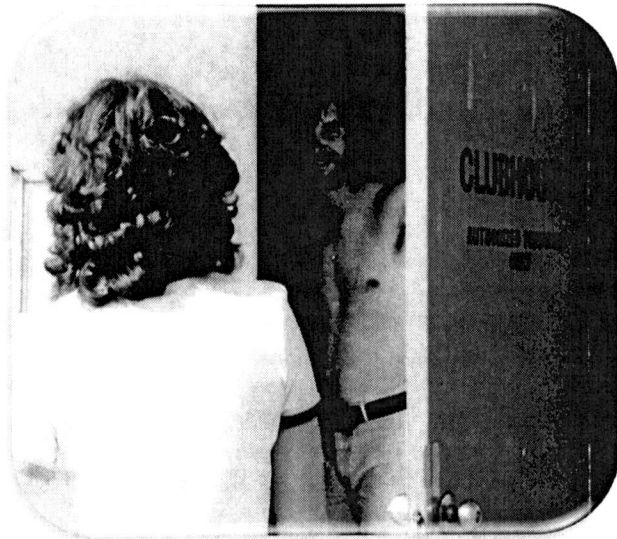

The cops and ushers working the lonely section laughed when I explained why I had chosen such seats; we could have sat anywhere in the ballpark. But when Kong knocked three home runs that day, and I retrieved the second one, I had the last laugh. Somehow, after the game, I was able to talk myself past the players' entrance into the ballpark and just as quickly Kingman emerged from the visiting clubhouse. A couple of smaller kids followed me as I approached Kingman who seemed to be in a hurry to leave.

"Mr. Kingman," I said, "this is the second home run you hit today, would you sign it for me?"

Without answering me directly Kingman simply said, "just one" to our small group, grabbed the ball from my hand, signed it, and handed it back to me.

Two years later, I was assigned by my eleventh grade English teacher, Ms. Tower, to write about a significant day in my life. At that time, I couldn't think of a more significant day than the one at Shea when I got the home run ball. (It's still way up on the list.) I wrote a blow-by-blow narrative account of the day called, "Kingman's Shot," which received a perfect score. Ms. Tower even wrote the word "Great" on top of the paper. Here's an excerpt:

> *We had purchased the dollar-fifty grandstand seats, and every time Kingman came to bat, we would stand ready, in hopes that he would hit us a shot. During his second at-bat of the game, my dream was to be fulfilled. As he hit the ball, my eyes followed it. As it appeared I could sense the people all around me charging for the ball. I leaped over a few seats and grabbed Kingman's shot on a bounce. As I held the ball in my clutches, I wished the moment would last forever.*

This is when I began to make the transition from obsessed fan to writer. I have Kingman to thank for spawning my interest in writing about baseball. "Kingman's Shot" would be the first of a series of stories on Kingman that would propel me through high school and college.

Kingman would go on to lead the National League in home runs in 1979, with a career-high 48. He was on pace to threaten Roger Maris's then single-season record of 61 before being sidelined by a late-season injury that cost him the last 17 games of the season and continued to nag him the following year. He hit 18 home runs in 81 games in 1980, and after two-and-a-half seasons, Kingman had overstayed his welcome in Chicago, and the Cubs told the Mets they could have him back.

Kingman plodded along through an injury-riddled 1981 season, hitting 22 home runs in 100 games with a .221 batting average. He rebounded, so to speak, in 1982 leading the National League with 37 home runs while batting .204; the lowest average ever posted by a player to lead his league in home runs and/or by a first baseman with enough plate appearances to eligible for the batting title.

While I still followed Kingman's antics, by this time I hardly cared, having all but disappeared as a baseball fan for a few years, lured away from the game by the teenage pursuits of sex, drugs, and rock and roll (mostly the latter two). I checked in with Kingman and the Mets only sporadically in between acid trips and Frank Zappa and Grateful Dead concerts. I started to come back around in 1983 when the Mets made the great trade that brought all-star first baseman Keith Hernandez for relief pitcher Neil Allen. Hernandez's arrival was the beginning of a turnaround for the team that would culminate with the 1986 World Series championship. The arrival of Hernandez at first base would also relegate Kingman to the bench, and he was released unceremoniously by the Mets after the 1983 season.

The following spring, Kingman was back with me again in Arizona, earning a roster spot with the Oakland Athletics after an impressive tryout with the team at Municipal Park in Phoenix.

He appeared to be a good fit with the A's as the team's designated hitter, posting perhaps the three most productive seasons of his career. But his time in Oakland was also marked by a particularly disturbing incident involving his belief that female reporters should not be allowed in the clubhouse.

After refusing to speak with or even in the company of former *Sacramento Bee* reporter Susan Fornoff for the first three months of the 1986 season, Kingman had a wrapped package delivered to Fornoff in the Kansas City Royals press box. Kingman's gift to Fornoff was a live rat with a tag that read "My name is Sue," tied around one of its feet. Kingman was released by the A's at the conclusion of the season.

I can't remember if I was immediately aware of the circumstances concerning the story of Kingman and Fornoff and the rat at the time, but, in retrospect, I think it should have changed the way I felt about Kingman, although I'm not sure if it did then.

When Kingman was released by the A's at the conclusion of the 1986 season I was more concerned that he would not have the opportunity to reach 500 career home runs. He would again return to Phoenix in the middle of the 1987 season, signing a minor league contract with the San Francisco Giants Triple A affiliate Phoenix Firebirds in a last-ditch attempt to make it back to the majors.

Of course, I was there for the first and last game of his abbreviated six-week stint. In his first game back Kingman provided the fireworks on the Fourth of July. I was standing in line for a hot dog and a beer when I heard the crack of the bat and picked up the ball's flight as it soared high in the Phoenix night sky over the left field wall toward the Papago Buttes out onto Van Buren Street.

Kingman would hit just one more home run during the next four weeks and decided to throw in the towel after his final month in the minors. I received the news that it would be Kingman's last game while listening to the radio in my truck on the morning of August 4, and figured I ought to be there to see what kind of material it might add to my ongoing story. I brought the home run ball from 1979 with me. I had foolishly brushed clear nail polish over Kingman's signature, which was now cracking and turning yellow. I figured I would ask him to resign it. I also brought my original hand-written eleventh grade English paper, an extra copy to give to Kingman, and my friend Mark Fast. It was a rainy night, and Kingman was not in the starting line-up, he wasn't even in the dugout. There was a situation early in the game when the Phoenix pitcher, who had already given up a bunch of runs, was due to bat with the bases loaded and two outs. I thought it was the ideal time for Kingman to pinch hit. He was standing at the end of the tunnel where the players entered the field from the clubhouse behind a belt-high chain link fence looking out over the field, and like me, I'm sure he was thinking that he should be batting.

I still think he was trying to convey that message with his body language in the way that he was standing there in full sight of everyone. There were periodic rain delays throughout the rest of the night, and Kingman would occasionally emerge from the tunnel, but he did not play or even get an at-bat in his final game. It was close to midnight when the game was completed, and Mark Fast and I were among the very few fans that chose to stick it out. We waited by the players' exit in the parking lot. It seemed like 24 of the 25-man roster had left before Kingman finally came up the stairs. He was carrying a large Oakland A's duffle bag on his shoulder, which I imagine contained the contents of his locker and all of his big league memories. When I approached him, I think I caught him a bit off guard. I don't think he expected anyone to still be there.

"Hey, Dave, can you sign this ball for me? It's one of three you hit against the Mets on July 28, 1979. You signed it for me then but it's kind of fading."

He looked a bit incredulous and slightly perturbed, but I also thought I saw the beginning of a smile. I don't think he had planned on putting the big bag down until he got to his car, but he did, and he signed the ball again for me. I asked if he wouldn't mind writing the date on the ball as well but he said I could do that myself and started to walk away.

"Wait!" I said, "This is an essay I wrote in high school a couple of years ago about the day I got the ball, look," I said, "it's great," pointing to where Ms. Tower had left her mark. "Can you sign it, too?"

He autographed the essay, as well.

"Wait!" I said, one more time. "I made a copy for you maybe you can read it later."

He folded it up and stuck it on his back pocket. I figured there was a fifty-fifty chance he'd actually read it. (In retrospect, I don't think he ever did because I still think he would have acknowledged knowing who I was later, if he did. I mean c'mon, I was probably his biggest fan. I know I was his last. You think he'd remember this exchange on the last night of his career.)

A couple of years later, I wrote about that night for a creative writing class at Scottsdale Community College titled, "Kingman's Last Shot."

A classmate, who happened to be on the school newspaper staff liked the story and asked if I would be interested in writing about sports for the paper, which led me to enroll in a news writing class the following semester.

I began writing sports stories for the school paper and even served as sports editor for the next three semesters. Later, when I transferred from Scottsdale Community College to Arizona State University, I registered for a creative writing class not knowing that renowned baseball novelist Mark Harris (*The Southpaw* and *Bang the Drum Slowly*) would be the instructor. While at ASU, I also took a class in baseball fiction. I don't know if it was because of my obsession with Kingman or that the material seemed to flow so freely but again I chose Kingman for an assigned paper on heroes.

> *Of the hero types discussed, I think Kingman best fits the Adonic mold.*[1] *We had trouble getting to know him, and when we did catch a glimpse of his persona it was not always favorable.*

After graduating from ASU in 1993, I parlayed my journalism degree and a referral from Mark Harris into a job as research editor at a new baseball history magazine called *The Diamond*, which had its offices in Scottsdale. Although the magazine would fold in the wake of the players' strike of 1994, after just nine issues, I still had a nice office to work from in January of 1995, when it was announced that Kingman would receive $829,849 in collusion damages as a result of his loss of job for the 1987 season. The news happened to coincide with a charity fundraiser Dream Game that Kingman would be participating in a few weeks later in Phoenix.

I converted some of the material from "Kingman's Last Shot" story into a local newspaper preview piece for the game and attended the fundraiser's gala banquet where the jersey that Kingman wore on that last night was being sold in a silent auction for the fundraiser. I can't remember what the starting bid was, but I do recall that I kept upping the ante in $10 increments and that I was bidding against just one other person who seemed to want the jersey as much as me. In the end, I outbid former Firebirds' owner Martin Stone, placing my final $135 bid as the auction sheets were being lifted from the table while my good friend Mark Fast set a pick on Stone. During the banquet, I also was able to get Kingman to autograph a copy of my story in the local paper. When the Dream Game was played the next day, I opted to sit outside Phoenix Municipal Stadium on a sloping desert hill, accompanied by nothing but a six pack of beer, in hopes of catching another one of Kingman's shots.

---

[1] Adonic mold – "a rebel...who does not uncritically conform...he represents a sort of middle way between animal indulgence...and authorized forms of behavior...hence he lives in a world of tension, pain, struggle and hope." *Seeking the Perfect Game, Baseball In American Literature*, Codelia Candelaria, Greenwood Press, 1989.

Fan Interference

He came close, launching one of his patented long fly balls that hit the wall in left field, right in front of me, but did not make it over.

A few months later, I contributed an editorial piece on Kingman and the collusion damages award to *USA Today's Baseball Weekly*:

> *Surely the 6-foot-6 slugger, still lithe at 210 pounds, was on a pace to hit 58 home runs during the next two seasons to reach the coveted 500 mark. He was only 37 when his career came to its abrupt halt...Now that it has been revealed that collusion cost Kingman his job and the magic 500 home run plateau, does it mean it cost him his spot in the Hall of Fame?...Another thing that must be understood about Kingman: His home runs didn't just clear the fence. They cleared buildings and neighborhoods. They are the stuff of myths and folklore, and that is his greatest contribution to the game.*

In 2006, I updated the Kingman narrative in a story for the San Francisco Giants spring training program:

> *I still think of him often. It's been 35 years since Dave Kingman's major league debut with the San Francisco Giants in 1971 and 20 years since his topsy-turvy career came to a close in 1986. During the time between, the 6'6" free-swinging slugger hit 442 home runs for seven different teams. As a young baseball fan in the 1970s I saw many of them in person and still recall the breathtaking majesty of Kingman's towering blasts. Kingman put the long in long ball.*

A couple of years ago, I caught up with Kingman at one of the aforementioned autograph tables during a spring training game at Hohokam Park in Mesa. I introduced myself just as I did this past spring; I mentioned the home run ball from 1979, and some of the writing I had done on him since. He didn't acknowledge having any memory of our previous meetings, which I thought was kind of peculiar. I thought for sure he must have remembered that last night of his career in Phoenix, or that he may have seen or read the *Baseball Weekly* piece or *Giants Spring Training Magazine* story. Perhaps he does know who I am and thinks I'm just another asshole writer.

After seeing Kingman on the first day that I was in Arizona for the Cactus League season this past spring, I caught up with him again, sitting at the autograph table at Scottsdale Stadium on his last day in town. I told him I just wanted to say hello and goodbye and mentioned a presentation I would be making about him and the influence he had on my career at the fiftieth anniversary of the New York Mets Conference at

Hofstra University. He smiled and was polite but he didn't seem all that interested.

I gave him a copy of the photograph taken of the two of us together a few weeks earlier and even autographed it for him at no charge.

Originally appeared in issue #21, Fall 2012.

Part II: Because We Hate You — Fury Has Many Faces

Mike Faloon vs. Barry Bonds

Mike Faloon

Two weeks ago, fellow *Zisk* editor Steve Reynolds and I went to Shea to see the Mets play the Giants. The Mets brushed aside the Giants 3-0 behind a four-hit shutout from Kenny Rogers. Rogers neutralized the Giants' offense racking up nine strike outs and yielding only one walk. A major part of Rogers' success was keeping Barry Bonds in check. The numbers glowed on my scorecard: Bonds, 0-for-4, three strike outs.

Rogers' dominant performance was worthy of much post-game discussion but eventually talk turned to Bonds' surprising ineptitude. A trio of Ks was not what we expected from a hitter of his magnitude. Then I remembered a Giants-Mets game I'd seen last year. Bonds did little at the plate and was the third out in a triple play. It was a thing of beauty. Bonds was on second. He moved to third on a ground ball. The next hitter sent a grounder down the first base line. As the Mets started a routine 3-6-3 double play Bonds bolted for home. He got nailed at the plate for the third out. For such a smart player it was an uncharacteristic display of bad judgment. Combining the two games, I had seen one of the game's best hitters go 1-for-8, whiff three times, and stumble into a triple play. Was this a coincidence or, more likely, did I have Barry's number?

When I got home, I dug through scorecards from previous years. I discovered that what I had witnessed over the past two years was nothing new. Between 1995 and 1999 Barry Bonds and I have squared off four times. Aside from an occasional bit of productivity—an RBI here, a stolen base there—Bonds was not the same hitter. My intimidating gaze has shaved nearly 50 points off his batting average (Career without

Faloon Factor = .290, Career with Faloon Factor = .244). Also, I am responsible for a nearly 100% increase in his strikeouts (Career Strikeout Rate without Faloon Factor = 13% of at-bats, Career Strikeout Rate with Faloon Factor = 25% of at-bats). Pretty remarkable for a player who has not struck out more than 100 times in a season since 1986, his rookie year with the Pirates.

    I haven't played baseball since the sixth grade. I bruise playing a simple game of catch. So how am I so effective against a perennial all-star such as Bonds? That I cannot reveal. Fans in every NL city would be able to contain Bonds on a comparable level and that would introduce an unfair competitive advantage. I recognize there may be skeptics, but I'll let the numbers speak for themselves. When I'm in the stands, Barry Bonds, future home run king, future Hall of Famer, hits like Mark Belanger. So, a word of wisdom to all NL managers, when you have to pitch to Barry Bonds there are two surefire solutions: face him in the playoffs or leave a ticket for me at the box office.

Originally appeared in issue #2, Fall 1999.

Yes, I've Heard, They Suck

Dr. Nancy Golden

I was at a going-away party for one of my co-workers when the familiar needling started up again. "Hey, Nancy, how 'bout that game last night?" There was no need to ask which game. Whenever there's a Yankee loss there's never a need to ask which game has just been happily brought up in conversation. The questions continued: "So who do you think will win tomorrow?" It was a Yankees-Mets subway series, so I spouted off something about the Mets choking, or whatever standard fare I launch into when trash talking about baseball over beers. My tirade was met by a blank stare from both of my co-workers.

"Oh, I don't follow the Mets, you know," explained George.

"I don't even follow baseball," said Craig.

And that's when it really hit hard. People will go to extraordinary lengths to rile me as a Yankees fan.

Since I live in Washington, D.C., where most people are just passing through, almost everyone I know here roots for a different team. My office alone has wide multi-city representation, and while I like to think that we all talk trash about each other's teams, it's recently dawned on me that in reality, it's just me who talks trash about their teams, and they, collectively, about mine. For instance, my co-worker Joe, whose Atlanta Braves had taken a precipitous fall from first to last place, escaped the 2006 season relatively unscathed from harassment, even though his office is much more centrally located than mine and, in my eyes, roots for a team that is at least as hateable. Dan, who roots for the Tigers, received nothing but support after so many years of suffering, and Mike, whose Nationals could barely piece together a win, didn't merit the effort. And yet people who barely even follow sports will seek me out to discuss a Yankees loss.

At times, I've wondered if it's just me. But people don't rile me this way about the other teams that I root for. Hating the Yankees is simply something that brings the rest of the world together, fans and non-fans alike. Perhaps in the same way that loving the Yankees brings the majority of New Yorkers together. (Sorry, Mets fans, you know it's true.) I recently lost an argument about unwise spending practices of big market teams to a nine-year-old, whose father had taught him that hating was wrong—except in the case of the Yankees. ("Dana," I told him, staring down at his NY baseball cap with the extra-curvy Y, "I don't know what your *dad*'s been telling you, but nobody in New York really likes the Mets." One of us was going to leave crying, and it wasn't going to be me.) I'm even amazed by the sheer effort expended in hating the Yankees. There is no shortage of Yankee-hating websites (rather uninspired, if you ask me . . . and slightly homophobic) and many books devoted to the history and fundamentals of that hatred. In fact, if you type "Yankees" and "hate" into amazon.com, you'll come up with products to purchase in the categories of Books, Automotive, Home & Garden, Apparel, and, of course, Music, because if you feel that strongly, you gotta sing about it. (Incidentally, similar searches for "hate" and "Brewers" or "Astros" turned up no relevant matches.) C'mon, people, there's a whole world out there! Come down to D.C., I'll show things we can all hate. I just can't muster up the same degree of hatred for my rivals as love for my own team. It would mean thinking about my rivals that much. Hell, I even considered rooting for the Mets after the Yankees got knocked out last post-season until I encountered the overwhelming vitriol of the Mets fans after the Yankees' elimination (present publication included).

These days, most guys on the team aren't even career Yankees that came up through the farm system. Last season, they were probably regular working stiffs for some other team who had a good season and were bought out by the highest bidder (i.e. Steinbrenner). (Hey, would it be better if he bought himself another yacht?) And yet seemingly as soon as they join the Yankees, they become "Evil," as if their new contracts have them slaying bunnies at the pediatric cancer ward on off days. My co-worker Don, who, in the spirit of full disclosure, is a Red Sox fan and probably knows a thing or two about being evil, told me about the discomfort he felt going into a fellow co-worker's office after he learned he was a Yankees fan. "From then on, it was like he was wearing The Mask," he told me, referring, of course, to the one worn by Darth Vader. "And then I learned you were a Yankee fan, and well, it just sucked the wind out of my sails."

While I find all the attention fascinating, none of it really fazes me. I've been cocky since Jim Leyritz's home run in Game 4 of the 1996 World Series, and there's no end in sight. I grew up in the '80s, which highlighted a 17-year post-season dry spell and earned me every ounce of unrelenting smugness I continuously display, regardless of the circumstances. So I can live with the constant and sometimes random chorus of "Yankees Suck" in the background: at the Mets game, the Nats-Phillies game, even the Capitols-Sabres game last month. I actually think it's telling that you're all still thinking about them when they're not even in town, not even playing the same sport. Know what's even more telling? Two people telling me last season that they wanted to lay off the Yankees bashing now that their teams were winning. Please, spare us your pity. For rest assured, we'll be drinking beer and cursing out your right fielder from the stands while we cry on our 26 World Series rings.

Originally appeared in issue #14, Spring 2007.

The Last Days at Fulton County Stadium

                                    Sean Carswell

Probably nobody would've gotten kicked out if I hadn't been running my big mouth. I had a lot of beer in me, though. And there's just something about the Atlanta Braves. They bring out the asshole in me.

My accomplice, like half the women of my generation, was named Jennifer. As far as friends named Jennifer go, this one wasn't in my top five Jennifers. Definitely in the top ten, though. She was a decent enough girl. We had enough in common, like that we both had the day off and we both wanted to get drunk on our day off and we both figured a Braves game was as good of a place as any to get drunk. So there we were, getting drunk and watching the Houston Astros take the Braves to task. Jennifer tapped me on the shoulder and said, "I gotta go to the bathroom." I nodded and kept looking down at the field. Jennifer didn't stand up. "No, really," she said, "I'm gonna go to the bathroom." She sat there looking at me until I snapped out of it and realized that she was giving me some kind of stoner hint that she wanted the one-hitter so that she could smoke pot in the bathroom.

"Oh, okay," I said. I pulled the one-hitter and the lighter out of the pockets of my plaid cotton shorts and I put them in her hand. She left.

I looked around the Fulton County Stadium. In a month, the Braves were leaving it and moving to Turner Field. In general, I was pretty pissed off about the move because I worked in a restaurant in downtown Atlanta, right by Fulton County Stadium, and I made most of my money off Braves fans on their way to Braves games. When the team switched stadiums, I was going to lose my job. Jennifer was going to lose hers, too. But, to tell the truth, that's not really what I thought about. I thought about good times at Fulton County Stadium, like all the times my buddy Pete would bring his camera bag to games and we would fill his empty film canisters with whiskey and get drunk as hell on one whiskey and Coke apiece. Or that sixteen-inning game that I went to with my sister and her boyfriend that finally ended when Deion Sanders outran a bunt, stole two bases, and scored the winning run on a routine infield grounder.

After my wave of nostalgia passed and Astros retired the side, Jennifer came back glassy-eyed. She handed me the one-hitter and said, "We better be cool about that. I think the security guard down by the bathroom is on to us."

"Damn it," I said. "I hate the Braves."

Fan Interference

I stuffed the one-hitter back into my pocket, about half-realizing that no more pot-smoking and the nature of my hatred of the Braves was gonna seal the fate of the crowd around me. Because my hatred of the Braves was something clean, something pure. And it wasn't because they were moving stadiums and taking my job with them. It wasn't even because I'd lost that same job two years earlier when major league baseball went on strike. No. I hated the Braves long before that. I hated them since I was a little kid and the only baseball games I could see on TV were Braves games. I hated them ever since the only choice for hero worship they offered me was a .281 hitting, John-Boy-from-*The-Waltons*-look-alike outfielder named Dale Murphy.

Hell, let's be honest. I hated the Braves when Murphy was still a .226 hitting first baseman.

Let's be even more honest. I hated the Braves so much that they were my favorite team. I could never muster the passion or fury rooting for a baseball team that I had rooting against the Braves. I looked up at the scoreboard, and realized the fifth inning was about to start already. More than half of my heckling time had passed, and I'd done almost no heckling. I drank my beer and watched John Smoltz jog out to the pitcher's mound and thought of ways to get cracking.

Jennifer settled into her seat and picked up her beer. After a minute of silence, she asked, "What did I miss?"

"The Astros ran off the field. The Braves ran on. Everyone played catch."

"That all?"

"That and I remembered that the Astros used to be my favorite team," I said. "When I was a kid growing up in Florida, the Astros would spring train right by where I lived. My dad would take me to games. The Astros sucked then, but, man, they were my heroes when I was eight years old."

"Really," Jennifer said. "I thought you told me you hated baseball."

"I don't hate it. I love to hate it. There's a difference."

I glanced back down at the field. Derek Bell, one of the two Astros whom I'd heard of prior to the game, stepped up to the plate. I shouted out, "Give 'em hell, Derek Bell."

A guy two rows in front of me—whose name, I later found out, was either Baumer or Bomber—turned and gave me a dirty look. I smiled. He turned back and yelled, "Go to hell, Derek Bell." I looked at the back of his t-shirt, where he had a silkscreened picture of Bill Clinton with his nose growing like Pinocchio's.

Jennifer nudged me. "You pissed off the young Republican," she said.

"Have you ever heard that 'Johnny Smoke' song by the Butthole Surfers?" I asked Jennifer.

"No," she said.

"Do you want to know how it goes?"

Jennifer shrugged her shoulders, not really knowing where I was going with this. "Sure."

It's a weird, chanting song. Very repetitive. Full of barnyard noises that I didn't have the ability to make. Still, I started to sing, loud enough for the two rows in front of me to hear, "Johnny Smoltz, oh Johnny Smoltz. Oh Johnny, Johnny, Johnny, Johnny." Jennifer smiled. "Sing with me," I said. And I guess she'd had enough beers because she sang with me, "Johnny Smoltz, oh Johnny Smoltz. Oh Johnny, Johnny, Johnny, Johnny."

We kept singing it until Derek Bell cracked a double off the left field wall and Bomber the young Republican yelled, "Fuck!"

A little bit of anger from a Braves fan fueled me. The fact that Jennifer was so clearly going to be a co-conspirator kept me going. We talked about watching baseball as kids. Jennifer's father was a big fan of the Minnesota Twins, even though her family was from South Carolina, because he thought that Rod Carew was the best. I told her that, when I was growing up, my best friend used to practice Rod Carew's batting stance in the mirror. That he always thought the key to good hitting was getting down in the crouch. She had no idea what I was talking about, so she just said, "Baseball was better when we were kids. I don't know what happened. I don't know if it's me or the game that changed."

"You just gotta root for the past," I said. And, as if he were helping me out, Smotlz threw a wild pitch that advanced Bell to third base. "Smoltz, you suck," I screamed. "Put in Phil Neikro."

"Smoltz, you throw like a girl," Jennifer screamed, not really catching on to my joke.

A sorta hick-looking dude in front of me turned around and said, "Phil Neikro? That old boy's gotta be about sixty by now."

"And he still throws a better knuckleball than John Smoltz," I said.

Bomber the young Republican turned around and said, "Smoltz isn't a knuckleballer."

I glared at him through my one sober eye, the eye I could still keep all the way open and said, "Not the way he throws, he ain't."

The hick-looking dude started cracking up at this. "Goddamn, you're having a good time. I need to hang with you." He introduced himself to me and Jennifer. Said his name was Shane. He introduced his grandfather, an old, smiling fellow wearing dirty jeans and a John Deere baseball cap. The grandfather didn't say anything, just lifted his beer to us. "I got stuck hanging out with old Granddad," Shane said. Old Granddad's smile faded a little, and he kept watching the game.

In time, I convinced Shane and Jennifer to chant our "Johnny Smoltz" song, and we came up with new ways to annoy the young Republican. When the Braves third baseman, Chipper Jones, stepped into the batter's box, I yelled, "You suck, Bob Horner." Which is what I always yelled at

Fan Interference

the TV when the Braves' third baseman came up to the plate in 1978. I figured, so what if it isn't 1978 and Bob Horner hasn't played pro baseball in a generation. When the young Republican told me to get out of the '70s, I knew I'd gotten him fired up. I waited until the Braves catcher, Javy Lopez, struck out. I started screaming, "You're no Biff Pocoroba!"

"Biff Pocoroba sucked," Bomber said.

"And Javy Lopez isn't even that good," I said.

This cracked Shane up. He told Bomber, "You walked right into that one." Jennifer and I laughed.

Bomber told Shane, "Shut up, you fucking redneck."

"Calm down, Bomber," the young Republican's young Republican friend told him.

"No, man, fuck this redneck," Bomber said.

"What the fuck did you say?" Shane asked. Bomber didn't turn around.

I decided that this was a good time to quit stirring up shit. I finished up my beer and noticed that Jennifer was empty, too. It was getting close to the end of the sixth inning. Beer sales would end in the next few minutes, so I told Jennifer that I was gonna head down to the concession stand. "Be careful," she said, I guess thinking that I was speaking in code and really planning on going to the bathroom to smoke pot.

I walked down the ramp towards the beer stand and noticed that the security guard did seem to be watching me. I wasn't sure if Jennifer had made me paranoid or not. I took a right turn and headed for the bathroom. The security guard ambled in the same general direction. I figured that he wasn't checking me out or following me or anything, that his movements in my direction were merely coincidence. And I really did have to take a leak. I walked into the bathroom and up to a urinal.

As I was doing my business, I got that weird feeling like someone was watching me, which isn't a good feeling to have when part of your genitals are exposed in a public place. Not that I was exposing myself. I was well hidden by the urinal, but still, I didn't like that feeling that someone was watching me, so I glanced around the bathroom really quickly and, sure enough, that damn security guard was standing right by the bathroom door, watching me piss. "I hate the Braves," I mumbled.

I was so angry that I forgot about the beers and went back to my seat empty-handed.

Jennifer asked me if I forgot something. I was too flustered to answer. I tried to mumble something about how having a grown man follow you into the bathroom to watch you pee just throws off your whole afternoon, but I couldn't think of the right way to express it, and anyway it didn't matter because a beer guy was coming down the aisle just as I was about to talk. I flagged him down.

The beers were three-fifty a piece. I reached into my pocket and saw that I had a twenty and a five. The beer guy asked me how many I wanted. I did some quick math and said, "Six, please." He started to pour them out.

"What are you going to do with six beers?" Jennifer asked.

"Drink 'em," I said, but the truth was that I hadn't thought about how little time was left in the game and how much beer that really was. I'd just figured out how many I could get with what I had, and I ordered that. When the guy finished pouring the beers, I gave him the twenty-five bucks and told him to keep the change.

Now that I had six beers, I gave one to Shane because it sucked that he'd just been called a redneck, and I gave one to his grandfather, because he seemed like a cool old guy, and Jennifer and I kept two each. "Cheers, folks," Jennifer said, tipping back the first of her drinks.

"Happy Fourth of July," old Granddad said, because, though I'd completely forgotten about it, it was the Fourth of July.

I leaned back, feeling that balance again. The good and the bad. A security guy watches you pee and that sucks, but you get a beer and that's good. Bomber calls Shane a redneck and that sucks, but he gets a beer and that's good. The Braves are my home team and that sucks, but it's a nice day and I don't have to work and there's all that cool green grass down below me, right here in downtown Atlanta, and I'm in that special place where it's okay to be drunk in the afternoon. I felt so good that I started to tell Jennifer about my favorite Astro when I was growing up: J.R. Richard. To hear me tell it, Richard was almost seven feet tall and he threw ninety-five-mile-an-hour curve balls and you could see batters shaking in the batter's box when they had to face him. "He was the best," I told her. "Better than any of these million-dollar Braves pitchers. He threw the ball so fast that you couldn't even see it. He threw so hard that, even if someone could hit the pitch, it would break the bat." And so on. A whole load of bullshit.

Jennifer laughed at how ridiculous it was and I kept going about how I'd met J.R. Richard and got him to sign my copy of *Sports Illustrated* that he was on the cover of—which actually was true. I even told her about his tragic demise, the stroke he had in the middle of the 1980 season, his painful and mostly failed comeback attempt. Jennifer expressed the right amount of sympathy. I paused to drink.

Shane turned back to look at me. "Man, I'm jealous of you," he said. "You get to have all this fun with a beautiful girl and all I got's my goddamn granddad."

I looked at Jennifer and she looked at me and we both looked at Granddad but he didn't look at anything but the field. I didn't know what to say, so I kept my mouth shut. Same with Jennifer. I felt bad for old Granddad. He seemed like a nice guy. He'd even wished me a happy Fourth of July. And my grandfather had never once taken me to a baseball game, or anywhere else. Hell, my grandfather never did anything with me except make fun of me. To be honest, I would've been just as happy to be at that game with a grandfather who was actually grandfatherly as I was at that game with a top-ten-but-not-top-five-favorite Jennifer. So I was at a loss for words. Shane kept looking at me and Jennifer. Finally, Jennifer said, "Why don't you just watch the game, dude?"

Shane turned forward to watch the game. Just as he did this, Jeff Bagwell took John Smoltz downtown. The soon-to-be home run sailed towards us. The ball didn't have enough steam to make it up to the cheap seats where we were sitting, but it was high enough that some fans around us jumped out of their seats. One of these fans knocked into Shane's arm, and Shane's beer spilled all over Bomber.

It was too much for the young Republican. His team went down by three runs just as he got drenched in beer. He jumped up and shouted, "You fucking asswipe. You stupid fucking redneck."

Shane was ready for this, though. He was still stewing over the first time he'd been called a redneck. He leapt to his feet and said, "Maybe an ass-kicking would straighten things out."

A few people told them to calm down. Granddad even stood up to hold the guys at arm's length from each other. Bomber slapped Granddad's hand out of the way. "That's it," Shane said. "Step downstairs and we'll settle this." He stormed down the aisle, towards the bathroom.

Bomber started down the aisle, but then cut across a row of fans so that he could walk down a different exit ramp than Shane had gone down.

The Braves retired the side. We had the seventh inning stretch. Everyone sang "Take Me Out to the Ballgame." The Braves had a scoreless bottom of the seventh, leaving one runner on base. The Astros went three-up, three-down. During this time, four things happened in the cheap seats in front of me.

One, old Granddad decided to go hunt down Shane and pull him out of trouble.

Two, Shane returned without old Granddad and asked Bomber's friend what happened to Bomber. Bomber's friend said, "I don't know. Sit down."

Three, Bomber came back. The security guard who'd watched me take a pee was with him. Bomber pointed out Shane. The security guard said, "Please come with me, sir."

Four, old Granddad came back, looking very confused. Bomber was in his seat, but Shane was gone. Old Granddad looked right at me and said, "Have you seen my grandson?"

I didn't have the heart to tell him. I didn't have time to tell him, anyway, because Bomber was saying, "He went bye-bye." Just like old Granddad was senile or a small child, Bomber kept saying, "He's all gone. He went bye-bye."

The old man's face kinda sagged and looked like it aged a bit. He took a slow look at all that outfield grass, then started walking down the aisle. Bomber waved to him. "Bye-bye. Bye-bye."

In a way, it broke my heart and in another way, I wanted to launch over the seat and scrape my knuckles on that smug little bastard. I didn't do either. I just watched the old man's slumped shoulders as he walked away. At first, I thought he should've stuck around for the last inning and a half. He could've hung out with me and Jennifer. I would've split my last beer with him. But, of course, he couldn't do that. And something about the way he trudged down the stairs of that aisle and out of the game made me see how I kinda felt inside about baseball. Because I wanted to stick it out to the end of the games, but somewhere between Biff Pocoroba and Javy Lopez, between Phil Neikro and John Smoltz, I lost something big. Sure, I was about to lose the stadium that meant baseball to me, and, sure, I'd lost the inclination to worship twenty-five-year-old men just because they could throw and catch and hit. But it seemed like something bigger was riding on that old Granddad's shoulders. Like neither of us had been kicked out, but in a way, it was time for both of us to leave.

I didn't leave, though. I just sat there until I finally said, more or less to Bomber, "Man, I hate Braves fans."

I don't know what Jennifer was thinking during this time, but whatever it was, it motivated some action out of her. She threw her mostly empty plastic beer cup at Bomber, nailing him in the back. The dregs of her last swallow of beer and bits of backwash splashed up onto the silkscreened, big-nosed president. Bomber spun around, fists up. Jennifer just said, "Sit down, asshole."

There wasn't much left for him to do. It wasn't like he could run and tattle to the security guard over that one. Besides, a few guys behind me had taken up the battle and started yelling, "Down in front," and other variations with the same sentiment, but more profanity. Bomber sat down.

And that was it. In another month, the Braves would leave that stadium and take all their million-dollar men and spineless yuppie fans and pee-watching security guards with them. I'd stop going to games and start looking for a new job and find other excuses for getting drunk in the afternoon. In the meantime, there wasn't much left for me to do except finish my beers and watch the sun set over one and a half scoreless innings.

Originally appeared in issue #8, Spring 2004.

Duckie Nation: Two Writers and Friends, One a Yankee Fan and the Other a Red Sox Diehard, Discuss the Very Nature of Their Disagreements Through the Lens of Pop Culture

Dan Dunford and Ari Voukydis

"Springtime comes, and the leaves are back on the trees again." So begins a relatively obscure song by Wilco side project, Loose Fur, alternately called "Laminated Cat" and "Not For The Season." If you think about it, it's a wonderful sentiment for the Northeast, especially at what feels like the tail end of an excruciatingly bitter winter. However, said sentiment is followed by an afterthought of intriguing nature, as the next line of the song notes that, with the leaves back on the trees, "The snipers are harder to see."

It's as though the verse was written by the collective voice of the Boston Red Sox fan base.

The first sign of spring for many of us in the seasonally desolate Northeastern United States comes courtesy of baseball, when across this continent (and one city in Asia), the opening pitches of the season have been ceremoniously tossed from the outstretched arms of politicians. After all, to quote both Don Henley and Roger Kahn, the players who participate in our national pastime are "the boys of summer." If they're playing ball, that means two things: summer is approaching, and Boston fans are filled with discontent and paranoia.

This year is no exception, courtesy of the New York Yankees' recent acquisition of shortstop Alex Rodriguez. For those of you unfamiliar with Rodriguez and his recent saga, let me draw a parallel. Alex Rodriguez, this winter, was much like Molly Ringwald's character Andie Walsh in *Pretty In Pink*: gorgeous and available. Ultimately, it boiled down to two candidates for his affection and services: the honorable, yet geeky, Duckie (Jon Cryer in the movie, played in this saga by the Boston Red Sox) or the "hunky" Blane McDonagh (Andrew McCarthy/the 26-time World Series Champion Yankees). As in *Pretty In Pink*, the hunk gets the girl. But, unlike the movie, the geek had a real chance to score with the gorgeous girl in the baseball world—in fact, one might parallel what happened to the Red Sox to an alternate version of *Pretty* where Duckie gets into some heavy, heavy petting with Andie and even gets to see her imaginably perky nipples. Yes, folks, it was that close for Alex Rodriguez and the Boston Red Sox. They almost "did it."

Cut to the next morning, and a satiated Alex Rodriguez is smoking in bed—this bed is located in Yankee Stadium's Monument Park, next to the Babe Ruth and Lou Gehrig plaques.

You'd view something as optimistic and beautiful as spring through the twin eyes of bitterness and paranoia, too, if you were a Red Sox fan. (I'm not, but I've been told that I'm pretty "empathetic" for a man, whatever the hell that crap means.) I mean, hell, you do everything short of lip-synching "Try A Little Tenderness" to try to get the prize, and you lose out to the hunk—every year since 1918.

To which I reply, well, so what. Ask any aficionado of Reagan-era teen cinema what they remember about *Pretty In Pink*, and the odds are good that they'll talk about Duckie. Why? Well, it's probably because Duckie carves out the most resonant persona of the movie—in losing, ultimately, he wins the hearts of the viewers. Similarly, the Red Sox have created a dazzling history colored by failure and near-success, from the trade of Babe Ruth through the presumably soul-crushing Aaron Boone home run. Much like Duckie losing Andie to Blane in *Pretty In Pink*, the Red Sox' failures in baseball have been colored by the successes of the archrival Yankees. One wonders what happens to Duckie after the credits roll on *Pretty In Pink*. I think it's safe to assume that he eventually did win the heart of some lucky girl and probably managed to mold himself a remarkable life. Similarly, I'm pretty sure that the Red Sox might someday mold themselves into a champion of some sort or another, if they can only escape the shadow of the Yankees.

The kicker here, echoed in the last scene of another great '80s-era teen movie, *The Last American Virgin*, and the truths at the heart of any unrequited love stories of the era and beyond, is that this will probably never happen. Everybody loves Duckie, but he never succeeds while we're watching him. And, now, we look at Duckie and see that his back's perpetually pinned to the wall—and that wall might as well be the 37-foot behemoth that stands in left field of Fenway Park. I have many friends who are Red Sox fans, and, in a way, I root for them to someday understand the remarkable feeling that you get when your team wins it all. Despite my status as a card-carrying Yankees fan, I'd be the first one to call them and congratulate them if their team ever won a World Series. Ultimately, though, I guess I never expect to make that call. After all, the Red Sox are the human, baseball-based personification of unrequited love. Call them Team Duckie, and remember—if you, too, were doomed to a lifetime as runner-up, you would also see the leaves on the trees and think about hidden snipers.

—Dan

Fan Interference

Dear Dan,

I enjoyed your latest article about Alex Rodriguez and the New York Yankees vís-a-vís *Pretty In Pink*. I believe that you were correct in your assertions, and for all the wrong reasons. It is a matter of public record that:

1) In the original script to *Pretty In Pink*, it is Duckie who ends up with Andie. That's how John Hughes wanted it. During the original screenings, however, the test audiences were creeped out by the "correct" ending because they felt it implied—to put it in a Bushian context—"class warfare;" that the rich were evil and that love, as an ideal, belonged not to the rich but to the integrity punks/nerds. Thus, the ending was changed so that Andie ends up with Blane. If you don't believe me, look it up.

2) I am not making this up. This is a matter of public record.

3) With this in mind, rent *Pretty in Pink* again. The whole plot leads, inexorably, to Duckie and Andie getting together. The hastily added "go to him" part is obviously hastily added.

4) Duckie ends up with Kristy Swanson—not so bad, but not "what the founders had intended" as constitutional scholar Larry Tribe might say.

5) No man with integrity watched that movie and rooted for Blane. Every guy rooted for Duckie. If you rooted for Blane, you probably didn't see the movie in the theaters. Also, you're a douchebag.

6) The moral of the revisionist *Pretty in Pink* is that the rich always win. Moreover, the earnest, punk rock working-class is reduced to flashing a shit-eating grin and settling for the vacuous consolation prize. (Kristy Swanson as Manny Ramirez? Don't ask me, kitten, I only work here.)

7) Let me ask this directly: When you first saw *Pretty in Pink*, were you rooting for Duckie, or Blane? The Red Sox are Duckie. The Yankees are Blane. Steinbrenner is Steff (James Spader's character). If you root for Blane and Steff, then you missed the point.

8) Pokey Reese is Annie Potts.

9) Okay, I'm just making stuff up now.

10) The point is: Blane is the enemy. Steff is the enemy. The Yankees are the enemy. Honestly, how long do you think Andie and Blane really lasted?

11) This one goes to eleven: Rooting for the Yankees is like rooting for the house in blackjack.

—Ari

Dan Dunford and Ari Voukydis

Dear Ari,

While it may be a matter of public record that Duckie was intended for Andie, and it may be at the heart and soul of everybody with half of a heart/brain who watches the movie to believe that Duckie belongs with Andie, it never actually happens. Ask anyone who's ever seen the movie, which is the ultimate public record of *Pretty In Pink*.

I refer you, then, to the countless preseason predictions of writers over the years who, in their own hearts and first drafts (and regardless or not of their affiliation as a member of Red Sox Nation) scripted a season where the Red Sox won it all. I hate to point this out, but there have been several seasons where everything has been scripted toward the inevitable conclusion of a Red Sox title. Then, a horrible tacked-on ending spoils the whole thing. The weird little kink endings to seasons—the ones that have shattered your heart so many times that I hesitate to bring them up—don't they jibe all the more with the "hastily added" assertion about *Pretty In Pink*?

That said, did I—and everyone, really—root for Duckie? Absolutely.

And, if you rooted for Blane, were you a douchebag? I think that's a little harsh—I'd go with "more superficial." What I disagree with is your contention of (paraphrase) "Yankees as Blane, Steinbrenner as Steff." Here's why. It's never that simple. (Of course, you want to codify the parallels between *Pretty in Pink* and the Sox/Yankees battle to make it so that the owner of the Bronx Bombers gets played by professional asshole James Spader. Well played, Voukydis.) But, realistically, we know that in this type of argument and relationship, we're never that removed from it. As fans of our team, we're not watching the movie objectively, we're living it. We are minor, background players, already allied. And, just like in real life, you go with what you know. If you're born and raised next door to Blane, you're more likely to root for him—no matter what the objective reality of the situation. In simple terms, you get caught up. It's life, and it's living. If that means that the Yankee fan base (as opposed to George Steinbrenner) are a collective Steff, then so be it. That's how the cookie crumbles. But, remember, we're just looking after what we know. You would, too, if you were born "on this side of the tracks."

And, as hot as Kristy Swanson is—and she still is (see *Playboy* layout sometime last year, if I'm not mistaken)—she's the consolation prize. The ALDS trophy, if you will.

While Andie and Blane might have never had a wonderful lifelong companionship together, all we can bank on as truth is that they wound up together. In a John Hughes movie, and a John Hughes world, that's the ultimate form of currency. It's the end of the movie. When the screen fades to black, and the lights go on, that's how things are.

We love Duckie, and we root for him, and we see ourselves in him—and, for Christ's sake, there's true and tremendous honor in being Duckie—but his fate is sealed as soon as the movie ends, no matter what the original screenplay might note.

—Dan

Dan,

My point was that your *Pretty in Pink* analogy is, in fact, perfect. Furthermore, in being perfect it underscores the inherent loathsomeness of the New York Yankees. Every time we watch the movie, we don't really believe in our hearts that the ending will magically change; that hey, this time maybe Duckie will get the girl. But though we know the story by heart, we still root for Duckie.

Again: we know he doesn't end up with Andie. But even so, we root for him. It would be amoral to rent *Pretty in Pink* and root for Blane because hey, we know he wins and everyone loves a winner—even if the winner was determined, literally, by choosing money over integrity.

But you know who does that? Anyone who bought their first Yankees cap after 1996. Anyone who abandons their hometown Tigers (or whomever) and gets a Jeter starter jersey and then yells "1918" at me on the street. The signing of A-Rod draws a line in the sand. If you were not a Yankees fan in the '80s, or at least early '90s, it is corrupt to be one now. One thing I pity about lifelong Yankee fans like Mr. Dunford is that they can never trust the company they keep: are the people in the seats next to me, behind me, around me real fans? Or are they the kind of mercenary poseurs who will root for nobody but the overdog? We Sox fans don't have that problem. If you jumped on the Sox bandwagon when they were winning Series after Series, you are very old and probably easy to spot.

The Red Sox Nation will always root for Duckie. It is our nature. And perhaps, this year, some new director's cut will be released and fans will get to see the movie the way it's supposed to end. I wonder: will the nouveau Yankees fans hide their caps, remove their blazers and ties, and claim they were with the good guys all along? What if the Yankees lose several years in a row? What if they lose 84 years in a row? Think they'll still be there? We will. The Nation will. The Nation is. Because the ship will one day be righted, the injustices corrected, the piper paid, and when that happens, a whole lot of Yankees fans—as Steff says to Blane—"won't know whether to shit or go sailing."

—Ari

Originally appeared in Issue #9, Fall 2004.

Part III: Personality Trumps Performance — How > How Well

The Hack Man

Ken Derr

"What becomes a legend most?" Well, when it comes to baseball, everybody has his own criteria. Some focus on clutch playoff performances. Others look at consistency. For my greenbacks, though, a legend has nothing to do with the numbers. Hell, anybody can get lucky in the post-season, and if you believe the sabermetrics geeks, the playoffs are all about luck anyway. No, to attain mythic status, one must perform with style, and it sure helps if that panache has a touch of the middle finger in it. To paraphrase then—who becomes a baseball legend most? Why, the Hack Man, of course.

Jeffrey Leonard was born in Hate City, Philadelphia, in 1955, the height of the Cold War—both seem appropriate to the man who would later be known as "Penitentiary Face" for his sullen scowl. Ironically, Leonard was signed as an amateur free agent by the Dodgers, but wisely made his way out of that great void and ended up in Houston, where he was named *The Sporting News*' Rookie of the Year after he hit .290 with 23 steals for the Astros in 1979. But moving out of a cultural vacuum and into a figurative one (the Astrodome sucked the life right of the game) was no way to make yourself a star, so when Jeffrey was traded, along with skill-deficient Dave Bergman, to the Giants for the work ethic-challenged Mike Ivie in 1981, it was just a matter of time before new nicknames were born.

Leonard bided his time by being aggressively mediocre for most of his years with the Giants. His stare was scarier than Dave Stewart's, but he couldn't match Stew's playoff heroics or his falsetto. He was known as the "Hack Man" for his approach at the plate—an occasional homer, a complete lack of discipline, and a long line of strikeouts. No matter. The Giants, after years of bumbling ineptitude, finally returned to prominence under the Hum Baby tutelage of Roger Craig, whose down-home country manner probably did not sit well with old Penitentiary Face. But baseball is not about making kissy face—it's about winning. So when the Giants finally won the West in 1987 and left to face the Cardinals, few knew that a legend would soon be born.

Leonard changed his Giants uniform number from 20 to 00, perhaps a sign of the nullity of human compassion lurking in his heart, or maybe just a count of San Francisco Giant championships. Maybe that was the catalyst for what came next. Or it might have been the sea of St. Louis red hurling abuse in his general direction, fueling his lust for hate and his compulsion to enrage entire cities. Who can say, but when Leonard homered in that first game, it was not the majestic flight of the ball that suggested a legend in the making. No, it was his trot, the now famous One Flap Down, one arm held against his side and the other extended (one finger would have been, too, in a perfect world). That alone would not have been enough, but he homered again in Game 2, down went the flap, and Cardinals fans began welling up with indignation. How dare he disrespect the house that Bud built?

When the black and orange returned to Frisco for Game 3, Giant outfielder Chili Davis (who, when asked by reporters earlier in the season what he did differently to break out of a miserable slump, replied, "I had 15 Scotch and sodas") referred to St. Louis as a "cowtown," which didn't assure the boys a guided tour of the Arch upon their return to Bovine City for Game 6. Of course, Leonard homered in Games 3 and 4, and his One Flap Down tour of the bases could not have lasted long enough for the hometown faithful. Four games, four homers, all punctuated by the best thirty-second bird in Giants history. So when the Giants returned, up three games to two, the suave fans of heiferland taunted the Hack Man: "Jeffrey Leonard eats quiche!" and "Leonard is a fruit!" Could they possible turn Penitentiary Face into America's least likely poster boy for tolerance?

Well, what happened in those next two games is buried so deeply that it must be lurking in the same murky strata of my subconscious as the event that stole my childhood, the Immaculate Reception. I do remember watching the games in Boulder, Colorado, where I was pretending to attend grad school. Three days later, I dropped out, drove straight to Vegas, and woke up the next morning in the backseat of my VW Rabbit in the parking lot of a stateline casino covered in hundred dollar bills, Colt 45 empties, and soiled underwear. Jeffrey Leonard did everything he could to get the Giants to the World Series, but like my post-graduate career, things ended ugly.

The Hack Man came to spring training in Scottsdale the next year even meaner than before. A buddy of mine was also there, and he somehow got his hands on one of Jeffrey's cracked bats. Where the etched name should have been, it read, FUCK YOU, and it was inverted so it sat at the eye level of the catcher and the ump. Old Testament rage was chewing him up, and he would never approach his '87 greatness again. The Giants eventually traded him to Milwaukee for the poor fielding and non-hitting Ernest Riles. Leonard later briefly rejuvenated his career in Seattle before hanging up the scowl.

The Hack Man spent most of the '90s as a minor league coach and hitting instructor, and would briefly resurface in sports pages in 2001, when Kevin Mitchell instigated a brawl against the team Leonard was managing in the Sonoma Independent League. In 2002 the Giants got their revenge against the Cardinals, sealing the deal when another mean-spirited bastard, Kenny Lofton, who had nearly started a brouhaha of his own earlier in the series after a brush-back pitch, drove in David Bell with the winning run in the bottom of the ninth in Game 5. The *San Francisco Chronicle* looked up Jeffrey during the series, taking him for an unpleasant stroll down memory lane: "That series brings back bad memories for me. I still look at that MVP trophy (Leonard was only the third player in postseason history to win the MVP award while his team lost the series) and have bad feelings. I was never an individual player. I was a team player. I remember holding that trophy during the interviews, saying, 'I want a ring. I want a ring.' Candy (Maldonado) messed up two fly balls, and it killed us. If they needed me to rile them up to play, they shouldn't have been playing." And so it's not just me who suffers acute, pancreatic pains whenever I hear the name Oquendo. It's not just me who wakes up in a cold sweat screaming, "Death to Maldonado, Death to the Candyman!!!"

Jeffrey Leonard may now hold the coveted position of head baseball coach at Antelope Valley College in Lancaster, Calif., but goddammit, the man still cares about the past. He took on an entire city and met its rage with one singular gesture, and the obnoxious flair that forever blurs the line between asshole and hero. What becomes a legend most? One flap down, baby, one flap down.

Originally appeared in issue #8, Spring 2004.

Jose Valentin's Moustache

                                            Jake Austen

Sports fans in cities around the country get excited over different things, be it Big Mac home runs, Shaquille's dunks, or Tiger Woods's Dockers. To me, nothing had been more exciting sportwise in years than the 2000 season of the Chicago White Sox . . . and not because they had the best record in baseball for most of the season. Rather, it was because of something that was right under someone's nose all season, but it took me a while to notice it.

As I do each season, I was obsessively following every Sox game in 2000, but a number of factors have made it difficult to get super into the team for quite some time. Of course, there is the fact that the strike was for the most part our owner's fault, and there is also the awful new stadium that replaced the then oldest park in the world. But really it was more the bad personnel moves that made it hard to totally dig the team. Since firing Jeff Torborg (whose son became a pro wrestler who wore KISS makeup as his gimmick), they have gone through a series of managers who were either schlumps or assholes, and that made it hard to believe the team was headed for greatness.

More importantly, the free agent situation was pretty ugly. Personally, I have nothing against Albert Belle's personality or performance, I like the dude. But the problem is that Frank Thomas (personawise, stats not a factor here) is dull and not particularly pleasant, so adding Belle to Thomas is just redundant from an entertainment standpoint. They also signed Jaime Navarro who was a dick and was also one of the worst pitchers I'd ever seen. Meanwhile, Robin Ventura, who always showed heart, and Ozzie Guillen, who was incredible to watch as he'd fuck around with the runners on base, attempt decoy plays all the time, and generally exude personality, were both canned.

But things looked better the last couple of years. The new manager had a lot of dignity and seemed to have a chance to guide kids to success and the team was stocked with super young farm products. So I was digging the 2000 Sox, but there was still some lingering ambivalence from the preceding years of unpleasantness. I was having a hard time making a true visceral connection with the team. Then it happened. I was visiting New York and had just seen Sebastian Bach's triumphant Broadway turn in *Jekyll & Hyde*. As I walked into Times Square, I expected to find the Sox score easily accessible as they were playing the Yankees. Sure enough, the score was scrolling on the ESPN Zone electronic marquee, and it was a close game. We took a subway to where we were staying and the game was still going on. I was excited, but as I said, not entranced in the way I had been in my younger days. Then I noticed it.

Our new shortstop Jose Valentin was having a good year (he'd already hit for the cycle) so I liked him, but didn't feel a connection. Then, perhaps because whomever directs the Yankees broadcasts has a different philosophy than the Chicago TV crew, I noticed something I hadn't before. Jose Valentin has the most incredible "manly" Latin lover moustache I'd ever seen. It alternates between looking like it's made of the same substance as the black lines Valentin paints beneath his eyes, and looking like it belongs on the construction worker from the Village People (more so when JV's wearing his batting helmet). Take me *out* to the ballgame indeed! That thing is a marvel of human achievement! All of a sudden, I was connected again with the team in a way I hadn't been since the early '90s. I can't really explain it, but that jet black something-or-another that hovers above his lip was so absurd in a fun way that it somehow brought back the pure joy I used to feel while pretending that baseball was important.

My pre-strike, pre-ugly new stadium, pre-zillion dollar contract love of the game *was back*! That road trip became a milestone of the season, as the Sox swept the Yankees and some other teams and never looked back on their way to a division title. But to me it was even more important. The 2000 team became one of my all-time favorites because every member of this super young group of guys seemed great to me in their own way. Unlike previous seasons where I'd really had favorite players, that year the entire team was my favorite, with no real individual standout. But I owe the perspective to enjoy it the way I did to one man…or rather, to one man's patch of facial hair.

Thank you, Jose Valentin's moustache.

Originally appeared in issue #4, Summer 2001.

Batman: Making the Case for the Akron Aeros MEP

Mike Faloon

One of the most difficult aspects of following a minor league team is the high turnover of players. This is especially true when a good minor league team, like the Akron Aeros, is feeding a dying major league team, like the Cleveland Indians.

Despite this, every Aeros home game I've seen in the past two years has delivered entertainment. Sure, the players are great, especially the 2002 club, but they represent only a small part of the Aeros' guaranteed ability to entertain.

The bulk of the credit goes to the team's adult batboy. Or, rather, their batman. Or, to get it right, Batman.

Clad in an Aeros uniform with "Batman" blazing across the back, donning wrist bands and glasses that border on being Sabo-esque, Batman puts on a show each time he steps onto the field. My wife and I became fans at our first Aeros game.

Most batboys pick up a stray bat and scurry back to the dugout. Batman uses a stray bat to kick-start his show. He passes the bat between his legs, twirls it behind his back, and then uses the handle to scoop up a batting helmet. He moves so fast you're certain he'll impale himself but he's as accurate as he is fearless.

In between innings, as the public address system cranks out the hits, Batman steps onto the dance floor. He snaps his fingers to "Runaround Sue," struts to "Hungry Like the Wolf" and unleashes a wide array of full-body spins, side-to-side head bobs, and a full range of arm movements. And, like any successful interpretive artist, he's not bound by his material, choosing to air guitar to the piano-driven "Great Balls of Fire."

Like a seasoned pitcher, Batman knows how and when to pick his spots, never getting in the way of the game. And he supplements his role as showman with that of ambassador. He strikes up conversations with the umps when he brings out fresh balls or a between innings beverage. He guides the first base coach to the coach's box as if he's bringing a plane in for landing. He chats it up with the opposing players, sitting in their dugout while the game is in action. Watching Batman break out his dance moves, the visitors bust out in laughter. But Batman is unfazed.

My theory was that he didn't care if people were laughing with or at him, if they were laughing he felt he was doing his job.

Without planning to do so, I put this theory to the test at the last Aeros game we saw before moving away from Akron. I went down to field level to snap a picture of Batman. As I readied for another shot, Batman saw me looking up at the scoreboard.

Batman: Who's Cleveland playing tonight?

Zisk: Boston, I think.
Batman: Huh, it looks like they're in Cincinnati.

Zisk: Oh yeah, it's interleague tonight. By the way, I've always enjoyed the way you entertain the fans.
Batman: Thanks. (Offers to shake hands)

Zisk: By the way, what's your name?
Batman: Brian.

Zisk: I've always known you just as Batman.
Batman: (Walking back to dugout) Batman is my stage name.

That's a man who knows where it's at, thus substantiating my theory that Batman is the Akron Aeros' Most Entertaining Personality.

Originally appeared in issue #6, Fall 2002.

The Wham of Sam

Jake Austen

Every spring I throw down $20 worth of sports book in Vegas: $5 on the White Sox to win the World Series, $5 on the Bears to win the Super Bowl, and two $5 bets on anyone that's 350 to 1 or so (the Devil Rays and Saints this year). Well, this year, I didn't really feel good about the Sox. It was not a bad feeling about their chances really. (I *always* believe the Sox will come through, no matter how bad they suck.) But for the first time in memory I didn't really *care* about the Sox. It's a strange feeling to be a diehard who sees things get so hard that something dies, but the Sox have driven me there. Though I used to go to 30 or more games a season back in the beautiful, crumbly old Comiskey Park, the antiseptic, super ugly new stadium, with quadrupled ticket prices, and an unsittably steep upper deck really has no appeal to me. But even after moving there the Sox always maintained the tradition of fielding a personality filled team, and that's way more important to me than winning. But over the last few seasons, the management has decided to go the opposite way. Gone is hardcore punk vocalist Scott Radinsky. Gone is moody, nervous Wilson Alvarez. Gone is playful jokester Ozzie Guillen. And though I have nothing against Albert Belle as a player or a person, adding a guy who plays and interacts with his surroundings with no emotion or personality to a team that already has Frank Thomas is like having oil and oil salad dressing.

I made no Sox/Series bet this year. But I needed to have some Sox-related action and I saw a sure bet. Way near the bottom of the "1998 Most Regular Season Home Runs" betting odds was one of my all-time fave Sox stars, Sammy Sosa at 30 to 1 (well below McGwire who was like 5 to 1 or something). Now that was a bet I liked!

Sammy Sosa was one of the best Sox ever. Sure he never hit more than 15 homers for them, but when he got his 150 strikeouts in 1990 he swung so hard on every pitch it was awesome! And sure he was Mendoza material average-wise, but that didn't mean much to us Southsiders. I'll never forget, after going to dozens of Sox games with me the summer after our senior year in high school, my girlfriend noticing all the visiting Boston players' averages and asking why they were all in the never-before-seen *three* hundreds?

And it wasn't just batting magic with Sammy. He had the strongest arm we'd ever seen. However, he'd often miss third (from right) and throw the ball into the stands! One time in an "important" tie game, extra innings with a man on third and less than two outs, the Sox moved Sammy to center with the intention of him fielding the ball no matter where it went . . . and it worked! Speaking of center, as an observant fan there was amazing tension between him and his then (and current with the Cubs) center fielder Lance Johnson. First of all, during pitching changes Sammy and left fielder Ivan Calderon would meet in Johnson's center grass and talk *en Espanol* while Lance just stood there a few feet away, no one to talk to. But the best ever was a time when Lance made the third out getting caught stealing at second. He stood there waiting for Sammy to bring him his glove (as is customary) but Sammy ran past him and gave him this attitudinous shrug. Lance stood there, hands on hips, shaking his head, as peacekeeper Robin Ventura went out of his way to bring Lance his gear. And if all that mega-ego didn't make you love Sammy, he had a bigger Jheri curl than Marlon Jackson on the Victory Tour.

Now how does all that relate to this season? Well, it doesn't. Being traded from the White Sox to the Cubs, from a team playing in a ghetto-located, half-empty stadium, whose fans are working-class goons, to America's most beloved team, who play in beautiful Wrigley Field, in upscale Wrigleyville to a packed house of Yuppie goons, allowed Sammy to reaccess his persona, and I'll be damned if he didn't do the most brilliant job of it I've ever seen. Gone is Latin Machismo Sammy, all ego and gold chains, and born is All-American humble sincere Sammy. I guess it's significant that he got way better, too, but that's less than half of the magic, as far as I'm concerned.

But I guess his home run stuff is as good as any place to start. Even though the popular novelty T-shirt, "I'd Rather have a Sister In a Whorehouse Than a Brother Who's a Cubs Fan" is still seen around New Comiskey, on occasion, the fact is that Sox fans don't necessarily hate Ernie Banks, Billy Williams, Ryne Sandberg (okay, maybe they hate him) or even Wrigley Field, it's the cell phone carrying, briefcase-holding, don't-pay-attention-to-the-game-as-you-socialize-about-the-workplace fans that receive the Southside's ire. That said, I usually go to a few Cubs games a year, especially since Sosa and Lance Johnson, two of my Sox faves, joined the team. This year, at an early season contest, I saw one of my best Cubs game moments yet. Late in a game (that the Cubs had pretty much lost by the fourth or fifth), Sammy cranked one out, a line drive over the left field bleachers, where I was sitting in the back row. Throughout the game there had been this one guy with a glove waiting on Waveland for a home run. This Sammy dinger flew right to the guy without him even moving a step. From very few seats (and not on TV) could the path of that ball be seen, so I was really fortunate to have kept my eyes on it. Of course, I also had to sit in the bleachers with some of the dumbest frat boy stupid motherfuckers on Earth, engaging in verbal abuse with women that I think could legally be defined as rape in most states. But then again, Sammy hit another in the ninth, and all was good and well.

After those two, Sammy went on a tear. He broke the record for most home runs in one month and did all kinds of great stuff. Despite him not being on the Wheaties box or on *Sports Illustrated* with "Big Mac" and Junior, my bet started looking more and more realistic. I might finally cash in a sports book ticket! But as Sammy and McGwire got closer to 61 homers, the really good stuff started. It became apparent that though McGwire might be the better home run hitter, Sammy was doing some things right that were *way* more important. While McGwire cranked them out, he did it in an ugly way. With his beady-eyed, red face bearing down on the pitcher, and his intimidating batting stance, there was always an aspect of crushing the pitcher's weak shit to McGwire's achievements. Sammy, on the other hand, developed an approach that balanced all-business game play (his total concentration batting style), with enough flair to give the fans something to love while not showing up the opposition (his little skip at the beginning of his trot, as opposed to, say, Griffey or Bonds freezing after the swing and not leaving the box). But what really put Sammy over was his new public personality, and as the cameras stopped focusing on Griffey and got Sammy in their sights, that's when the show began.

It turned out that what America wanted, or what "saved" baseball, wasn't athletes being real, or athletes being true, but it was athletes acting like 1940s athletes. Instead of the in-depth answers and deep thoughts that ESPN and other sports shows would have you think the public wanted, what people really desired was a return to athletes saying things like, "Kids, always say your prayers and brush your teeth." It wasn't until McGwire saw Sammy giving those interviews that he lightened up and started doing them, too. He stopped losing hair, and everything became happy and great and All-American again. Each insisted that the other one was the greatest and that they wanted the other one to do great. Each gave the perfect answers about the Maris and Ruth legacies. Each gave the proper respect to the team, and the management and God and whoever. And that turned out to be what *everyone* wanted. Then Sammy started taking it to another level. The real glory of the season was when the off-field Sammy Sosa started to become Sammy Davis, Jr.!

It started off subtly, so subtly I didn't pick it up at first. He wore non-prescription designer glasses (not sunglasses) that looked like Sammy's. He started to display a Sammy-esque sincere-sounding insincere humility. He started to work the interviewers like a seasoned Vegas pro. And then he went all out . . . the jokes! Sammy would tell a joke, for example the "baseball has been very very good to me" bit from *Saturday Night Live*, then he would cock his head to the side and let out this huge, open mouthed laugh—fake but totally believable, like Sammy Davis Jr's. And if that didn't convince you of the show bizzyness of it all, he would tell the same jokes with the same boffo cocked-to-the-side laugh in different cities, and it always worked.

I'm not saying Sammy wasn't sincere about being a good guy or anything, he was just playing the game by the rules that many overlook. And despite the scripted aspect, he displayed plenty of true life moments during the season, as well. When McGwire hit number 62 against the Cubs, the camera went on Sammy, and though the announcers didn't mention it, he was *pissed*! Minutes later, he was hugging Mac, but you could see how much he wanted it for himself on that first shot. McGwire's bouncing around and celebrating seemed kind of forced, as he hugged the Maris family, grabbed his fat son like a weekend-custody dad overcompensating, and gave his beady-eyed thank you speech. Conversely, when Sammy hit his 61st and 62nd a couple of days later, after his curtain calls, as was his ritual, he sat in the dugout, poured some water on his head, and got into a mode of deep focus and concentration rather than a forced joyous celebration mode. This too-real behavior didn't fit the script, and announcer Chip Carey insisted that the close up of Sammy showed him shedding a single tear, although it was obviously the water he had just poured over his head dripping down into his eyes. But despite the moments of his true personality shining through, the post-game Sammy was able to keep up perfect banter and sound bites and never invoke any of the ugliness, stupidity, or criminality associated with sports these days.

As summer went on, I was stricken with Sammy-Fever. I watched or listened to every at bat of every game and was riveted, and unlike all the times in the past when I got obsessed with some odd thing, there was a lot of payoff this time! I started having anxiety dreams of him catching up to McGwire. I would do mathematical calculations all game, every game of how many batters above the minimum needed to reach base for Sammy to get five, six, or more at bats, and I'd check the paper every day to see if "Dumbass" (as I called McGwire) hit another homer.

As the end of the season approached, though, it became apparent that it was more important that he get into the post-season than win the home run title. He wanted that title bad, but the fact that he had said over and over in his perfect little post-game press conferences that the most important thing was making the playoffs made it imperative they did, or else despite the huge numbers, a dark cloud would hang over him. Thanks to the Mets' futility, it happened, and thanks to the serendipity of a one-game playoff between the Cubs and Giants, the Cubs actually got to act like they won a round of the post-season. But from my perspective, what became more important, more than beating McGwire, or even going to the post-season, was him going ahead of McGwire, at any point, after number 61. And when Sammy hit number 66, he did it. He became the first baseball player ever to hit 66 in a season, and even if someone else did it 45 minutes later, the fact that no one had done it for the previous 100-and-something years was pretty great. In that way, it was almost best that he ended the season with 66—that was his number. McGwire deserved to have the title, he really was the Home Run King. He averaged over 60 homers for three seasons in a row. That's unbelievable. However, though he would have probably passed 66, I think those last four were only semi-earned. Though I don't think anyone put any pressure on him, I do believe that the Dominican manager[1] of the team pitching to McGwire to end the season feared that if his pitchers didn't serve up fat ones to Mac that he would be perceived as having national loyalties to Sammy, and there would be repercussions. But whatever. Sure, I didn't get my $150, but that only lasts about five minutes in Vegas, anyhow.

I have a fine postscript, as well. I was awoken one morn with a tip that Sammy would be addressing the city council, and the mayor would be declaring it Sammy Sosa Day. I had an in, so I got to go to the reception, and though I didn't get a photo with Sammy, I did get a nice picture of the cake and an autographed baseball card. The most interesting aspect of this event was that Sammy actually had become a *super*star, and the media crush following him around was amazing, like nothing I'd ever seen before. It was a bigger, more insane treatment than Walter Payton, Andre Dawson, Carlton Fisk, Scottie Pippen, or anyone else this side of Michael Jordan received. And the cake was delicious!

Originally appeared in issue #1, Spring 1999.

---

[1] Expos manager Felipe Alou *–Ed.*

Baseball Is Just Baseball – An Interview with David Shields

Mike Faloon

Baseball is Just Baseball – The Understated Ichiro is a fascinating book. In it, author David Shields collects the most interesting quotes from Ichiro's rookie MLB season (2001). But there's more than meets the eye, both in the way in which the quotes are presented and, as he reveals in the following interview, the way in which Shields thinks about those quotes. Long story shorter, here's what happens when an uncommonly intelligent and insightful writer gets completely wrapped up in the exploits of an uncommonly talented and enigmatic player.

Zisk: I really enjoy the book a lot.
David Shields: Thank you very much.

Zisk: The introduction is excellent.
DS: That was important to get that right, somehow set the tone. For all of last summer, Ichiro, it was very weird, he kind of dominated my summer. From gathering the quotes, to writing that article about Ichiro (for *The New York Times Magazine*), to cheering on the Mariners. It was very strange how totally he occupied our house for that summer. I remember on June 7th saying to someone, I've got to put together these quotes of Ichiro, every day I'm struck by these hilariously funny and subversive and anti-cliché quotes of Ichiro, and then Adam (from TNI Books) published the book two months later, it was amazing.

Zisk: That's remarkably fast.
DS: It really was. We were very aware that it was a special season, and we thought if we had a chance to gain some attention this was it, right now, so Adam and I went into overdrive. It was a really interesting project.

Zisk: How would you characterize the extent to which you followed the Mariners before that?
DS: Pretty much of a fan. I don't know if you know some of my other books, I wrote a book called *Black Planet*, which has a subtitle *Facing Race During an NBA Season*. That book is sort of about me being a Gary

Payton fan. My first novel, a book called *Heroes*, is about a sports writer in the Midwest who's obsessed with this college basketball player. It's clearly a theme that pervades my head. I'm definitely a sports fan. I keep trying to not be but that seems to be part of my make up. I'm definitely a baseball fan, but that year was amazing. It really had a nice feel in Seattle that if you walked around at night you'd hear the radio coming out of houses and you know, you drove around and you heard people cheering. It was a shame it ended so abruptly although you were probably happy if you were a Yankees fan.

Zisk: No, I live in New York but hate the Yankees.
DS: Good for you. To me it's bizarre anyone who'd be a Yankees fan. I was born and raised in L.A. and my dad was raised in Brooklyn so I have this anti-Yankees thing. To me it's weird to root for the Yankees so I'm delighted you're not.

Zisk: One thing I noticed about the book is that all of the quotes are from March through June, the first half of the 2001 season.
DS: Good point.

Zisk: So now you've had the second half of last year and most of this year, how does that alter or add to your perception of Ichiro?
DS: During that time, I had these huge cardboard boxes of everything Ichiro had ever said. I had Japanese grad students translating these things from Japanese for me. Since the book got published, I haven't been paying quite as careful attention to Ichiro's utterances, but I feel like in the last year I've become more convinced of the argument in the book. To me, the argument the book tries to make, kind of a delicate thesis, is: is it just bad translation? Is Ichiro oblivious of American clichés? Or are there some people who want to make every utterance that Ichiro makes into some kind of Zen wisdom? At the time I published the book, I was honestly open to saying perhaps it's just bad translation. But over time, I've become more than ever convinced that Ichiro really is this amazingly alert and in-tune person whose gift is the way he does exist within the moment, is completely oblivious to abstraction, to obsessing on the past, to worrying about the future, and is just amazingly present. He has all kinds of gifts. He has great eyesight, great eye-hand coordination. He works very hard at his craft, but I think one of his main gifts is that he's really amazingly in the present moment. Like a ball is coming to him and he actually watches the ball. He doesn't sort of watch the ball; he really, really, really watches the ball. I think that a lot of Ichiro's sayings, a lot of their core is him taking sports writers' clichés and refusing to answer on the grounds that the cliché happens to be based on, and instead trying to affirm, you know, I'm just in the present

moment. The best example I can think of occurred after the book got published and he made this great catch, I think to help achieve win number 113 or something, and they asked him, "When did you know you were going to catch the ball?" And Ichiro said, "When I caught it."

Zisk: *Laughs*
DS: I'm glad you laugh because people say, "What's so funny about that?" He's supposed to give them all this melodramatic Sturm und Drang and instead he's just there in the moment. So to me it's really this sort of wisdom book about really paying attention to where you are, whether you're an athlete or a bus driver or a writer or whatever. It's really about being there, you might say.

Zisk: When you say that it reminds me of the Peter Sellers movie (*Being There*).
DS: The title of my article for *The New York Times Magazine* was "Being Ichiro" so I guess they were trying to make that connection, too. Some people want to say he's some kind of idiot savant, that American writers like me are making too much of him, that he'll say, I want some lunch, and I then pretend that's brilliant Zen statement. In the last year, his play, his demeanor, and his statements do nothing but confirm my sense that he is indeed the sort of Zen craftsman or Zen artist that I want to claim that he is. Absolutely nothing has happened that diminishes that sense for me.

Zisk: If you were to take a book of quotes from any other baseball player it wouldn't be this engaging.
DS: No.

Zisk: And there are plenty of intelligent guys who give good interviews, but nothing Tom Glavine says makes you scratch your head or think about the game in a different way. And Ichiro's not the first person born in Asia to come to a lot of attention in the U.S., so there are precedents on many levels, and no one is like him. Some of his quotes are as simple as the one you just mentioned—I knew I was going to catch it when I caught it—but there are others like, I like the fans, I appreciate them but I don't play the game for them.
DS: Exactly.

Zisk: I didn't expect a quote like that.
DS: I know. Just when you think you have him typed as some sort of polite Japanese player, he'll say something fairly aggressive in his assertion of his own right to be left alone. He's very hard to track in that way. When the book came out last year, I developed a little talk about it

and there are ten themes cascading through the book, and I try to pattern them so they're sort of presented in mini-clusters, sort of Zen moments, when he refuses to be a symbol of Japanese baseball, there are all kinds of others.

Zisk: Yeah, one of the things I was curious about in reading the book I noticed the quotes were not in chronological order. Is that what you had in mind, what you were just referring to?

DS: Without being too grandiose about it, I do think of the book as kind of an act of composition. It's not just me slapping together about one hundred and ten quotes. Adam and I really spent a lot of time trying to get the quotes right so that they felt like they have a rhythm, some kind of pattern and, yeah, chronological was the last thing we wanted to do. I'm sort of digging out my notes here. What are some of the patterns to it? There's this whole focus on sort of fighting the hype in which they'll ask why he wouldn't appear on the cover of *Sports Illustrated* and he says, "Because I haven't done anything yet." Then there's this one where he uses humor. They ask him what his acupuncture stick is called and he says, Wood. He's constantly trying to take away abstraction from the eyes of the questioner and say, "Listen, it's just a piece of wood. You may want to gloss it all with all these sort of Asian stereotypes and have me do this whole shtick about being Asian but I'm just going to tell you that it's a piece of wood." One thing that I think is really nice about him, he's really aware of the limits of communication. I did a short interview with him for my *New York Times Magazine* piece and he's really aware that in a twenty-minute interview you're not going to get to know each other very well. You can't even begin to know me in twenty minutes so let's not pretend. He has a sense of how profound and difficult human communication is and he just has a wonderful sense of, I'll try to answer your questions, but I'm not going to pretend we're going to become best friends in twenty minutes. Whereas someone else would go through this shtick where you're trying to bond in this sort of symbiotic way and the journalist is getting what he wants and the athlete is getting what he wants. The key to his appeal is that, to me, he really is this pretty mysterious person.

Zisk: Even though he is so well-known around the world, an international figure.

DS: Right, and I think that's really true of most really iconographic people like Madonna or Elvis Presley or even Jesus. They're real contradictions, and that's a point I try to make in my *New York Times Magazine* piece. I try to argue that a lot of icons, I talk about Michael Jordan perhaps, Elvis Presley, Madonna, Jesus, Ichiro, obviously you can think of exceptions that don't prove the rule, but I think that a lot of them, they embody contradictions in this very complete way. They're both total rebels and completely conventional. You can't really solve their mysteriousness because to me the moment you can really name what they are, they lose their hold on you. I think Ichiro is really very much like that.

Zisk: Did you receive any feedback from either Ichiro or the team?

DS: No. Just like when I published my book about the Sonics, absolutely zero response from the team. If you're not sort of writing the totally standard thing, it doesn't really register for them. A few other themes that strike me as important about the book are his emphasis on process, you know, don't focus on the product, focus on the process. The way he tends to value experience over expectation and the way he urges kids to find something passionate to believe in. The way he tends to refuse being viewed as a symbol whenever someone wants to turn him into a symbol of Japanese baseball he tends to definitely refuse that gesture. I've gone into a bunch of schools and those are the themes I talk about. To me it's a book of wise sayings that kids can apply to their own lives.

Zisk: How about the feedback from readers?

DS: I've gotten a lot of wonderful comments out of nowhere, people just loving the book. It's sold pretty well. It's published by Adam's small press, TNI, and sold more copies than some books I've published with major corporate publishers. It was published in Tokyo, and it was on the paperback best-seller list in Japan. It's been fun, and, for awhile, there was a guy who had a stand near Safeco and he was selling the book like a couple hundred yards from Safeco Field, it was neat. Days I would go to the game and walk by his stand, you felt very much a part of the community; it was sort of cool. And he would tell me, 'We sold eighteen this week,' or whatever. It was sort of a wild idea I had and two months later there it was on a stand right next to the guy selling popcorn.

Zisk: I was surprised that as a position player Ichiro received much different treatment than Japanese pitchers who have come to play in the U.S. There seem to be a lot of, "We can accept Japanese pitchers but Japanese position players won't be able to cut it." It seemed racist, "Asians are too small to come up against big, bad Americans," almost a Eugenics thing. And there was a quote in the book where (ESPN commentator) Rob Dibble said, I'll run through the streets naked if he (Ichiro) hits better than .280. These comments sounded similar to those made when blacks began playing in the majors in the '40s, and I'm wondering what you thought of that.

DS: Definitely, Ichiro faced a little bit of fairly overt racism when he played the first couple of weeks against the A's in the Oakland Coliseum and people were saying things like, Remember Pearl Harbor, and stuff like that. And they were throwing quarters at him and making derogatory remarks and gestures, all kinds of stuff. He sort of amazingly refuses to ever engage in self pity or, you might say, play the race card even when it seems completely justified. But through humor and wit, he beautifully transcends it and shows these people to be just completely inferior to his intelligence because he just says, "Oh no, those weren't quarters, that was rain coming from the sky." And in so doing, to me, he brilliantly retires the issue and transcends it. He has a wonderful way about him. Other players like him; he tends to be funny and self-deprecating. He's sort of a show off and he's not how Americans view Asian players typically. He can be exhibitionistic and demonstrative, and he's sort of a showboat at times. It's almost like he says, from the moment he arrives, "I'm not going to be your Japanese houseboy, I'm just not going to do it. I'll either be funnier than that, I'll be more aggressive than that; I'll be more subversive than that, I'll be wittier than that." In a way it's very assertive, I'm not going to play that role for you. So even though he's very different from say, Gary Payton, the trash-talking Seattle Sonics player, in a way he's just as subversive of American sports clichés, and I think that was sort of my connection to him, that I'm really interested in language, in people, you might say, screwing up the language. Gary Payton screws up the language in a certain way, Ichiro screws it up in another way. He's really amazing.

Zisk: Another factor was the number of games in a season. In Japan they play about 130 games a year and MLB plays 162, Do you have the stamina to hold up for an American season? He downplays that, too, and it goes back to what you said before, weighing experience over expectation—I'll let you know in game 131.

DS: Exactly. There was a moment around early August or so where he really seemed to be tiring, and perhaps they figured him out blah, blah, blah. Bust him inside with fastballs and throw these curves on the outside that he doesn't have the strength to hit out and just when your worst fears were starting to be realized, he went on this amazing streak where he batted about seven hundred with runners on base, it was unbelievable. Just when you needed him to prove the doubters wrong, that's exactly what he did. Again, if you asked him if that's what he's doing, he'd say, "Of course not." But then he'd sort of wink at you. The way his performance and his articulation are at complete variance really fascinates me because you know that's what he's doing, trying to prove these naysayers wrong, but ask him if that's what he's doing, and he would dearly deny it. It was fascinating to watch. He's like a great performance artist who always keeps you from seeing, almost like a striptease artist, you never quite see what you want to see. (Laughs) He's always keeping you off balance a little bit.

Zisk: The other day I was watching an Andy Kaufman video . . .
DS: I'd love to see that.

Zisk: He does this amazing bit where he's a character playing a character playing a character and yet none of them seem like the real guy.
DS: And it's crucial that you can never quite touch ground, crucial that you never feel quite safe.

Originally appeared in issue #6, Fall 2002.

PART IV
THOSE WHO STUDY HISTORY WANT TO REPEAT IT—
LOOKING BACK AGOG AND AGHAST

Mitch

Ken Derr

In the annals of great sports losers, the Cubbies and the Bosox get all the slobbery press. Us West Coasters are fed a steady diet of sappy pieces about those "loveable" laughing stocks an entire nation is supposed to get all weepy aw-shucksy over every year when they fall face first in the grime, and every year I refuse with more vitriol than ever. Why? Because we have our own soul crushers on the bay, god damn it, and they're Giants in heartbreak only. Since they left their old Polo Grounds stomping ground, the Frisco boys in black and orange have failed to deliver a single championship to the faithful. These days, it's even more difficult to prop yourself up on the couch and submit to September disappointment, because outside of Richie Aurilia and Dusty Baker (sad to think that the manager, for god's sake, is the most popular member of a sports organization), the Gyros are decidedly unlikable. You can root for Barry Bonds because he transcends the game, but he's one miserable human being. Jeff Kent's most endearing moment was that cockamamie story about falling off his truck while washing it at the do-it-yourselfer. His moustache speaks for itself.

Alas, it wasn't always so in Giantland, for while they never quite reached the level of screwball team character of those A's asylums of the 1970s, they once produced a few first-class nutcases. Gaylord Perry delivered more gobbers than all of London in '77. Who can forget the Hack Man, Jeffrey (don't call me Jeff) Leonard, and his patented One Flap Down home run trot? But for my dime, the greatest spaz in Giants' history was Kevin Mitchell. Now Mitch only played five of his fifteen seasons with San Fran, but oh, the memories. Legend has it he started in baseball to escape the mean streets of San Diego, where he absorbed three gunshot wounds while running with the notorious Syndos gang. He also brawled with Daryl Strawberry during a pickup basketball game, and clearly the Straw never got over that. In his first year as a major leaguer, few remember that Mitch started the Mets' game-winning rally with a two-out single that Buckner later lost. He was then unceremoniously traded to the Padres, where he was pegged the local boy to turn that sad train around. It didn't quite work, though, as he began running with the homies and "lost his focus."

He was traded to the Giants, and I remember exactly where I was the day he played his first game—drinking tequila in the parking lot of a Jackson Hole motel, playing Frisbee with my little brother, and wondering whether we should drink beer or vodka next. The Giants were in Chicago (it's no accident that the Cubbies and Red Sox play prominent roles in this story—losers find each other), and we sat riveted in front of the set as the big man hit two out on Waveland Ave. We were plastered in the early afternoon, riding that rare wave of intoxication, motel summer, and freshly traded player done good. Mitch was in our drunken hearts forever.

Never one to shy away from drink or a large buffet, Mitchell continued to put on weight during the '88 season, finally resembling a sumo bulldog with a gold tooth. He slumped during that year, but his greatest moments were yet to come. My all-time favorite baseball highlight is still Mitch, probably hungover and half-asleep in the outfield, breaking late for a fly ball into the left field corner. Either incapable or unwilling to break stride, he overran that white spec and then reached back with his *bare hand* to make the catch. He could have dropped dead on the spot and his godliness for late-night *This Week in Baseball* watchers would have been assured. I still think they ought to place a marker on that spot that reads, "Home of the Last Baseball Badass." Mitch went on to hit 47 homers and drive in 125 runs in 1989, winning the National League's Most Valuable Player award. Along with Will Clark, he also led the team to the World Series, which, in true Giant fashion, was overshadowed by a devastating earthquake that rocked the Stick and delayed the Series. The team never recovered, and neither did Mitchell.

He was eventually traded to the Mariners. He showed up 30 pounds overweight and never found a home in Starbucksland. He did pretty well in Cincinnati, but did not make headlines again until he signed in '95 with the Fukuoko Hawks in Japan, becoming the highest paid player in the history of that league. Trouble bubbled again when the team refused to let Mitch return to the States for knee treatments, so he went AWOL for ten weeks, hanging in the old hood, quaffing down Scotch and sodas for "physical therapy." He finally went back and hit a cool .300 for the season, but he came back to America for good the next year. The nation of Japan breathed a collective sigh of relief.

His last MLB seasons were relatively undistinguished, as he bounced from Cleveland to Boston and finally ended his career here, in my hometown of Oakland. And while we heard rumors that Giants' manager Dusty Baker wanted to give Mitch a tryout, Kevin never made it back to the majors after that final season with the A's. He did, however, make it back to the sports pages. In 2000, he joined the Western League's Sonoma County Crushers, and in one game, after Solano Steelhead Jim Converse's pitch sailed behind Mitch's back, he charged the mound and popped Converse in the mouth. A brawl ensued, and after Mitch "engaged" some Steelhead fans, he strolled over to the stands and punched Steelhead owner Bruce Portner in the face. The owner pressed charges, which did little to deter Mitch's boys. The Crushers fought with fans two games later in Yuma, Arizona, while Kevin sat out his nine-game suspension. Did I mention the manager of the Crushers was Jeffrey Leonard, the Hack Man? Two years later, Mitchell took over as Crusher manager, and it didn't take him long to live up to his team's name. In yet another game against the Steelheads, the new manager attacked Steelhead third base coach Larry Olenberger for allegedly stealing signs, and was ejected. His spot at the helm is said to be shaky.

Kevin Mitchell won the highest prize in professional baseball, and he missed part of spring training after surgery to repair a tooth damaged by a microwave chocolate doughnut. He has a mean and violent temper, and he loves his grandma more than anyone else in this rotten world. He invented more excuses to get out of games than Kenny Stabler in the exhibition season, and his smile makes children burst into giddy laughter. Giant fans are used to losing. But it sure makes the medicine go down easier if it's taken with a spot of insanity and a gold-toothed smile. Thanks for the memories, Mitch. Have a trough of drinks on me.

Originally appeared in issue #6, Fall 2002.

Adrián Beltré's Right Nut

Todd Taylor

It's safe to say that no dude likes getting hit in the nuts really hard.

On Wednesday, August 13, 2009, during the ninth inning, Seattle Mariner third baseman Adrián Beltré Pérez attempted to field a routine ground ball off of the White Sox's Alexei Ramírez. The ball took the unkindest hop of all. With great force, it smashed into Beltré's right testicle. Although Beltré was able to recover the ball (the one in his mitt), his throw to first base was far off the mark, resulting in an error.

"It hurt pretty bad," Beltré said about the ball's impact. "It was hurting me pretty much the whole game after that."

After the ball-to-ball contact, Beltré played five more innings and had three more at-bats. He was suffering from a yet-undiagnosed tear in his testicle, which had become contused from the blow. (Picture one of the claymation California Raisins doing an extended blues sax solo.) In the tenth inning, Beltré tackled the White Sox's Scott Podsednik on a pickoff attempt from catcher Rob Johnson.

Blood continued to coagulate in Beltré's scrotal sac through the fourteenth when Beltré singled and then dove back into first base during a pick-off attempt. The game ended with a Ken Griffey, Jr. single and Beltré scoring the game-winning run.

Poor workmen blame their tools. Professionals play through pain and act like nothing's out of the ordinary. Beltré left the field stoically and assessed the damage in the clubhouse. "When I looked down, after the game, it wasn't a pretty sight. My testicle got the size of a grapefruit." The average, unwhacked-by-great-force male testicle is approximately the size of an unshelled almond, fig, or robin's egg. Beltré iced his injury. He was put on the disabled list. Surgery was scheduled.

Beltré is a man who needs room to boogie. He had not been wearing a cup when the accident occurred.

Adrián, a native of the Dominican Republic and born in Santo Domingo in 1979, had signed with the Dodgers organization when he was fifteen years old. During his youth and when he played on the Liceo Maximo Gomez High School team, he had never worn a cup. "When I came through the Dodger camp, they forced me to use it," Beltré said, "but I told them I can't play like that. I feel like I can't move."

Beltré advanced to the majors, debuting with the Dodgers in 1998 at the age of nineteen. He didn't view wearing a cup as a minor inconvenience. It sucked. He felt it as an unnecessary hunk of plastic in a restrictive place that prevented him from playing his best game. Beltré's a steely dude. He isn't a whiner. The cup wasn't just a minor inconvenience. Prior to the 2001 season, while in spring training with the Dodgers, he suffered the after-effects of a botched appendectomy. While healing from a second operation to close the wound left by the first, he fielded ground balls while wearing a colostomy bag.

C-bag? No problem. Cup? No ma'am.

And so, for over an entire decade, the quick-fielding Maginot Line-style hands of this third baseman were all the protection he had needed to stop all balls advancing into his groinal area. Thousands of balls had hurtled toward him at over one hundred miles per hour from one hundred feet away. In 2007, he won a Gold Glove.

But if decade's-worth of watching *America's Funniest Home Videos* has taught me anything it is that it only takes one direct shot to the snacks to convert one man's private tragedy into a nation's laughter.

Mariners' manager Don Wakamatsu used Beltré's misfortune as a public service announcement directed to aspiring baseball players. "This guy is not a guy that hadn't played a long time in the majors. But sometimes you think your hands are so quick, it will never happen to you. The word is—no matter how good you are—that one chance is not worth taking. Wear a cup."

Beltré's confidence in his skills and his freedom of movement had far eclipsed concerns for his nuts' safety and continued sperm production.

"If it happens every ten years and you get hit there, it's not bad," Beltré reasoned. "I have never been hit right in the spot (before). It's been close, which hurt, but not right on one of the testicles. A cup just got in the way . . . I made a play and dove and it hurt more when you had the cup on than without it. I never liked it . . . I couldn't run. I couldn't move."

In the two weeks that followed the incident, while on the fifteen-day disabled list, the final diagnosis was good. Although there had been internal bleeding and there was a tear on the testicle wall, there was no permanent damage. All systems go. Clean bill of health. Unshelled almond-sized testicle once again.

Upon Beltré's return, Wakamatsu insisted his third baseman wear a cup to facilitate a complete recovery.

When reporters asked if Beltré—father of two—would consider "cupping up" upon his return, his response was similar to that of old bikers when requested to voluntarily wear helmets "for safety's safe:" a fuck you that almost sounds like a yes.

On Wednesday, September 2, 2009, in his first at-bat after the errant ball, Ken Griffey Jr. got the stadium to play Tchaikovsky's "Nutcracker Suite" as Beltré stepped into the batter's box.

As for the cup?

"I wore it for a couple days," Beltré said, "so they think I'm wearing it. After that, I stopped. At the end of the year, I was back to normal."

Beltré is currently swingin' in the breeze once again with the Red Sox.

Postscript: A Short History of the Jock Strap and the Cup
Adrián Beltré had a five-year, sixty-five million dollar contract with the Mariners. A fancy jock strap with an ergonomic cup runs around fifty bucks. It's reasonable to assume that finances weren't the reason he didn't wear one. It was freedom. Freedom of movement. Freedom to play baseball in the manner most comfortable to a player, regardless of the risks involved. Freedom from the Man cupping several precious ounces in the name of security from future attacks. What is comfortable and right for one man may not be for another. What is important is the right to choose and the pursuit of happiness, be it commando-style or hardened protection. In contrast to Beltré, pitcher Tom Seaver of the NY Mets used the security of two straps, plus a pair of jockey shorts, all sandwiching a plastic cup fitted inside the second jock. During his career, he threw 3,640 strikeouts with his "kids" wrapped up like a mummy during Halloween.

Let's set down the equipment basics. What's referred to, almost interchangeably as "the jock strap" or "the cup," is actually a two-part system. "The cup" is a piece of hard material used to physically shield the genitals from impact. Such cups normally define a cavity area which is designed to encase the male genitals. The original designs look like urinals and bananas. The new ones—like the NuttyBuddy and the Shock Doctor—are more contoured and form fitting. The NuttyBuddy, in particular, looks as if you cupped Michelangelo's *David*'s groin with loving, careful hands, and formed a PG-rated bump of plastic in that private place.

"The jock strap" is a garment that houses and positions the protective cup. It was traditionally a knit pouch held up above by a wide elastic waistband and below from two leg straps going upward from the groin. Jock straps have, in recent years, been largely replaced by compression shorts (stretchy boxer briefs) with a pocket for the cup to be inserted into and look a lot less like the wearer is in a Cameo video or an extra on *A Clockwork Orange*.

In 1874, Charles Bennett was approached by the Boston Athletic Club to design an undergarment that would help alleviate the blistering and chafing which resulted from the friction between a bicycle jockey's dangling testicles, the bicycle's seat, and the violent jostles provided by Boston's rough, irregular cobblestone streets. The thin material of a union suit wasn't limiting the sway of a heated scrotum against the surface of an unforgiving seat. A device was needed to comfortably hold the genitals close to the body so they didn't bounce around—and get crunched—during vigorous athletic activity. Bennett adapted the idea of women's girdle, but for dudes, positioned a little bit lower. Athletic supporters were born. The garment's original trademark name was the Bike Jockey Strap. Its insignia was a penny-farthing's spoked wheel. Over time, the undergarment became known simply as a jock. Bennett's invention was a continued success. In 2005, after over 130 years in production, Bike had made its 350 millionth jock strap.

Unlike the reasonably verifiable origins of the jock strap, there is very little corroborating evidence—or even a claim about—who first inserted a cup into the jock. Specifically designed to lessen the impact of hard objects hurtling at high speeds to protect the male genital area, there is speculation that it found its way into hockey rinks soon after Bennett's invention. However, *The Cultural Encyclopedia of Baseball* credits White Sox catcher Claude Berry with introducing "the safety cup" to major league baseball in 1904. Berry's cup was made out of steel.

To this day, Major League Baseball regulations state that only the catchers are required to wear a protective cup. It is voluntary compliance for all other players, primarily enforced by their ball clubs in the name of safety, prolonged productivity, and the protection of valuable assets.

Originally appeared in issue #19, Fall 2010.

KY Jelly and Moral Responsibility

Ken Derr

All this talk about cheating in baseball is wearing me out. If these boys want to play their homoerotic games in the privacy of their own stalls, who am I to say Lyle Alzado? Yeah, maybe some drug-twisted version of Ronnie's trickle-down theory could ensue, and soon sixth graders will be creamin' and clearin' and mainlinin' dinosaur hormones and highlighting *I Was a Grade School 'Roid Monster* instead of *Island of the Blue Dolphins*, but until then, can we descend self-righteous mountain?

Okay, so I'm kidding. But let's drift back to a happier time, when cheaters took pride in their art and bragged about getting away with it. Take Gaylord Perry, The Expectorator. Perry believed in the spittle, the grease and the KY. He used to touch himself all over his cap and face before each pitch, even if he wasn't doing any doctoring. Like any great seductress, he believed in the power of mystery, and if the hitter thought Gaylord might be illegally liquefying that next pitch, it might just be the psychological edge Perry needed. It was illusory cheating as weapon—can you dig it?

Perry was not, however, just a greasy gimmick. He could get folks out, and he has the numbers to prove it. He won 314 games in his 22-year career, and he was the first pitcher to win the Cy Young in both leagues (1972 with the Indians and 1978 with the Padres). He and his brother Jim won more games than any sibling combo except the Niekros, and we all know their sandpaper story didn't end well. In 1983, Perry became the third pitcher to pass Walter Johnson's strikeout record of 3509 Ks (along with Steve Carlton and Nolan Ryan). He pitched a no-hitter in 1968, and he was inducted into the Hall of Fame in 1991. Not bad for a man who once reportedly approached the makers of Vaseline about endorsement possibilities but was rebuffed with a one-line postcard reading, "We soothe babies' backsides, not baseballs."

One story about Perry had nothing to do with slime, but with his alleged feebleness at the plate. In his rookie season in 1963, legend has it that Alvin Dark boasted they'd put a man on the moon before Perry hit a home run. Well, within minutes of Apollo 11's historic touchdown on the lunar surface, Perry launched his own rocket over the wire fence at Candlestick Park. When Perry was asked about this later, he said, "Alvin was right. But only by an hour."

Unlike today's phony denials and "integrity of the game" histrionics, most folks just smirked and looked for one-liners when commenting on Perry's antics. Catcher Gene Tenace said that Perry's pitches arrived with so much goop that he couldn't get the ball to leave his hand when he tried to throw it back, so he made trips to the mound on the pretense of talking strategy, just to give the ball back to his pitcher. Billy Martin once joked that when you walked by Perry, you smelled a drugstore. Gene Mauch argued that they should attach a KY tube to Gaylord's Hall of Fame plaque, but shockingly, the powers-that-be refused. Perry titled his autobiography, *Me and the Spitter*, for god's sake. I'm betting we won't be seeing Ivan Rodriguez's *Me and the Juice Up My Ass* any time soon.

Maybe it's the shamelessness of Perry's confessions that's so endearing. Jose Canseco's self-righteous rat tour and the sanctimonious defensiveness of the accused ring so hollow compared to Perry's, "Aw shucks, see if you can catch me." Try to imagine Sammy Sosa calling up Balco to do commercial spots and then winking at Bud Selig and saying, "Test me. I dare you." Gaylord didn't care. Try to imagine Roger Clemens saying, "I'd always have grease in at least two places, in case the umpires would ask me to wipe one off. I never wanted to be caught out there with anything though, it wouldn't be professional." When Gaylord won his 300th as a Yankee, he sported a T-shirt after the game that read, "300 is nothing to spit at." This from a man who wasn't busted for using grease until his twentieth season in the show.

So maybe he's not the finest role model for our kids in the "everybodygetsatrophyera," but at least he didn't wrinkle his face with indignation and trot out his lawyers every time somebody suggested he was lubing pitches. Instead, he used the hype surrounding his transgressions to his advantage. In an age defined by hypocritical moral huffery and holier-than-thou posturing, there is something refreshing about a man who looks like grandpa after a three-day moonshine-bender rubbing KY jelly on a ball so it to dances away from ripped 22-year-olds and then winking about it. And yeah, sliming a baseball doesn't lead to roid rage or shrunken testicles or brain fever. The physical and emotional costs of steroids can be horrific, so maybe the haha has been drained from the issue. But I can't help thinking that if Melky Cabrera dropped trough at his first spring training press conference and cracked, "Wanna check my tracks?" somewhere Gaylord Perry would be chuckling.

Originally appeared in issue #10, Spring 2005.

A History of Cheating in Baseball

John Shiffert

Poor Ozzie Guillen. Everybody's on his case. He's politically incorrect. He's insensitive. He has his spikes in his mouth so often he's qualified to go to dentistry school. Even his GM, Ken Williams, isn't happy with him. And now, he's been accused of stealing signs. Of cheating. Tsk, tsk, tsk.

Although the St. Louis Cardinals are only the latest outfit to complain that Ozzie and Co. were getting their signs in U.S. Cellular Field—maybe from a center-field camera—they were among the most vocal, to the extent that the *St. Louis Post-Dispatch* picked up the story. Maybe the Sox' 20-6 and 13-5 wins over the Redbirds during interleague play in June had something to do with that. Nonetheless, the Sox' manager was unfazed by the flap, answering the Cards' charges in, of all places, the *Chicago Sun-Times*.

"They couldn't see the scoreboard because there were so many numbers up there," he said, laughing when asked about the *Post-Dispatch* report. "The way we swung the bats, it looked like it. But what happened [the other day]?"

Guillen was referring to the Sox' 1-0 victory over Cards' rookie Anthony Reyes, who threw a one-hitter, allowing only a Jim Thome homer. It could probably be said, in fact, that Reyes only made one bad pitch the whole game. However, an inside fastball to Jim Thome is a *very* bad pitch, and one that he doesn't need a sign for.

So what happened after the Sox had molested the Cardinals staff for 33 runs in two games (giving Mark Mulder a bad enough beating that he went on the DL—actually, he had a shoulder injury)? The *Post-Dispatch* quoted an unnamed Cardinal who said the team changed signs after the fifth inning of the 13-5 rout. Interestingly, the *Post-Dispatch* noted, Chicago was 40-for-88 with 15 extra-base hits and 33 runs before the change, and then went 4-for-36 with one run scored afterward. However, in the White Sox response on their website, it was pointed out that the sudden Chicago offensive drop-off also coincided with the Cards removing Jason Marquis, who the Sox were using for batting practice, from the 13-5 game.

On his part, Guillen did not make any pejorative comments about the *Post-Dispatch* or its writers. (Of course, Jay Mariotti writes for the aforementioned *Chicago Sun-Times*.) In fact, he said he was not offended by the allegations and generally made light of the matter.

Now, whatever you may think about Ozzie Guillen, his making light of the sign stealing allegations is just following a great baseball tradition. "Cheating" has been an integral part of the game since the Knickerbockers lost control of their gentleman's pastime back around 1858 or so. And, making light of cheating allegations has been just as integral to baseball. In fact, really good cheaters are often celebrated after a fashion. Going contrary to the rules in some form is so ingrained in baseball that it's practically not cheating, it's sort of legal cheating. For that matter, even the *Post-Dispatch* article referred to the Sox' alleged actions as "gamesmanship" and not cheating. Now, before everyone gets on their high horse about baseball rule-breaking, be reminded that baseball is not the only sport where this happens. Ever see a soccer player cheat down the sideline ten feet on a throw-in? Or move the spot for a free kick closer to the goal? Or take a dive when an opposing player makes a tackle? For that matter, ever see a hockey player take a dive on incidental contact? (The Philadelphia Flyers' Bill Barber made a career out of this move.) Or a punter fall down when an opponent gets to close trying to block the kick? ("Don't rough the punter!")

You get the picture. Such is the nature of sports. It is very common to try to get away with something. So common that to even consider trying to thoroughly review all the means by which baseball players and teams have "cheated" over the years is utterly foolish. Having said that, some of the more common have been rule bending, using ringers, cutting the bases, impeding baserunners, faking catches, fixing the field, altering the ball, altering the bat, and sign stealing.

Baseball barely had codified rules before players started figuring out ways to bend them. Although they weren't the first team to do so, the original Cincinnati Red Stockings, during their undefeated 1869 season, took advantage of the fact that the infield fly rule hadn't been invented, turning double plays on deliberately dropped infield pop-ups with runners on base. Somewhat later in the nineteenth century, the loosely-written substitution rules supposedly led to an instance where King Kelly jumped off the bench toward an errant foul fly, and called out, "Kelly now catching," snaring the ball and getting an out his team would otherwise not have made.

Ringers, or revolvers as they were called at the time, were a common dodge back in the really early amateur and proto-professional days, when there was no reserve clause and players jumped from team-to-team in mid-season. Rules were passed that theoretically prohibited players from appearing for two different teams within a set period of time, but that doesn't mean it still didn't happen. One of the most famous cases took place in 1871, when catcher Scott Hastings, the Rockford Forest Citys' regular backstop in 1870, played a game in April 1871 for the New Orleans Lone Stars. Hastings then returned to the Forest Citys by May 6, for the start of the National Association season. This was clearly against the N.A. rules, which prohibited a member of any club from playing with another club for 60 days. Despite the fact that other N.A. teams protested Hastings' use, Rockford kept using him, thus setting up forfeits for 25 of their games.

Cutting the bases and impeding baserunners were among the favorite tricks of the Old Orioles of Baltimore. Or rather, the Orioles were best-known for these tricks, even though a lot of players on other teams did it as well. You see, there was only one umpire per game in the 1890s, and he couldn't keep an eye on the runners, the fielders, and the ball all at once. Hence, if the ump turned his back, a runner would say, bypass third base on his way from second to home. On the other side of the ball, the Orioles were notorious for giving opposing baserunners the hip (or worse), making the journey around the bases somewhat perilous. The best-known of those Old Orioles, third baseman John J. McGraw, added his own touch to this form of "gamesmanship." When a fly ball was hit with a runner on third, McGraw would hook his fingers in the baserunner's belt, thus making it sort of tough to get a good jump after the ball was caught. The story goes that Pete Browning "cured" McGraw of this foible by undoing his belt, and running home holding up his knickers with his hand. (Cute, but likely apocryphal, since, except for three games in 1894, McGraw and Browning were only in the same league for the 1892 and 1893 seasons, and McGraw played a total of just three games at third in those two years.)

Faking catches, although still practiced, had its heyday in the pre-lighting era. Nowadays, any outfielder who traps a ball, either on the ground or against the fence, will hold up his glove to "show" he's caught the sphere. In the old days, when games were often played in twilight, fielders would sometimes try to really brazen it out. Once again, King Kelly is the subject of one of these stories, wherein he was supposed to have leaped high at the fence to catch a potential game-winning twilight home run. Upon being congratulated when he came to the bench, he demurred that the ball went a mile over his head. Better documented, more dramatic, and less certain instances of this sort of gamesmanship took place in the 1912 and 1925 World Series. In the former, it was thought that Josh Devore made a running catch in deep right center field to save Game 3 for the Giants against the Red Sox. It was getting dark, and a mist had settled over the field when Devore made his "catch" and continued on running into the center field clubhouse. Did he really catch the ball? The batter, Forrest "Hick" Cady, was called out, but who really knows? In 1925, the Senators' Sam Rice dove into the stands to apparently take a home run away from the Pirates' Earl Smith. However,

Fan Interference

since Rice didn't reappear out of the stands for what seemed like an eternity, the Buccos quite naturally made a big stink on the play. All Rice would say at the time about the play was that the umpire said he caught the ball, so he must have done so. This one raised such a ruckus that Rice left a letter with the Hall of Fame, to be opened after his death, explaining the play. In said letter, he claimed that at no time did he lose possession of the ball. Maybe, but a story told by a fan years later claimed that Rice had temporarily knocked himself out on his dive into the stands, and that the fan took the ball and put it in Rice's glove!

Fans aren't the only non-players to get involved in legal cheating. Groundskeepers, at the behest of management, have been doctoring their home fields since the Old Orioles days. At that time, the Baltimore ground was hard as a rock around home plate, so that the home team could beat down on the ball, producing an unplayable bounder—the famous Baltimore Chop. Oriole Park also had the foul lines raised, so the O's bunts would stay fair. This particular trick lasted a long time—for years Connie Mack Stadium in Philadelphia had Ashburn's Ridge, the same raised foul line that aided and abetted Richie Ashburn's bunts. The ultimate piece of home field gamesmanship came from the fertile mind of Bill Veeck, who designed a movable chicken wire fence for the Milwaukee Brewers' Borchert Field, a fence that could be rolled in or out across the top of the normal right field wall, depending on whether his team or the opponents' had more left-handed power. At first, pulling this little stunt between games, Veeck decided the ultimate in accommodating fences would be to do it between innings, in other words, the fence would be rolled out when the opposing team was at bat, and rolled back when the Brewers were up. There was no rule against such a maneuver, until Veeck tried it one day, and it was prohibited the next. Veeck later had more success with field-doctoring in Cleveland, supervising the condition of the infield of Municipal Stadium so that each of his four infielders—Ken Keltner, Lou Boudreau, Joe Gordon, and Eddie Robinson—would have a segment to their liking.

The most common, and most famous, means of cheating became just that after baseball banned trick deliveries and foreign substances on the ball after the 1920 season. So common, in fact, that there's just no point in even trying to list all of the accused spitball, scuffball, greaseball, and the like artists who have practiced their craft since that time. However, let's tip our caps to Gaylord Perry, Hugh Casey, Don Drysdale, Tommy Bridges, Joe Page, Claude Passeau, Lou Burdette, Doug Corbett, Don Sutton, Mike Scott, Preacher Roe, Rick Honeycutt, Nelson Potter, Dizzy Dean, Phil Regan, and Whitey Ford. It's worth noting that Perry, Drysdale, Sutton, Dean, and Ford are all in the Hall of Fame. It may be that this form of cheating is becoming passé, however. The advent of the split-fingered fastball and the circle change having given pitchers two legal weapons that act a lot like a spitball or a scuffball.

If pitchers can alter the ball, it seems only right and proper that hitters can alter the bat. Another practice with a long tradition and, like altering the ball, one that wasn't always outside the rules. In the nineteenth century, Hall of Famers George Wright and Cap Anson were both associated with bats that now would get you tossed out of a game, Wright with a plugged bat and Anson with a laminated bat. Then there was a gentleman that played in the 1920s who has a bat from that era on display at the Hall of Fame, a bat where the wood of the round end doesn't match the barrel. That's known as a plug, Babe.

Prior to 1940, the rules just said a bat had to be made out of wood. Now, the rule says they have to be one piece of wood, a rule that Norm Cash, Billy Hatcher, Graig Nettles, Amos Otis, Albert Belle, Wilton Guerrero, and Sammy Sosa, among others, have ran afoul of, usually with either cork or superballs (ah, the wonders of modern toy technology). Another early Hall of Famer who broke the all-wood rule, George Sisler, drove nails into his bat and filed off the ends. That's a no-no, George.

Finally, we return to sign stealing, another vaguely illegal methodology in baseball that has been around forever. Now, having a coach or a manager—Charlie Dressen and Del Baker come quickly to mind—who's good at stealing signs on the field is okay. But, if you use technology and do it off the field, that's not considered kosher, at least by the aggrieved parties. There have been more instances of this than you can shake a Louisville Slugger at, including one mentioned by Jim Brosnan in *Pennant Race* (when the Cubs were giving signals from the Wrigley Field scoreboard), the aforementioned Mr. Veeck admitting in *Veeck...As in Wreck* that the Indians stole signs from the scoreboard in 1948, and the 1951 pennant race, wherein it has been broadly claimed that Leo Durocher's Giants were stealing signs from the center field clubhouse in the Polo Grounds.

There's no doubt that the practice has been around for a long time, since at least 1900. Maybe the most inventive example, and one of the first recorded instances, took place in mid-September 1900 at Philadelphia Park, when a Cincinnati infielder thought he had caught his spikes on an underground vine. Close examination showed it was an electrical wire that ran from a plate buried in the third base coaches' box to the Phillies' center field clubhouse. In said clubhouse was backup catcher Morgan Murphy and a telescope. He was reading the opposing catcher's signals and relaying them, via electrical impulse, to the coaches' box, where the third base coach could pick them up via his metal spikes. While it's a good bet this device wasn't used during rainy games, the National League requested that this new form of communication cease and desist immediately. As for the Phillies' owner, the devious Colonel John Rogers (well, he was a Philadelphia lawyer)... he thought this ploy was perfectly fair and legitimate. Your turn, Ozzie.

Originally appeared in issue #13, Fall 2006.

Winning Is Everything, You Asshole

Ken Derr

In 1967, Charlie Finley moved his lowly Kansas City Athletics to Oakland. In the next 13 years, he would forge a path of triumph and terror through this fair city unlike anything since Ted Hendricks and John Matuszak took that pub crawl. Finley was an egomaniac who drove a stake through the heart of his best players if they dared get more attention than he did. Paradoxically, the Swingin' A's also won three consecutive World Series under his reign. Along the way, he tried to spice up the game in Veeckian fashion with orange baseballs, designated runners, Charlie O the mule (a more fitting mascot there never was), a mechanized rabbit that popped from the ground with new balls, neon uniform colors, a 12-year-old M.C. Hammer listed as Vice President of the organization, and many more. Almost everyone who met him attests to his charms when he needed something from them, but if there was a pettier or crueler professional sports owner in the last 40 years, he's going to have to duke it out with Charlie in the grave.

Whenever a player got too big for his britches, Charlie would puff out his concave chest and drag that man down. For instance, in 1970, A's ace Jim "Catfish" Hunter took out a $150,000 loan from Finley for a 500-acre ranch he wanted to buy near his home in North Carolina. Hunter was to pay back Charlie $20,000 a year at 6%. That year, Finley proceeded to call Catfish every day he was scheduled to pitch to ask about the loan. He was relentless. Hunter became so upset about the harassment that he fell into a horrid slump and failed to win a single game in August, and this from a consistent 20-game winner and universally beloved prince. Catfish finally sold off 400 acres and paid back the loan in full, because he was afraid his career would be ruined if he didn't escape Charlie's badgering. That cantankerous alpha male had "won" again, but always at the expense of everyone around him.

Reggie Jackson, as most folks know, has a gargantuan ego. Even Reggie's narcissism, however, was dwarfed by Charlie's. In 1969, Reggie hit 49 homers and received a tremendous amount of media coverage, so Jackson's agent demanded a considerable salary increase. Charlie refused and instead offered five grand more, stating that only seasoned veterans deserved large bumps in salary after they had produced consistent seasons. Reggie was incensed and held out for part of spring training, but he eventually got eager to play. Finley finally agreed to a $10,000 increase, still some $30,000 less than Jackson wanted and the market called for, but Finley vowed to teach that ungrateful bastard a lesson. He had Reggie benched against left-handers for most of the season, pinch hit for him at critical times and even threatened to send him down. Jackson hit .237 with 23 homers in 1970. I suppose one can say that Charlie won that personal battle, and that made him happy. But with Finley, happiness never lasted long.

In 1971, Finley hired irascible Dick Williams to manage the team. Early in spring training, Williams called a meeting. He had heard that in previous years, players had gone behind the manager's back to Finley if they had problems, and Williams wanted to set the record straight: "Here is the phone. If you want to call Charlie, go ahead. But that's the last time you're going to call him. I'm the manager, and if you have any problems, you come to me." Williams earned the respect of his players, and the A's won their division, only to lose to the more experienced Orioles in the playoffs. Charlie seethed.

In 1972, however, the championship run began. The A's again took the division title, and in the ALCS, they faced the Tigers, led by the fiery Billy Martin (who would later become the A's manager, establish his own brand called Billyball, and set records for whiskey shots in the Oakland Marriot, but that's another story). Martin and Finley had bad blood over an alleged contract offer that Finley made to Martin to manage the A's in 1970, which Martin claimed Finley reneged on. Finley, of course, said Martin backed out. Earlier in the season, the two teams had brawled when Tiger pitcher Bill Shayback plugged Campy Campaneris and Angel Manguel in consecutive at bats, apparently to let Charlie know that nobody messes with Billy, and he was playing hardball. So the stage was set for fireworks, and it didn't take long, when in Game 1, Martin ordered Tiger pitcher Lerrin LaGrow to hit Campy in the ankle to take out his legs. Campy took a different kind of offense and proceeded to fling his bat at LaGrow's head, just missing the stunned hurler. Less psychotic heads prevailed, but after the game, AL President Joe Cronin suspended Campy for the series. LaGrow and Martin got out of jail free, which incensed Finley, who claimed the league had a vendetta against him. Proving LaGrow's pitch was intentional was far more difficult than convicting Campy when his bat is flying through the air, so there it was. Campy's suspension, though, put a crimp in another of Finley's moonbeam strategies. Each A's second basemen was a weak hitter, so Williams would pinch hit for him and then replace him at second, only to pinch hit again when the replacement next came to bat. With Campy out of the series, however, Dal Maxvill had to move to short, which forced Williams to use catcher Gene Tenace late in Game 3. Tenace then dropped a sure double play throw that would have given the A's the sweep. They went on to win the series in five games, but

Williams vowed to abandon Finley's directives forever.

Reggie Jackson pulled a hamstring in Game 5, which kept him out of the upcoming World Series, but the A's weren't done sticking pins in themselves. Starting pitcher Vida Blue relieved late in Game 5 to save the game for John "Blue Moon" Odom, and afterwards, he asked Blue Moon why he couldn't finish what he started and put his hands around his neck in the universal choke sign. Odom attacked Vida and they fought briefly before teammates intervened. Clubhouse violence was a primary motivator for the kings of dysfunction, and so the A's were now officially ready for the Big Red Machine.

Going into the '72 Series, no one gave the A's a chance against the team most tongue-waggers considered the class of the league. The Reds had superstars in Johnny Bench, Tony Perez, and Pete Rose, and they were scoring runs in bushels. But unlikely star Gene Tenace hit two homers in the opener off Gary Nolan to help the Oaktown boys shock everyone and take Game 1, which prompted the always gracious Rose to state, "I'm not impressed by the A's. They have nothing." The brilliantly mustachioed Rollie Fingers saved Catfish's gem in Game 2 after Joe Rudi made one of the most miraculous homer-saving catches of any World Series, and suddenly, the A's had a flabbergasting 2-0 lead in the Series. The Reds managed to win Game 3, 1-0, but all anyone remembers is what transpired in the eighth. With the Reds threatening and Fingers at a 3-2 count to Bench, Dick Williams visited the mound. As he returned to the dugout, he pointed at first base and put up four fingers, signifying that he wanted Fingers to walk Bench intentionally. The A's catcher put out his right hand to indicate the free pass, and Rollie threw a strike right down the middle, ending the inning. The A's lost the game, but won the highlight reel.

Tenace hit another homer in Game 4 to help the A's win 3-2 and put them in an unthinkable position—taking out the Machine in just five games. The Reds rallied, however, sliming out a 5-4 victory. Before Game 6 in Cincy, a woman waiting to get into the Stadium overheard a man say, "If Tenace hits a homer, he won't walk out of the park." She alerted officials, and the police found a loaded gun on the nutbag, prompting Reggie to tell Tenace after the game, "Hey, if ya got to go, Gene, at least it will be on national television." Obviously shaken by the insanity running through the city Jerry Springer would soon run, the A's fell quietly, 8-1, setting up the ultimate finish. In Game 7, the A's used their best starting pitchers to subdue the Shrinking Red Machine and eke out a 3-2 victory. Oakland finally had its championship, and pitcher Kenny Holtzman explained why: "Finley kept us all hungry and at each other's throats and at his, too. That gave us the edge we needed to win." Finley would dance on the dugout with his wife that night causing many viewers to throw up in their mouths, but the fun was just beginning.

    Nineteen seventy-three began typically, as the A's traded for perennial grouch Billy North, who had nearly come to blows with Leo Durocher in Chicago. North and Reggie were at each other immediately, and it probably didn't help that they were dating the same woman. One night, it exploded in a clubhouse scrap, but details were kept relatively secret. When asked later who had won the fight, North smirked, "I played that night, and Reggie didn't." But clubhouse brawls only fueled the fires of resentment, and the A's again won their division, led by their three 20-game winners: Vida Blue, Catfish Hunter, and Kenny Holtzman. Again they squared off with the Orioles, but this time they were the defending World Champions, and they were stupid with confidence. That didn't stop more fisticuffs, though, as Rollie Fingers and John "Blue Moon" Odom clashed after the A's blew Game 4. Catfish calmly stepped in to shut them out in Game 5, however, to send the A's back to the World Series, where they would meet the New York Mets.

    The A's took Game 1, but all hell broke loose in Game 2 in what would become one of Finley's lowest moments. In the eighth inning, reserve infielder Mike Andrews, who had played sparingly but was inserted into the game late, made errors on two consecutive plays to cost the A's the game. In the clubhouse afterwards, Finley met Andrews with a contract stating that Andrews was physically unable to play, which had already been signed by the team doctor. Andrews was fine, but Finley wanted him off the team at once, and he also wanted to get another player on the roster, which he couldn't do if he kicked Andrews out of the clubhouse for incompetence. The next day at practice, the A's players arrived wearing black patches with Andrews' number 17 on them, and threatened to boycott the Series if he was not returned to the lineup. Commissioner Bowie Kuhn may have ironically saved Finley further embarrassment by reinstating Andrews himself and reprimanding Finley for embarrassing his own player. The A's won Game 3 and the Mets got Game 4, which was most notable for Met fans giving Andrews a standing ovation when he pinch hit. The Mets took Game 5, but the A's came back to win the last two to secure their second straight championship. Once again, however, nothing went smoothly in the East Bay, as manager Dick Williams announced on national TV after the game that he was resigning effective immediately. The man had just guided his team to the World Series title, and he wanted the hell out, arguably the greatest indicator of how miserable it was to work for Charlie Finley.

    Finley replaced Williams with Alvin Dark, who had almost been run out of baseball in 1964 after he suggested in an interview that blacks and Latinos weren't as smart as white ballplayers. Dark had found God since then, though, and this now devout Christian, who had run off with a stewardess while married with kids, now had the unenviable task of replacing the man who had commanded the respect of the rowdies who were riding more than a little high on themselves after two titles. Dark was just happy to be back in baseball, and he was Charlie's lackey. When Finley suggested they find themselves a speedster as a designated runner, Dark suggested Herb Washington, whom he had seen win the 60-yard dash in an indoor track event. That year, the A's were not as dominant during the regular season, but they still managed to take the division with 90 wins. Again they took out the Orioles in the ALCS, and then it was time for the A's singular brand of twisted fun.

The A's were to take on the L.A. Dodgers, but more trouble was brewing. Rollie Fingers was going through a nasty divorce, and he was near the emotional boiling point after weeks of his teammates' ribbing. Before a Game 1 workout at Dodger Stadium, "Blue Moon" Odom made a classy comment about Fingers' inability to keep a woman. Fingers erupted and punched Odom in the face. Odom retaliated by head butting Fingers' chest. Obviously, the A's were ready, and they took Game 1. The Dodgers had a 3-0 lead in the ninth of Game 2, but the A's rallied, scoring two on a Joe Rudi single. Alvin Dark then replaced Rudi with Herb Washington, hoping the designated speedster could steal second. Dodger iron man reliever Mike Marshall, however, had other ideas. He stepped off the mound three times. He threw quickly to first almost nailing Washington, and then, just as Charlie's prized recruit took his lead, Marshall winged a quick throw over and picked him off, effectively ending the experiment that had never worked in the first place. The Dodgers won, 3-2, but it was their last hurrah. The A's won the last three games of the series, sweetened in Game 5 when Bill Buckner, who had been talking trash about the A's the whole series, idiotically tried to turn a double into a triple in the eighth inning of a one-run game. The A's had won three consecutive World Series, the most unlikely of dynasties, but it would all come to an inglorious end.

Despite one of the greatest and most improbable runs in baseball history, few of the A's players were happy, and almost all reasons pointed in one direction: Charlie Finley. Catfish Hunter had never forgiven Finley for the loan incident, and when Charlie failed to make a payment on a life insurance policy for Hunter that was part of Catfish's contract, Hunter contacted his agent in September of their '74 drive for the title. Catfish did not want to do anything until after the World Series, but then, after much legal wrangling, Marvin Miller, executive director of the Players Association, claimed that Finley had breached Hunter's contact and that he could become a free agent. More negotiations, threats, and insults ensued, but ultimately, Peter Seitz, the only independent member of the arbitration committee, ruled Jim "Catfish" Hunter an unrestricted free agent. Baseball would never really be the same again. Once Hunter was free to negotiate, he learned how valuable he was on the market. He eventually signed a $3.75 million deal with the Yankees over five years, which may not sound like much by today's standards, but his previous year's contract was $100,000. Amazingly, the A's still won 98 games and their division the next year, but this time, they did not have enough in the playoffs, and the Red Sox swept them in three games.

Between the 1975 and 1976 seasons, Seitz made another ruling that was probably even more critical to the future of the game than the Hunter decision. Seitz ruled that the reserve clause in players' contracts bound them to their teams for only one year beyond the contract. They could become free agents after that. The writing was on the bloodied clubhouse wall, and Charlie Finley's bare bones operation had to come crumbling down. Finley's first move was to trade Reggie Jackson and Ken Holtzman to Baltimore. Then on June 15, the day of the trading deadline, he sold Joe Rudi and Rollie Fingers to the Red Sox for $1 million each. Then he sold Vida Blue to the Yankees for $1.5 million. The players were in a state of shock, especially since the A's were scheduled to play the Red Sox. Rudi and Fingers switched uniforms and clubhouses and then sat on the opposite bench. Three days later, Bowie Kuhn declared the sales null and void, and Finley countered with a $10 million lawsuit against Kuhn. His claim, however, was denied in U.S. District Court. Meanwhile, Finley wouldn't play the players he had sold. "You don't belong to me," he said. When the players threatened another boycott, Finley backed off. Through all the chaos, the A's still put together a respectable season, falling just two and a half games shy of another West Division title. The damage, however, had been done. Fingers, Rudi, and Sal Bando were gone as free agents after the season. Vida Blue was traded to the Giants after one more season. Billy North was traded to the Dodgers. The next year, the A's lost 108 games. In 1980, Finley would sell the team to Levi's owner Walter Haas, ironically one of the game's most decent men, and the reign of terror was over.

Charlie Finley "presided" over one of the greatest dynasties in baseball history, but he also helped create the conditions that led to the explosion of free agency, George Steinbrenner, and the Yankees' resurgence. Finley ruled in a time when owners were still feudal lords who were not shy about reminding their serfs who was master, but when the times began to change, he refused to. He was creative and charming and one miserable son of a bitch if you crossed him, and he minded the ship for one hell of a ride. It's hard to imagine a ragtag bunch of under-paid, under-shaved and under-disciplined players winning three straight these days. Given the money in today's game, the stakes are just too high. So while it's nearly impossible to find anyone who has much good to say about Charlie Finley's integrity or business acumen, maybe we can remember him as the creator of such absurd conditions that only absolute

Ken Derr

failure or mad success could follow. Finley united his players against him, and that brought out the best in them, which is one of the most perverse success stories the game has ever known.

Originally appeared in issue #9, Fall 2004.

Disco Demolition Night

Todd Taylor

Civil Rights...and Explosions

Bill Veeck, Jr. was owner of the Chicago White Sox in 1979. Veeck had been a journeyman baseball club owner and a staunch supporter of civil rights.

In 1947, Veeck hired the American League's first black player, Larry Doby. A year later, he signed 42-year-old Negro League pitching legend Satchel Paige to a contract, making Paige the oldest rookie ever to play professional baseball. Although Veeck had an artificial leg, he participated in a day-long civil rights march in Selma, Alabama, in March 1965, without the use of crutches. Fellow baseball club owners often derisively likened Veeck to circus huckster P.T. Barnum: a sucker for a good promotion.

Veeck's accomplishments forever changed the face and tenor of baseball. He was the first owner to introduce fireworks displays after games. At Comiskey Park, he developed and deployed the "Monster," which was an enormous, garish, Willy Wonka-inspired scoreboard. It came with sirens, sound effects, flashing lights, and multicolored pinwheels. It also shot fireworks whenever the White Sox hit a home run. As a fan of the fans, another Veeck innovation was the picnic area in the ballpark. He created this by replacing portions of the left field walls with wire screens and setting up picnic tables under the seating areas.[1]

On May 2, 1979, the Detroit Tigers vs. Chicago White Sox game at Comiskey was rained out. American League rules called for the game to be made up at the teams' next meeting in Chicago.

The '79 Chicago White Sox were "second-rate," to put it nicely. More bluntly, they sucked pretty hard. At 40-46, they were twenty-two games out before the All-Star break. Average attendance was slightly more than 10,000 fans.

On July 12, the White Sox were scheduled for a twilight doubleheader against the equally struggling Detroit Tigers to make up for the previously rained-out game. The preceding night's game had drawn only

---

[1] Bill Veeck, in 1960, added player's surnames on the back of their uniforms. Veeck also installed a shower behind the speaker horns in the center field bleachers for fans to cool off on hot summer days.

Todd Taylor

15,520 fans.

Veeck put his son Mike—and White Sox marketing director—in charge of getting asses in seats. Bill didn't balk or blush when his son brought up the idea of a promotion, an event hyperbolically billed to "bring an end to the disco era." Bill lived in hyperbole when it came to promotion. It didn't sound like that big of a deal.

Mike Veeck had been listening to a 24-year-old DJ, Steve Dahl, on the radio. Dahl was planning to blow up disco records in a shopping mall.

"I called him at 10:05 a.m., as soon as he got off the air," Mike said, "and offered him the chance to do that at Comiskey Park. He was going to do it in front of three thousand kids. It didn't take long to convince him he could do it in front of forty thousand kids." The planned promotion was a joint effort between the White Sox and Chicago radio station WLUP-FM, The Loop, and also involved station Promotion Director Dave Logan and Sales Manager Jeff Schwartz.

The promotion promised the presence of Steve Dahl and the official "Rock Girl" of the station, Lorelei[2], who was featured in all of the radio station's advertisements. Disco had become a personal battle for Dahl, not just an abstract potshot or a woefully easy musical target. Previously, Dahl gained popularity in Chicago at FM rock station WDAI. In 1978, WDAI abandoned its AOR rock format. It embraced disco and changed its name to "Disco DAI." This prompted an abrupt and unexpected end to Dahl's show and employment at the station. He and the station parted ways on Christmas Eve in 1978. Happy holidays, Steve.

Disco's ubiquity couldn't be denied. *Saturday Night Fever*, the Bee Gees, and Donna Summer swarmed the airwaves. Kermit the Frog sang "Disco Frog" on *Sesame Street*. That same year, a band called Chic[3] rode the very top of disco's rollercoaster. Their debut single, "Le Freak," sold a million copies within a month. It hit number one in America, where it remained for six weeks. According to *Billboard*, it was the third most popular song of 1979. (One of Chic's founders, Nile Rogers denies that Chic was disco. Rogers stated that, "People couldn't tell the difference between us and Lipps Inc." Fair enough. I still can't tell the difference. I'm no discomusicologist.)

After parting ways with WDAI, Dahl landed on his feet at WLUP. The Loop's format had recently changed from light to hard rock. Dahl's fans followed him and echoed his pro-rock, anti-disco sentiments. Dahl smashed disco records over his head. Dahl mugged for the cameras taking bites out of disco records.

---

[2] Lorelei Shark: "I even did a spot with Pete Rose and another with a baby orangutan." "Yes, I am those famous biting lips in *The Rocky Horror Picture Show* poster."

[3] Chic's Nile Rogers had been an active Black Panther at the age of sixteen. Duran Duran's bassist John Taylor had envisioned the band he was in as a combination of Chic and the Sex Pistols.

Fan Interference

Dahl also cited philosophical, dermatological, and classic Marxist reasons for his disdain for this particular genre of music: "Disco is a disease. It's a thing you have to be near-perfect to get into. You have to have perfect hair and a three-piece suit, and musically it's just the same song with different words . . . I'm allergic to gold jewelry, hate the taste of piña coladas, and I'm a cheapskate."

Dahl had formed an on-air anti-disco, card-carrying army called the "Insane Coho Lips." The strange name was an amalgamation of The Insane Unknowns[4], a well-known South Side street gang, and the Coho salmon fishing fleet in Burnham Harbor that Dahl passed every morning on his way to work. The Cohos lofted Dahl's "disco sucks" banner and zealously attacked a form of music they considered exclusive, expensive, and empty. They got their class war on by attacking the soundtrack to the hedonism of the elite. They also just liked having fun and laughing along with Dahl.

Disco-makers viewed Dahl and his listener-army differently. "It was the rockers versus the discoers," said Harry Wayne Casey, frontman of Florida band KC and the Sunshine Band[5]. "We were like Elvis in the fifties and the Beatles in the sixties. Of course there was a backlash. We changed music . . . I had two hits on the charts, 'Please Don't Go' and 'Yes I'm Ready.' . . . I just figured the guy [Dahl] was an idiot."

The meeting between the White Sox and The Loops' management went well. A name for the promotion was agreed upon: Disco Demolition Night. It was a simple promotion distilled to a short sentence: Let's blow up some disco records.

An Ounce of Precaution?

The plan called for admission at the doubleheader to be 98 cents for any fan who brought a disco record. The ticket price matched The Loop's frequency, FM 98. The hope was that 20,000 disco records would be collected by the ticket takers, placed in a big box in the outfield, and the box would be detonated between the two games by Dahl, signifying the hopeful and abrupt end to the disco era.

Disco Demolition Night overlapped the ballpark's Teen Night. The consensus was they needed more than Cub Scout and Boy Scout troops to fill the stands. It was predicted and hoped of the promotion would draw 25,000—10,000 of which would be new patrons to the old ballpark. Sox Park had a seating capacity of 52,000.

---

[4] The Insane Unknowns itself was an amalgamation. Two gangs, the Division Skulls and the Unknown Souls, merged in 1967, and called themselves the Insane Unknowns.

[5] KC and the Sunshine Band took their name from lead vocalist Harry Wayne Casey's last name ("KC") and the "Sunshine Band" from KC's home state of Florida, "The Sunshine State." KC originally called the band KC & The Sunshine Junkanoo Band.

"I was really just trying to get through the evening without being humiliated," Dahl said. "I mean, how many people could you draw? A few thousand? The park would still look empty."

"Rock Girl" Lorelei threw out the first ball.

Once the gates opened at the beginning of the first game, it quickly became apparent that Disco Demolition Night would exceed all attendance expectations.

"I remember forking over a Bee Gees disc for 98 cents and, as I recall, they actually gave back two cents in change when turning in the voucher with your dollar at the ticket box," said fan Glenn McCullom.

"We brought the *Saturday Night Fever* Soundtrack, a double record, which was good for two of us to get in," said K.M. Lisowski, another fan.

Attendees also brought along and strung up homemade banners, primarily made from bed sheets. On TV, the "Disco Sucks" battle cry could be clearly read from throughout the ballpark. Not televised were the "What do Linda Lovelace and disco have in common?" banner and the more political, fuck-you-Australia "Welcome Home Skylab" banner[6].

Fans made giant paper airplanes with the Lorelei posters and threw them onto the field. Other fans came ready for a battle against disco with bottle rockets and long cardboard tubes. The empty center of wrapping paper rolls served nicely as suburban bazookas. For reasons still unexplained, the second base umpire was particularly targeted for bottle rocket attacks.

Beer vendor sales were brisk. Brian Pegg reported that, "On Disco Demolition night, I sold forty-nine cases of beer. Ordinarily, twenty cases were considered an outstanding total for a single night game. Thirty to thirty-five would be pretty good for a doubleheader." Math showed that's just shy of two-and-a-half times the usual volume of beer sales at a typical game. Raging against disco proved a thirsty business.

After 20,000 disco records were collected for demolition, ticket takers let fans keep their records—proof of how unprepared they were by the boosted attendance. "So that was a bad start," Dahl admitted." And then things just kind of got worse from there."

In short order, fans glided records like Frisbees all through the park. The game was stopped constantly as disco records were thrown out on the field. Vinyl's sharp. It shatters, leaves ragged edges.

"They would slice around you and stick in the ground," Rusty Staub, player representative for the Detroit Tigers said. "It wasn't just one, it was many. Oh, god almighty, I've never seen anything so dangerous in

---

[6] Skylab was engineered to fail within five years. The day before, on July 11th, 1979, NASA's version of duct taping a pair of Chucks to get every last step out of them—called Skylab—broke up in the atmosphere and scattered its remains across the Australian outback.

my life. I begged the guys to put on their batting helmets." Defensive players. Guys in the outfield. Not just hitters. Ron LeFlore, a former convict and center fielder for Detroit, was visibly afraid. In the later innings of the first game, fans remember the Tigers running back to the dugout, then removing their helmets.

The Tigers were not the sole targets of the record fling-a-thon. Chicago pitcher Ed Farmer picked up a record that had sailed by closely to his face. He was confused. It was a Beach Boys record. It wasn't even disco.

Other fans suffered from the flight of records.

"Later that night," Sox fan K.M. Lisowski said, "my friend's husband got hit in the head with a 'Frisbeed' record, and I remember getting cut with the edge of a broken 45 that had been flung our way."

David Schaffer, director of operations for the Sox, said that security had been beefed up from thirty to forty-five men in anticipation of a large crowd.

Another miscalculation: This wasn't the typical baseball crowd. It was a rock concert-type crowd.

The White Sox lost to the Tigers 4-1 in the first game.

A Successful Disaster

The umpires ordered the grounds crew to clear debris from the warning track between innings of the first game.

By the end of the first game, the ballpark was filled well beyond its maximum capacity. On the books, paid fan attendance for the evening was 47,795. Over 12,000 extra fans crammed in. The majority snuck in though the Sox's porous security. The official tally didn't include the fans who brought ladders, formed human ladders, or shimmied up drain pipes into the park.

It was at this time that Mike Veeck, along with The Loop and the Sox organization, realized they had woefully underestimated the draw of disco's suckage. "It turned out there were 60,000 inside the park and another 30,000 to 40,000 on the streets around the park," Veeck said. "Traffic was backed up all the way out to O'Hare Airport. Who had any idea that many kids would come out? WLUP was a 5,000-watt station, it wasn't a giant."

The Chicago police department closed exits on the Dan Ryan Expressway at 31st and 35th streets to discourage late-arriving fans. Traffic gridlock stretched for miles around Chicago's South Side.

Dahl was dressed like Henry Blake from *M*A*S*H*. He wore an Army jacket bedazzled with fishing lures over a Hawaiian shirt. An Army helmet was strapped loosely to his head. He was ushered to the outfield in a Jeep with his second-in-command Garry Meier, Lorelei, and bodyguards. Dahl admits he hadn't prepared a speech.

"Steve started to get the crowd excited as only Steve could do, chanting 'disco sucks' over and over," Lorelei said. "I think that mantra was probably the kicker—the swarming sound was getting louder and louder. It was deafening." The crowd was going bananas in their seats.

The big box filled with the fans' 20,000 disco records had been brought out to center field. A short burst of fireworks were touched off in a row in front of the box. That lead up to an impressive percussive charge, which detonated a fireworks "bomb." Vinyl disco records were blown to bits. Some continued to burn after they landed in fragments on the field.

"That blowed up real good!" Dahl exclaimed.

Now Would Be a Great Time for a Plan . . . Run!

Dahl didn't really have a plan after the explosion, except to get off the field, maybe go home, maybe watch the second game. There was no advisement from anyone with a microphone to the fans to stay in their seats, to remain calm. Folks were riled up.

Here's a recap: big explosion; adrenaline-high levels of "disco sucks!" excitement in the air; a large, mostly empty, beautifully-lit, largely-untouchable field beckoning fans; crazy-low security; and a silence so pregnant that its water was about to break.

This is when the trouble began.

What started at 8:40 p.m. was a confluence of several key factors.

Outside the park, some of the temporary ticket booths—staffed with older people—were being rocked by disgruntled fans who couldn't get inside the park. Some of the yellow-jacketed security guards were moved off the field to take care of that issue.

"What happened next was the worst thing that could possibly happen," said Mike Veeck. "The crowd began thinking as one and they realized there were only thirty-five to forty police [security] on the field. When a crowd begins thinking as one, there is no such thing as 'crowd control.'"

Conservatively, on the field, it was one security guard per 1,333 fans. Not good odds for reestablishing order.

"It was like popcorn. Boom! Everyone jumped on the field," one fan stated. The fans' feeling of rushing the field was, "sort of like the pennant celebration we would never get."

The players who had returned to the field for pregame warm-ups for the second game quickly retreated.

"Before I knew it, I had a bodyguard on either side of me," Lorelei remembered, "Each grabbed one of my upper arms and literally lifted me off the ground, running with me toward the Jeep, throwing me in the back. Steve jumped in the Jeep and we started rolling. I looked behind me and understood why I was whisked off—crowds of people were streaming onto the field."

The Jeep drove out of the stadium and onto the street. It looped around and its occupants snuck back inside as 10,000 people ran onto the field.

Among the revelers was actor Michael Clarke Duncan (the big dude in *The Green Mile*), a Chicago South Side native. He was among the first fans to run onto the field and slide into third base. Other fans took the roles of umpires, calling both "safe!" and "out!" Fans took bases. (An usher salvaged first base.) Fans dug out home plate. The pitching rubber was stolen from the infield. Duncan admitted to stealing a bat from the dugout.

Bill Veeck's "Monster" flashed, "Please Return to Your Seats."

Harry Caray stared down in disbelief at the field from his broadcast booth as the batting cage was wheeled out to the outfield then trounced, disassembled, and set on fire along with the remains of the disco records and the big box. A shirtless fan climbed to the top of one of the foul poles. Another fire burned in centerfield. The head groundskeeper shook his head in disbelief as the benches from the special picnic area were dragged out into the middle of the field and set ablaze. Revelers jumped through that fire.

Harry Caray tried to restore order by yelling "Holy cow!" over the public address system. He then asked the crowd, "What say we all regain our seats so we can play baseball again?" When none of the excitable fans took their seats, a tremor of horror resonated in Harry Caray's voice. "People, people, please get off the field!" Jimmy Piersall, Caray's broadcasting partner, was openly disgusted and repeated over and over that, "These are not baseball fans here. These kids are obviously on something more than beer."

Unruly? Absolutely.

Chicago Sun-Times columnist Bill Gleason called the event "an unmitigated horror . . . They were vulgarians who came to Comiskey Park to be ruffians." But people weren't physically violent to one another. This was no replay of the 1968 Democratic National Convention bloodbath eleven years prior in the same city. Fans were really worked up; they got all hyper. Much of the crowd, once on the field, simply milled around aimlessly. Some sat in the infield.

Fans from the upper decks couldn't get down to the field. More than half of the fans on the lower deck didn't go on the field and began chanting, "Na na na na, na na na na, hey assholes, sit down."

Bill Veeck looked at a quickly dissipating silver lining. "The great thing was all the kids were stoned," he said. "Had we had drunks to deal with, then we would have had some trouble. The kids were really docile."

At 9:08 p.m., the Chicago police department's tactical force entered Sox Park and efficiently took care of business clearing the field. Within five minutes, they had the situation under control. The cops had no trouble dispersing the crowd. The police and players showed an incredible amount of restraint in their dealings with the unruly revelers. This was not a true riot. True riots offer resistance to law enforcement and provide cops ample opportunity to work on their batting averages. This event was a gangload of partiers not given enough supervision. It was a bunch of nutty kids.

After the police sweep, Bill Veeck returned to the playing field and grabbed a microphone. "Please keep your rain checks," he told the crowd. "We'll tell you what to do with them once we figure it out ourselves." Behind the scenes, Veeck was busy rescheduling the game as part of a Sunday doubleheader against the Tigers.

Surveying a field strewn with bottles, exploded cherry bombs, smoldering patches in the midfield, and broken disco records, The Tigers countered that the Sox forfeit on the grounds that the delay was not a result of "an act of God." Tigers manager Sparky Anderson was vehement that his players would not take the field in any case due to safety concerns.

Umpire crew chief Dave Phillips agreed with Sparky and stated, "The field is not in playable condition." Home plate had been uprooted from the ground and hadn't been measured. The grounds crew was showing no effort to put it properly back in.

The White Sox were ordered by American League president Lee MacPhail to forfeit the second game of the twi-night doubleheader. It was only the fourth forfeit in American League history[7].

At the end of the evening, six people reported mild injuries. One vendor broke a hip. Thirty-nine people were arrested for disorderly conduct.

The Sox lost both games.

Get Your Big Foam Pointy Finger Out

The local Chicago press wasn't kind to Dahl, the Veecks, or Disco Demolition Night. Predictably, the media asked, "What went wrong? How did this disturbance by youthful crowds happen?"

Channel 7's Rosemarie Gulley's insight was as good as any for this cocktail of hyperactivity: "The explosion, the heat, and a lot of drugs."

Other talking-head snippets called the promotion "a gimmick that's gone too far," and "They created a climate . . . (word not omitted, just a pause) . . . an error in planning." (End of statement, back to footage.)

Deputy Chief Charles Pepp invented one word and one new meaning

---

[7] Other forfeits include: June 4, 1974's ten-cent beer night fiasco and forfeiture in Cleveland and 30,000 Dodger fans throwing baseballs onto the field On August 10, 1995.

in his short explanation of the promotion. "It was a good *methology* to get a crowd, but it overworked." (Italics mine.) Bill Veeck echoed the chief's sentiment. "Sometimes a promotion can work too well."

Later, a report caught up with Dahl and his thoughts on the Demolition.

Reporter: "You don't feel culpable?"

Dahl: "I'm not a security guard."

Reporter: "Would you do it again?"

Dahl: "Yes . . . with more security guards."

Later, Dahl—in a less pragmatic mood—expressed some regret. "I've always felt bad. I'm a baseball fan. I've always felt bad that the second game was canceled."

Two days later, Comiskey Park hosted a large concert called The Loop's "Day in the Park," featuring Eddie Money, Molly Hatchet, Thin Lizzy, Santana, and Journey, further ripping up the outfield for the rest of the season.

It'll Be So Famous, It'll Be Infamous

Predictably, Disco Demolition Night[8] was criticized throughout the disco community.

Unpredictably, Sox promoter Mike Veeck was blacklisted from major league baseball. "After that, I didn't work for ten years," Veeck said. "The second that first guy shimmied down the outfield wall, I knew my life was over... It backfired, and I took the heat. And it cost me personally. I went down the sewer. I didn't work in baseball until nineteen eighty-nine."

Twenty-two years after Disco Demolition Night—in Miami, Florida on Thursday, July 13, 2001—Mike Veeck, then a marketing consultant for the Florida Marlins, asked Harry Wayne Casey of KC and the Sunshine Band, to accept his apology on behalf of the entire disco world. Casey accepted. "I feel redeemed," Casey said. "It gives closure to the whole thing . . . It wasn't a very nice thing to do. There was no reason or call for it. It was a direct hit on myself and other artists who did that for a living. I didn't bash his baseball team."

So, did Dahl kill disco? Maybe yes. Maybe no. Maybe both. Most likely not. Well, no.

"You know, I think that it was a fad," Dahl said. "And it was probably on its way out. But I think it hastened its demise. I don't want to take credit for killing it." Later, however, the Bee Gees personally told Dahl that he did, in fact, destroy disco.

It feels good to blame someone else and to know the exact moment

---

[8] Steve Dahl has copyrighted the term "Disco Demolition."

things started heading downhill for good. It's much easier than looking inside.

The disco juggernaut was still able to prance around in sparkly platforms and satin bodysuits behind bubble machines and into the national consciousness post-Disco Demolition Night. On Wednesday, October 17, 1979, the Pittsburgh Pirates won the World Series in the best of seven games against the Baltimore Orioles. The Pirates proudly blasted Sister Sledge's hit disco anthem "We Are Family" as their adopted theme song throughout the final game of the 1979 season.

Originally appeared in issue #20, Fall 2011.

Statutory Rate: *Zisk* Looks at Baseball Statues Bombarding Chicago

Jake Austen

Public art, from modest graffiti tags to grand Christo wraps, is wonderful because when it's really good it's a great thing and when it's really bad it's a great thing. That's because both extremes fulfill art's mission to illicit thought, reaction, and feelings. But when its really mediocre... ecch. In 1994, one of the better pieces of contemporary sports-related sculpture became in many ways the worst thing to happen to public art in Chicago. *The Spirit*—a dynamic sculpture of a Michael Jordan-esque figure (identified as Michael, but vague enough in its portraiture to have some universality) flying over an abstraction of hapless opponents—was placed in front of the United Center. The mildly ambitious statue was such a success that soon the firm that designed it, The Fine Art Studio of Rotblatt-Amrany, would come to design all the sports statuary in Chicago (and *many* around the country), and one artist, Lou Cella, would design and oversee the majority of them. The result is an infestation of bland, unchallenging, homogenous statues, the majority of them around Wrigley Field (Cubs statues are about seven feet tall) and on the lower deck walkway of U.S. Cellular Field (Sox dudes are approximately life-size). Though these $100,000 (according to the *New York Times*) pigeon toilets are not awful in any way, the churning out of these (a baker's dozen since 2000) means they are rushed, same-ish, and yawn-inducing. That said, in rating these statues (in baseball batting terms) there are more hits than outs. Play ball!

WHITE SOX CHAMPIONS PLAZA (2008, bronze/granite/a bunch of other stuff, 35th and Shields) by Julie Rotblatt-Amrany, Rotblatt-Amrany Studios, C. Don Williams, Danielle Kennedy-Battle, 360 Architecture

I loved the 2005 World Series champion White Sox and went to Game 2 and respect their awesomeness and think they deserve to be honored, blah blah blah... but this huge ugly mess honors no one! This sprawling, focus-free folly is a tiny plaza atop hundreds of red "fan bricks" (inscribed with purchased messages), punctuated by weird, stubby poles with the retired numbers of players, inscribed within a baseball diamond outline with a historical time line of the franchise, and dominated by a vertical baseball field-shaped obelisk featuring dozens of square bricks with the names of players, executives, and others, and lots of plaques commemorating lots of stuff. On the obelisk are a bunch of laser etched photo drawings of 2005 post-season memories, including a photo of Ozzie Gullen lifting the trophy, with the trophy being a 3-D sculpture jutting out the top, a laser photo of A.J. Pierzinski celebrating the victory, his 3-D bronze arm also jutting out, low relief bronze sculptures on the side of highlights and middlelights of the games, including Paul Konerko hitting his memorable, though not game winning, grand slam in Game 2, and Joe Crede hitting a far less memorable homer. Emerging out of the obelisk are the chest, head and outstretched arm of Juan Uribe making a catch in World Series Game 4, and a low relief El Duque getting pumped about tricking Johnny Damon into striking out with the bases loaded in ALDS Game 3, and a low relief of Geoff Blum's fourteenth inning game-winning three run homer. So this awful looking excess is not only an eyesore, pointless, and an insult to aesthetics and design...it also argues that Geoff Blum should be immortalized in bronze!

Official scoring: Rally killing double play grounder

HAROLD BAINES (2008, bronze, U.S. Cellular lower deck, right field) by Sean Bell

Baines' right leg can't be right. He looks so awkward and unbalanced and weak in this batting stance, that I just can't dig this sculpture. This very wrong right leg is so weird that the poor likeness and the oddity of the sculpted beard hairs are moot.

Official scoring: Ground out

JACK BRICKHOUSE (2000, bronze, 401 N. Michigan Avenue) by Jerry McKenna
This is the only portrait statue I'm listing that's not in or near a stadium. Longtime Cubs (and Sox) broadcaster Brickhouse deserved honoring, and this is a decent likeness, in a great location (near the Tribune Tower, home of the WGN radio studio). I dislike it a little because the base is too wordy, but mainly because it's a torso-only sculpture, the body disappearing into the base, which I find kind of grotesque.
Official scoring: Warning track fly out

CHARLES COMISKEY (2004, bronze, US Cellular lower deck, center field) by Jerry McKenna
The best reason for this sculpture to exist is to placate nostalgic fans sad that they sold Comiskey Park's naming rights to US Cellular. The reasons for it not to exist are that he was an owner, this is a labor town, and he was so cheap he caused one of the all-time best teams in baseball to throw the World Series.
Official scoring: Fielder's choice

MINNIE MINOSO (2004, bronze, US Cellular lower deck, center field) by Maritza Hernandez
There's nothing wrong with the sculpture overall, and the baggy 1950s uniform is pretty awesome, but Minoso has one of the most distinct, sculptural faces in baseball history, and this gets the face kind of wrong, and also can't seem to decide how old he should be, as his eyes make him look like 1970s novelty-out-of-retirement Minnie though the body suggests 1950s borderline-Hall of Fame Minnie. On the plus side, they did hire a Cuban-American sculptress.
Official scoring: Weak single

ERNIE BANKS (2008, bronze, Clark and Addison) by Lou Cella
Banks is a genial, wonderful baseball ambassador, and this passive, smiling figure in a non-threatening batting stance seems appropriate to his current public image. But considering his prowess I'm sure he looked more intimidating to pitchers than this. I feel justified reducing this home run hitting superstar to a single because when unveiled they originally left the apostrophe out of his "Let's Play Two" motto.
Official scoring: Single

BILLY WILLIAMS (2010, bronze, 1060 W. Addison) by Lou Cella
I haven't really been to Wrigley that much in the last few years, so I've never stared at this in person, but driving by it, this statue of Williams appreciating a fresh home run looks really good at the larger-than-life

scale the Cubs use. I think admitted Cubs fan Cella may put a little more soul into his Northside statues.
Official scoring: Solid single

CARLTON FISK (2005, bronze, US Cellular lower deck, center field) by Lou Cella
Pretty noble and bold looking. This is a truly sculpture-y sculpture, in the Greek god, heroic vein. Thematically, if not artistically, it's Michelangelo's *David* . . . but in a jockstrap, uniform, and catcher's gear, instead of naked.
Official scoring: Double

BILLY PIERCE (2007, bronze, US Cellular lower deck, center field) by Julie Rotblatt-Amrany
Like the Fisk statue, just straight up heroic and noble. Neither are masterpieces but they are effective tributes.
Official scoring: RBI double

NELLIE FOX (2006, bronze, US Cellular lower deck, center field) by Lou Cella & Oscar Leon, and *LUIS APARICIO* (2006, bronze, center field) by Lou Cella & Gary Tillery

This is a solid double for two reasons. First of all, it's Chicago's only two-man statue, as Nellie is seen flipping the ball to Luis. More importantly, you can't stand next to this sculpture for ten minutes without seeing a female Sox fan sidle up to the statue and have a photo taken with Little Louie's throwing hand cupping her breast! This is what public sculpture should be about, and is why I *love* lady Sox fans.

Official scoring: Base clearing double

RON SANTO (2011, bronze, Addison and Sheffield) by Lou Cella

This is a pretty great statue. The kinetic energy of the action pose is exciting (I'm too young to have seen Santo in his prime, so I can't vouch for its authenticity of pose), and though I'm not a fan of the red and blue color accents added to the bronze, it does remind us of Santo's amazing *color* man radio work—this is a guy who could work his own double amputation into play-to-play! I'm giving him a triple because he led the league in triples in '64.

Official scoring: Triple

HARRY CARAY (1999, bronze, 1060 W. Addison) by Omri Amrany & Lou Cella

Though I criticized the Brickhouse sculpture for being grotesque by having his body disappear into the base, the sculpture of the famously inebriated Cubs/Sox broadcaster is so intentionally grotesque that I have to endorse this monstrosity emphatically, as this is the most art-history minded work in the ever-growing Chicago baseball sculpture cannon. His body is emerging from a weird bronze mass in an interesting way, kind of referencing the giant, amorphous bronze ball sack of Balzac in Rodin's revered sculpture of the French novelist. Add to that the happy (?) faces of loyal Cubs fans emerging from the bronze goo from whence Harry comes, and you have an unmistakable echo of the screaming faces in Rodin's *Gates of Hell*! Plus, it's impressive to sculpt a bloated face in bronze. Fans have treated this sculpture like it's special over the years, leaving beers and brats below it like sacred offerings. More extreme fans have hung goat carcasses on it to exorcize the billy goat curse, and it was hit by a car once (though un-poetically, no drunk driving was involved).

Official scoring: Base-clearing triple

FRANK THOMAS (2011, bronze, US Cellular lower deck, center field) by Lou Cella and Oscar Leon

I'm not the biggest Thomas fan. Though I appreciated having one of the most gifted hitters of his era on the Sox, he had a coarse personality at times, and as much as I tried, I couldn't love him. But I love this statue, because by it being all about Thomas's ridiculous, bulging biceps this work has a bit of a Tom of Finland vibe to it, which is exciting because it makes it the only one of these statues other than Carey's that incorporates subtext, weirdness, and references outside of the cookie-cutter baseball context. The studly statue is not even super gay. Rather, it's just gay enough to challenge the status quo of boring baseball sculptures.

Official scoring: Home run

BATCOLUMN (1977, steel, 600 W. Madison) by Claes Oldenburg

This is pretty great public art. Because it's awesome and giant (over 100 feet!), stupid and absurd (it's a giant bat!), and it makes sense (Chicago loves baseball, has vertical skyscrapers, and is as phallic a city as any in America). And for our sake, the fact that it went up in '77, the year Richie Zisk was an All-Star mammoth homer-hitter for the Chi-Sox means this All-Star mammoth sculpture is pretty much a monument to this magazine's namesake.

Official scoring: Grand slam

Originally appeared in issue #21, Fall 2012.

Now These Were The Real Idiots

Jeff Boda

The touts who proclaim the 2004 Red Sox the strangest collection of misfits in recent World Series history obviously never followed the 1984 Padres. Now, there was a team of freaks. Political freaks, image freaks, unfortunate freaks. It had them all.

Growing up in rural Wisconsin, it made no sense for me to follow this team. But the baseball bug bit me in the spring of '84, when I was 13. I had just started receiving *The Sporting News*, poring over the box scores, back when the *News* was the bible of sports junkies everywhere, before the Internet and fantasy baseball made statistics and box scores instantly available everywhere and a necessity for shut-ins.

But I had to pick a team to follow, and I already had suffered through the disastrous post-World Series campaign of the Brewers, back when they still were in the American League. I had to pick a National League team, too, and the Padres sounded fun, with their taco uniforms, coming from a land that sounded exotic to someone who only twice in his life had left his cold, snowy, remote home state of Wisconsin.

I followed them off and on through the season, watching them advance to the playoffs against the Cubs. Down 2-0, they rallied to win the final three games (Cowboy that, my friend) before being crushed by the juggernaut Detroit Tigers.

They limped through the next season to an 83-79 record and slid downhill after that. But the memories remain, and oh what memories they are.

Three of their pitchers were members of the John Birch society. One of those later snapped his arm while throwing a pitch after attempting a comeback from cancer. Another Bircher died in a rehab center. Their second baseman was the first major professional athlete to die of AIDS in the U.S. Their all-American first baseman later was found to play the field as well as Wade Boggs. Their all-star right fielder holds a place in my heart as the best fat player of his generation.

Oh, and their utility infielder has released folk records. Can't make that one up.

The lineup:

General manager Jack McKeon. Cigar chomper. Trader Jack. Reckless in his approach.

Manager Dick Williams. Wilford Brimley's even more hard-assed twin, who helped egg on one of the worst beanball fests ever during a game against Pascuel Perez and the Braves in August of '84. Two bench-clearing brawls, three hit batters, six brushbacks, 19 ejected players and even five fans booted!

Catcher Terry Kennedy, left fielder Carmelo Martinez, third baseman Graig Nettles, center fielder Kevin McReynolds, and shortstop Garry Templeton. Good players, but nothing that weird. Sure, McReynolds drove Padres and, later, Mets fans nuts with his unfulfilled potential. Martinez could produce Manny-like gaffes and stumbles in the field. Nettles wrote one of the best baseball books in history, *Balls*. And Templeton will go down in history as the man who was traded for Ozzie Smith and flipped off the fans in St. Louis. But compared to the others, none of these players stood out. But Tim Flannery, the utility infielder? He's recorded seven folk records, and name one other former all-star who's also played the Quail Botanical Gardens.

And how can we not mention right fielder Tony Gwynn? A star point guard at San Diego State, he holds the school record for assists and later was drafted by the San Diego Clippers. The best hitter of his generation—yes, better than Wade Boggs—the 220-pounder also was the best fat player of his generation. Only two players after the Dead Ball Era weighed more than Gwynn and had 3,000 hits: Cal Ripken, who is five pounds heavier and five inches taller; Dave Winfield, about the same weight but seven inches taller.

But after that, the fun begins.

First baseman Steve Garvey: The smooth-fielding first baseman honed his image as an All-American boy, the wholesomest of baseball players, an endorsement machine because of it. Garvey later proved quite smooth with the ladies, too. After he retired, he was hit with not one, but two paternity suits, and his wife divorced him and wrote a scathing tell-all book. Unlike Boggs, he waited until after he retired before his mistresses were unveiled. Once touted as a potential candidate for the U.S. Senate, he now is serving penance on infomercials.

Second baseman Alan Wiggins. The saddest case of all the Padres. A leadoff dynamo, he propelled the lineup into the World Series, even though the Padres only hit 109 home runs all season, with McReynolds and Nettles tying for the team lead with 20 each. Wiggins struggled with drugs, mostly cocaine, throughout his career and was suspended indefinitely from baseball in '87 for repeated drug use. When he died at age 32 in '91, he was the first major athlete in the United States to die of AIDS (and probably acquired HIV from dirty needles while shooting heroin).

Starting pitchers Eric Show and Mark Thurmond and relief pitcher Dave Dravecky. All three members of the John Birch Society. Never heard of it? It could be because of a U.N. conspiracy. The far-rightist, anti-socialist group is based in Appleton, Wis., home of noted rightist nutjob, alkie, and R.E.M. song subject Joe McCarthy. To give you an idea of their extremist views, one of their books accused the Republican party of being controlled by elitist intellectuals. But being a Bircher wasn't the worst thing that happened to Show and Dravecky. Show, always a moody player (after Pete Rose got a hit off him to break Ty Cobb's record, Show sat down and pouted on the mound) and a diehard conservative, died at age 37 of a heart attack in a drug and alcohol center in California. Some reports said it occurred after he did a speedball. Dravecky, later traded to the Giants, underwent surgery for cancer in the arm after the 1988 season ended. In his second game in his 1989 comeback, his pitching arm snapped in two. And to make matters worse, he broke the arm again during the celebration after the Giants won the '89 pennant, then found out cancer had returned. In '91, his arm was amputated.

The team was tough luck, all the way around. People now want to remember Trader Jack for taking over the 2003 Marlins and managing them to the World Series. Me? I'll fondly remember him for assembling a world-class collection of oddities into the 1984 NL pennant winners.

Originally appeared in issue #12, Spring 2006.

Thanks, Kirby

Steve Reynolds

Just as we wrapped up issue #12 of *Zisk* in March of 2006, Hall of Famer Kirby Puckett passed away far too young at the age of 45 due to a cerebral hemorrhage. Much had been written about his sad post-baseball downfall in the years before his death. Since all that sordid business has been covered elsewhere (especially in that shocking 2003 *Sports Illustrated* cover article that explored his various indiscretions and the wide difference between his public image and his private life), I thought I'd share a personal note about the man and his relation to our little magazine.

   The first half of Puckett's too brief career spanned almost the exact same time frame as the first two phases of my baseball fixation. When he was first called up to the majors in 1984, I was fully immersed in the game and had been since I first started hating the New York Yankees in 1977. (My grandfather and grandmother were old Brooklyn Dodger fans, so the hatred of the Bronx Bombers dated long before George Steinbrenner had his first calm and rational disagreement with Billy Martin.) As Puckett improved his game so did my two favorite teams, the New York Mets and the Boston Red Sox, and I found myself digesting as much of the sport as I could. (And yes 1986 was a *very* difficult time for me, thanks for asking.) That passion somehow lasted into my first semester at Ithaca College in Ithaca, New York in the fall of 1987. (Historical note: it was at I.C. orientation that summer where I first met *Zisk* co-editor Mike Faloon.) I watched the World Series for the first time on a TV that was connected to—gasp—cable. As a Mets fan, I was ecstatic to see Puckett lead the plucky Twins over the Mets mortal enemy of that year, the St. Louis Cardinals, and grab their first ever World Series win.

   However, as college went on, it wasn't too surprising that I found new pursuits that consumed my baseball passion—mainly girls and radio shifts. In other words, I acted like a typical college student. I became a casual fan—I paid no attention to the regular season and checked in during the playoffs. (However, the only games I remember watching during those years are classics—the Kirk Gibson home run game in 1988 and the earthquake-interrupted A's-Giants game in 1989.) My baseball fandom wasn't the only thing that changed during those years. I grew out my hair, got into the Grateful Dead, got *out* of the Grateful Dead, and fell out of love with 75% of the bands I liked in high school after I heard the Replacements. In short, I started growing up.

I graduated in 1991 thinking I had a job in radio lined up. When that fell through, I moved back home and took an evening research job at the radio station where I'd interned one summer. It was, not shockingly, a pretty miserable job and not what I wanted to do. After three months, I quit and moved back to Ithaca with no solid plan for my post-collegiate life. That October, I was still out of work, so I basically lived on cash advances from my credit card. One fateful night, I went to a bar in downtown Ithaca called Plums with a couple of people still going to IC. We arrived just in time to see most of perhaps the best post-season game of all-time—Game 6 of the 1991 World Series between the Minnesota Twins and the Atlanta Braves. On that night, Kirby Puckett reignited my passion for the game that continues to this day (even through the 1994 strike *and* being a Mets fan from 2007 until the present). Puckett's amazing catch of Ron Gant's fly ball in the third inning and his home run to win the game in the eleventh were stunning to watch. I'm not sure if any baseball player has won such a crucial game practically by himself. My memory is foggy, but I'm certain there were no fans of either team at that bar. Yet the place exploded with joy when Puckett crushed the ball that landed into the left field seats. As someone who really was agonizing over what to do with his life, having that minute of pure euphoria was a sanity saver. I listened to a replay of the late Jack Buck's call of that play ("And we'll see you tomorrow night!") while composing this, and I got the same chills I did that cold fall night in Ithaca.

Thanks, Kirby—*Zisk* might not have been a part of my life without you.

Originally appeared in issue #12, spring 2006.

Ya Gotta Bereave

John Weber

Some people aren't supposed to age—or die. Like Captain Kangaroo. Or Johnny Cash. And certainly not Tug McGraw. Unbelievably, at least to the people of Philadelphia, the Tugger left this playing field on January 6, 2004, at the way-too-young age of 59 after a ten-month battle with a brain tumor.

I've been fortunate enough to see the life and career of Frank Edwin "Tug" McGraw from almost all perspectives. As a young, pennant-starved Phillies fan who watched Tug strike out Willie Wilson for the last out of the 1980 World Series. As a colleague who produced Phillies baseball on the radio while Tug was a popular TV feature reporter. As a journalist who interviewed Tug on his life and times. And even as a member of Tug's extended "family." The family of Phillies fans who truly loved and appreciated this man's warmth, humor, and dedication, the family who still finds the fact that Tug is gone just unbelievable.

Why did we love Tug so much? The World Series win? Sure, but Mike Schmidt sure isn't loved like Tug, and he had a little something to do with that championship, as well. Neither is Steve Carlton nor Manny Trillo nor Garry Maddox, all important pieces of that '80 squad. What made Tug stand out?

It was the twinkle in his eye. His banging his right thigh with his glove after a tough out. His exaggerated sighs of relief and patting his chest after wiggling out of a tough jam (and he sure *loved* to load the bases). Tug also worked his tail off on that mound, pitching through pain, through injuries, through overuse, through just about everything, especially in '80. If there's one thing that Philadelphia likes to see in their sports heroes, it's seeing them sweat. We want to see the effort. Mike Schmidt was never fully embraced by the Philly fans because he made everything look easy. We didn't see Schmitty sweat. Tugger, meanwhile, was usually drenched, and, most times, with a smile on his face.

And the things Tug would do for a laugh. There are so many moments, enough to fill the pages of this entire magazine and then some. For instance, in his first spring training as a Phillie, Tugger entered a game on St. Patrick's Day in a Phils uniform he had dyed green! Although the green uni didn't go over well with the umpires, they let him keep the green hat. That started a tradition of the Phils wearing green caps every

March 17th and auctioning them off for charity afterward. The day Elvis Presley died, the team was in Montreal closing out a series with the Expos. Tug showed up in the locker room with a complete Elvis outfit—right down to the hair. He then proceeded to wear the outfit on the flight to Chicago after the game! That started another tradition—Tug did his Elvis dress-up every year after that on the anniversary of the King's death.

There was one last standout public moment in the life of Tug McGraw. It was the final day in the life of Veterans Stadium. My dad and I went to the game together. It was a day filled with memories. After the game, there were a few things planned that would ensure the old girl's final day was long remembered. Like a parade of players, in uniform, from all of the teams that had competed in the Vet's history. All the players were introduced, one by one. The 1980 team came out. No McGraw. I had heard from my friends at the Phillies that, despite public proclamations to the contrary, Tug was not doing well at all, and they weren't sure he would make it to Christmas. I told my dad this, and concluded that he wasn't feeling well enough to participate.

After the player parade, the fans were promised three reenactments of memorable moments in Phillies history. Steve Carlton stepped to the mound and pretended to throw a record-breaking strikeout. Mike Schmidt stepped to the plate again, slammed his 500th home run all over again, and circled the bases (although he did the actual deed in Pittsburgh). And then a black sedan suddenly appeared next to the Phillies bullpen, cruising slowly toward the infield. The cheers were deafening as everyone in the park knew who was in that car. As Frank Edwin "Tug" McGraw exited that car between home and first and strode toward the mound, it really was 1980 again. He pitched from the stretch. The Vet was pandemonium. Tug threw that final imaginary pitch. An imaginary Willie Wilson missed it again. And Tug leapt into the air, just like he did on that incredible night. And as he came back to earth, every player from every Phillies team taking part in the day rushed toward him, engulfing him in a sea of red pinstripes, hugging him, patting him on the back, just trying to touch him, to grab a piece of magic.

It was another Tug McGraw memory no one in Philadelphia would ever forget.

Thanks, Tug, for everything you did—on the field and off.

Originally appeared in issue #8, Spring 2004.

Rusty Staub: Heroism from Left to Right Field
                                              Brian Cogan

Rusty Staub is a retired baseball player, but he is so much more than that. Rusty Staub is the last of the old-time unconditioned ball players, one that did not worry about minor details such as "conditioning" or "working out." Rusty Staub is many things to many people. A beloved ex-Met and beloved ex-Expo. During his tenure in Montreal he struggled to learn basic French and the locals nicknamed him "Le Grande Orange," not just for his flaming red hair, but also for his sheer enjoyment of playing baseball and playing it well. Rusty Staub was the kind of player who would have scoffed at steroids, he very likely figured that eating an additional rack of lamb or some bar-b-q, or even poutine (a beloved dish in Montréal) gave sufficient protein to get through game day.

There are many reasons to love Rusty. My main reason is that after years of being a sports fan, a baseball fan, and at the core of it, a Mets fan, I learned that acts of sports heroism were not achievable by us fans. Hitting massive home runs, going for the cycle, pitching perfect games could only be done by a few fabled individuals, those who lived high above us mere mortals in some kind of rarified world where foie gras was the main course and the bubbly flowed. Those were things for finer people, giants, immortals. However, as a Mets fan, I learned something different early on. That true heroism, really impressive feats, were those of getting up to the plate and actually facing a major league pitcher throwing a spherical object ninety miles an hour toward your head. Real heroism was catching a tiny speck in the corner of your eye while running backwards blinded by the glare of the spotlights. To me, heroism was just being able to play on a consistent level. To rise above our own inbred mortality and mediocrity, and to somehow manage to just live our lives and do our jobs, despite the obstacles time and nature place in our way.

That's why Rusty Staub is one of my heroes. He did not transcend time and nature, he fought them. He fought them and lost (as we all must do someday) and he accepted his fate with grace and equanimity. How many of today's top players can you imagine taking a back-up role and then not complaining when they were relegated to a pinch-hitting role just a few seasons after obvious greatness? Rusty didn't seem to mind, or at least if he did, he didn't gripe about it in the papers, didn't complain on ESPN (even if it did exist, we didn't have cable back then). He took it stoically. The late Dana Brand, a professor and writer who was essentially the Proust of Mets bloggers took this stoicism to be a sign that, as many of us suspected, Rusty was gay. It is true that a virile ball player is usually the target of *some* gossip about his private life. Pictures out at a nightclub with some floozy. A paternity suit here and there. But not Rusty. Rusty's private life, whether gay or straight, was his own. He was one of the last generation that thought that his hitting and fielding should speak for him, and for many years, it did. Even when he was breaking down, the only things Rusty ever wanted to talk about were either baseball, the many charitable organizations that he had founded[1] or his two restaurants, both now sadly closed.

While Rusty's first run with the Mets (1972-1975) was memorable, including some truly spectacular heroics leading up to the 1973 World Series, by the time he had returned in 1981, his time in baseball was clearly on the wane. There were some memorable moments, but Rusty was an aging ex-superstar (few remember that he was a six-time All-Star) who had come back to his second home (although he was only an Expo for four years, he was so beloved north of the border that they retired his number) to wind down his career as a player/coach. With the Mets he became a whiz at pinch-hitting. In 1983, he tied two major league records, with 25 RBIs as a pinch hitter and eight straight pinch hits in a row. In his last season in 1985, he only played in 54 games, hitting .267 (which by today's deflated standards, seems pretty reasonable), and was clearly on his way out. But still, Rusty had something in him that would not just give up. Rusty was almost done with baseball, but in his last season, baseball was not done with him.

While Rusty was nicknamed Le Grande Orange by the media in Montreal, by the time of his retirement, he was no longer the big yet fit young man who started with the Houston Colt 45's and came to prominence with the Expos. Rusty was a 41-year-old man who liked his meals and was not ashamed to say so. Rusty became a pinch hitter not just because of his skill at emergency at-bats, but because he was increasingly a defensive liability at his two positions, right field and first base. Perhaps he could have squeezed out a few more years in the American League as a designated hitter, but Rusty chose to end his career not as a slugger, feasting on the fastball pitchers of the American League, but a pinch-hitting specialist—one that few teams could (even to this day) hardly afford. But there is beauty in the pinch-hit. There is a certain nobility in being the man who sits on the bench all day, chatting to the rookies, joking with the pitchers on their off day, spitting

---

[1] He founded the New York Police and Fire Widows' and Children's Benefit Fund in 1985 with Paddy Burns. In the last three decades it has contributed over $114 million to the families of police and firemen killed in the line of duty. He also founded and runs the Rusty Staub Foundation, which also gives to charity.

sunflower seeds with the other guys when it was the Mets turn at bat. But even amidst all the joking, there was also a keen sense of immediacy. That at any moment, particularly in the later innings, the game may hinge on you snapping to attention. Much as an actor has to go from joking with the grips or flipping though a script to come alive as a character, Rusty could be called upon to perform at any moment. But unlike an actor who more or less knows when they are needed, Rusty had to find his rhythm and groove at any moment. When he was called into the game, usually at a crucial moment, the time for joking around was gone, Rusty knew that the team needed a hit, and whether he was ready or not, they were counting on him.

Despite the fact that Rusty was a quiet, unassuming, stoic player, ready at a moment to get up and use his twenty years of experience in the big leagues to get that one big hit in the late innings, usually then to be taken out for a pinch runner, his hitting was not the reason that Rusty Staub inhabits a special place in my heart to this day. Strangely enough, it was a play in the field that defines my idea of heroism. When I think of overcoming impossible odds, I think of a game played on April 28, 1985. The Mets were playing Pittsburgh in the seventeenth inning of an 18-inning marathon, Davey Johnson eventually ran out of position players.

Rusty had to stay in the game.

Johnson's strategy was admirable, considering Rusty's weight, age, and range. Rusty was moved back and forth between right field to left field, depending on if the hitter was right handed or left handed. The first time this happened, the fans merely shrugged, by the fourth or fifth time, they were cheering. I was watching at home with my brothers and parents and we started cheering, as well. It was a grand sight, Rusty constantly jogging across the field to switch positions. If he felt humiliated, or annoyed, he never let on. He stoically moved from left to right to left to right to left. Then it happened. It had to happen. It was as inevitable as the hubris of '80s movie foreshadowing.[2] There was a hit, and the ball was pulled to right field, where Rusty was now residing. Rusty ran as fast as he could run at that point in his life, which was not very fast. But nonetheless, he pursued that ball with the tenacity of a lumbering bloodhound gamely tearing after his last rabbit. All in all, he probably ran about 25 or so feet, before he caught the ball. We all jumped around the room hugging each other out of sheer glee. It was a brilliant performance. Rusty had done it, he ran, sweat pouring down his face, and he caught the damn ball! But that was really never in doubt. Just as the hitter (I can't recall who he was and it would spoil the magic

---

[2] An example would be where an older detective in an '80s movie announces how close to retirement he is. This means he will die shortly.

of the story to look it up) was destined to hit the ball into right field, Rusty was destined to catch it. He was always going to catch that ball, and in some rift in the time space continuum, thanks to the magic of quantum physics, Rusty is always catching that ball.

The fans gave Rusty a standing ovation. This may have been the greatest thing they had ever seen in baseball. Even his previous heroics and his overcoming injuries to play in 1973 were overshadowed by the sight of an aging, overweight Rusty, running (to my mind) in slow motion and, at the last possible second, catching the ball. It was possibly the greatest baseball feat I had seen up to that time in my life. Rusty Staub, despite his age, despite his weight, despite the fact that he knew this would be his last season, despite the fact that anyone else would have made that a routine play, made it spectacular. Rusty made it heroic because it was not just an aging Rusty out there making a catch, it was because unlike anyone else the Mets had that season, he was struggling to make an effort. He was straining to do something that would have been routine just a few years back. What Rusty Staub represented out there as he chased that fly ball down to end the inning was not a man with dwindling baseball talent. No, he was *us* on that field. He was the fans. He was all of our frailties, all of our middle-aged aches and pains and doubts and fears, and when we strain to move the couch and feel our age, feel our vestiges of youth and strength slipping away, we are Rusty running 25 feet in right field to catch that ball. I used to love watching Jose Reyes make a spectacular catch, or run the bases with love in his eye and a hurt look when he was prevented from going to third, but I couldn't feel for him. I don't have that kind of passion, that kind of enthusiasm for a sport anymore. My delight is not on stretching my body to the limit, but in overcoming the many age-related limits that have been imposed by relentless entropy. Rusty was me out there catching that ball; Rusty was you out there catching that ball, and when Rusty did catch that ball, as we knew he would, it was an achievement that made us feel that we could still manage one last small victory. That we could show the kids the old man still had some gas left in the tank, that we can still wink at the pretty girl behind the checkout line, and she'd still blush because we still had it. Rusty made that catch because he had something left to prove. And because we are all Rusty, we don't have to be stars anymore, we can accept the limitations of time with grace, knowing that we can still have our victories in life. They won't be major feats of strength and grace anymore, they will be small, but dignified. We will from time to time be put out of our element, and like Rusty, we will triumph. Then we will fade into the background, and let someone else, our kids perhaps, or at least the next generation have the spotlight. Some day, they, too, will be switching from left to right field in their last season, and we hope to god, that someday they too will make that catch.

Brian Cogan

Postscript: In April 2012, *Zisk* editor Mike Faloon and I attended the first academic conference on the New York Mets. It was held in tribute to the previously mentioned professor Dana Brand who came up with the batty and wonderful idea of a conference devoted to the Mets before his sudden death due to heart problems. Mike and I presented a paper on the "Mets as Punk Rock" and afterwards we stayed and talked baseball with some really knowledgeable fans. It was a great time, and Rusty Staub was the special guest speaker at the banquet later that night. Rusty gave a really interesting humble talk about himself and his career, and especially his charities, which were clearly his true passion. He had a firm handshake, and he seemed comfortable joking around with old teammates like Ed Kranepool and Bud Harrelson. After his speech, there was a Q&A session and he delightedly answered questions for half an hour. I had wanted to ask him about the Pittsburgh game, but was too shy. Luckily another fan was not, and before he had even finished the question, Rusty laughed and said, "Oh boy, here we go!" As I looked around at the chuckling crowd, I could tell that all of them remembered that game. I think that Rusty jokingly dismissed it by saying that he did what he had to do for the team and it was a "hell of a game." Around me, I could see the crowd nodding. Several hundred people were there, most of them die-hard middle-aged Mets fans, and they were united in remembrance not of a moment of transcendent victory, not of the '86 Mets or Bill Buckner's legs, or Mookie's smile, or Gary Carter's last bow, or Seaver going into the Hall of Fame as a Met. This was a crowd smiling and laughing because deep down we all had the same evocative memory; we all knew that we were all Rusty. Le Grand Orange smiled down from the podium at us, and we smiled right back.

Originally appeared in issue #21, Fall 2012.

PART V
F IS FOR FAKE NOT PHONY—
FICTION AND HUMOR

Don't You Know He's A 3,000 Man: Milwaukee's Proud Fake Baseball Tradition Lives On

Rev. Norb

I have never been completely sure what the point of portraying "real" sports franchises in fictional sports-based movies is supposed to be. Does basing a movie like *Major League* around a fictitious roster of a "real" team like the Cleveland Indians really yield a greater potential for suspension of disbelief than it would have had the movie been based on the unlikely exploits of, say, a team called the "Washington Wombats" or "Metropolis Manglers" instead? I mean, what's a greater leap of faith: Allowing for the existence of a completely imaginary MLB franchise, or pretending that Ricky "Wild Thing" Vaughn really pitched the Cleveland Indians to the World Championship in our lifetime? (Geez, next thing you'll be expecting me to believe that some day the Indians will be like three outs away from their first World Series title in 49 years, and then they'll blow it in extra innings against some fictitious team like the Florida Marlins or something.) I mean, dude, I can look it up: The Indians were never owned by an ex-stripper; haven't won a World Series since the year Israel declared independence; never called Charlie Sheen up from the bullpen. *There is duly notarized data which states otherwise*, and everybody knows it. So, I mean, what's the point? Who ya tryin' ta fool? And whose idea is it to use real teams anyhow? Do the moviemakers think using actual franchise identities attracts sports fans who might otherwise give the movie a wide berth, or is the appearance of legit sports teams mere product placement undertaken by the league? If the latter is the case, fans of the other 29 teams can add another charge of shameless porkbellying (or kosher equivalent) to Bud Selig's laundry list of crimes against the sport: The main character in *Mr. 3000* is—gasp!—a Milwaukee Brewer.

For those of you who neither know nor care (which I am estimating to be approx. 100%, +/- about 0.0%), *Mr. 3000* is a Hollywood motion picture released in 2004 (about 996 years too soon if the math can be trusted), starring from-what-I've-seen pretty much legitimately useless Chicago comedian Bernie Mac as Stan Ross, an arrogant ex-Brewer who believes he has retired with exactly 3,000 hits to his credit, only to find that, due to an accounting error, he actually only has 2,997. Sooo . . . having been chronically unpopular with the fans and writers throughout his career, Ross feels the magical 3,000 number is necessary to cement his inclusion into the Baseball Hall of Fame, and returns to the Brewers in hopes of getting the three remaining hits. That's ya plot, folks.

Counterintuitively, some (all?) of the crowd shots for *Mr. 3000* were filmed at the Brewers' stadium, Miller Park (the counterintuitive aspect stems from the fact that *Major League*, which, as indicated previously, featured the Cleveland Indians, was shot at the Brewers' old home, Milwaukee County Stadium, so you'd think that *Mr. 3000* would have been filmed entirely at Jacobs Field—but, like I said, I don't really understand why they use real teams in these movies anyway [I mean, did they use real teams in *The Bad News Bears*? In *Gus*? In *Son of Flubber*? Actually, I don't remember if they did or not. Perhaps I should be looking this stuff up.]). (But this, in fact, inflicts further questions: If they filmed *Major League* at Milwaukee County Stadium [which they did], if the faux-Indians crowd was primarily composed of Brewers fans [it was], and if they even cast the Brewers' radio announcer, Bob Uecker, as the Indians fictitious play-by-play guy, "Harry Doyle" [they did], then *why the fuck didn't they just make* Major League *about the Brewers instead of the Indians*??? [Then-division rivals, at that!] I mean, it would've saved them the expense of replacing the Brewers' green outfield cushions with Cleveland Municipal Stadium-style blue ones, at the very least. See, that's why Bud Selig is such a great Commissioner: 1. He ain't gonna take that shit; 2. He kept the blue cushions up after the filming was over. *Hey, free cushions!*) We'll let the continuity director explain how the home scoreboard for both the *Mr. 3000* faux-Brewers and the *Major League* faux-Tribe came to be emblazoned with a WTMJ ad. *WTMJ, your fictional superstation!* Needless to say, when presented with the chance for celluloid immortality that sitting in the stands during the filming of *Mr. 3000* would surely afford me, I wasted no (well, some) time in making plans to attend one of the filming sessions, finally settling on the final evening of filming, which was conveniently sandwiched around a "real" Brewers/Astros game. Actually, I had no interest in being part of the filming—I just wanted to go to that game because, as the last home game before Bob Uecker's induction into the Baseball Hall of Fame (3,000 hits be damned!), they were handing out coupons for two bucks off a beer so the whole crowd could get sloshed and toast Uke after the fourth inning. Hey, I'm value-conscious! Sue me!

The evening does not start well. In the Miller Park parking lot, I almost get into a fistfight with two carloads (well, one carload, one truckload) of burly dolts, who are irate at me over my perceived breaking of certain traffic protocols (hey, just because *you* want to be in the backed-up lane because you are *too fucking dense* to realize there actually *are* non-backed-up lanes doesn't mean I can't go in the not-backed up lane and you gotta pull out in front of me and yell "FUCK OFF!" or "BACK UP!" or whatever [although you gotta love the middle-aged redneck types who think their every hostile bellow is gonna send the bellowed-at party zipping off in reverse in a cloud of dust, hatpins and speed lines, as they do exude a certain fucked-up tragic beauty]). As I exit my car, the offended parties hurl a variety of bon mots my way, ending the merriment with "WHAT A FUCKING FREAK!!! I BET HE'S GOT TINTED HAIR AND AN EARRING!!!" I am legitimately offended. I don't have an earring.

Upon entry to the stadium, I briefly plan out potential courses of future action against my belligerent lotmates. My favorite involves going down to the "Stan's Stick" stand, buying one of the super-deluxe $57 wood bats with my name engraved on the barrel, striding calmly back into the parking lot, and, with no manner of advance warning whatsoever, suddenly start maniacally hopping up and down and shrieking "AY YI YI YI YI YI YI YI YI!!!" at the top of my lungs while smashing the shit out of the truck and car with the bat, tongue waggling, eyes bugging out like a Big Daddy Roth cartoon—then stopping just as suddenly as I started, calmly walking back to my car, and driving away—but then I find two stray beer coupons blowing across the ramp and am filled with nothing but thoughts of peace and love for my fellows.

The fourth inning toast is a great success, as I am getting fairly toasted. Bob Uecker, shown live (along with Brewers neo-glory years GM Harry Dalton) on the Jumbotron during the toast, takes his microphone and imitates the Pope dispersing Holy Water into the crowd at Mass. I am in stitches: Bob Uecker would even be funny as a goddamn *mime*.

Brewers win. Having spilled my last beer, following a leap to the feet during a particularly adept play by Brewers third baseman Wes Helms, I retire to the Fridays Front Row Sports Grill for a cold one (I wind up drinking five pints of Miller in twenty minutes. Hey, Bob would want it that way! Plus he can give me a benediction with his microphone), where I run into Justin (Screwballs/Yesterday's Kids/Obsoletes—plus he's the guy who engineered my album *Earth's Greatest Rocker!*) and Tito (longtime associate of the Screwballs/Yesterday's Kids/Obsoletes camp).

Rev. Norb

We wanna stick around for the filming, but are quite unsure what exactly is happening, and what this will entail on our part, so we figure we will drink and watch the filming for a while that we might get our Wild Hollywood Bearings squared away. The acoustics at Friday's, located above left field, are horrible. The lady running the filming appears to be saying things of some import, but all we can hear is Charlie Brown's teacher. People start taking turns singing the beginning of the national anthem. Some are cheered; some are booed. We have no idea if the crowd reaction is part of the script, or some manner of peer review. We debate the deep philosophical question of whether a rendition of "The Star-Spangled Banner" sung by an actor in the process of portraying a character singing "The Star-Spangled Banner" is actually an official performance of our national anthem or not (results inconclusive). Large squadrons of faux-Atlanta Braves and faux-San Francisco Giants take the field. We yell a variety of brainless epithets at them as they jog past our perch. The Jumbotron plays a previously shot scene where Bernie "Stan Ross" Mac, clad in period-specific '90s Brewers garb, receives the world's least convincing brushback pitch from a Boston Red Sox hurler, and retaliates by hitting the next offering squarely into the offending pitcher's nuts. If said footage is any indication of the quality of the project as a whole, I fear the term "Sub-*Major League II*" may be making its way into the contemporary lexicon shortly.

Stan the Man Ross cometh by golf cart. He waves to the crowd, who fill most but not all of the lower deck between first and third base. We decide this is our cue to join the masses (well, that and I had quickly drank myself flat broke), and make our way out and over to the field. A Brewers security doofus stops us and informs us we need "tickets" to get in. *Fuck you! I know the rally rabbit!* Confused but essentially apathetic, we pull out our ticket stubs, which seems to work (we later decided that, having never signed even the most basic of paperwork, we likely weren't supposed to be there) (ohmigawd, renegade extras!), and meander down to about the fourth row, right behind the backstop. These are, by far, the best seats I've ever had or am likely to ever have at a Brewers game. God bless you, Bernie Mac! You saved Christmas!

The filming, as one might expect, consists of endless variations on one theme: Bernie Mac is on deck, Guy in front of Bernie Mac finishes his at bat, Bernie Mac strides to the plate, Bernie Mac argues balls and strikes, Bernie Mac strikes/pops/flies out, Bernie Mac yells at umpire, Bernie Mac trudges dejectedly back to dugout, guy after Bernie Mac in the order begins his at bat, cut. We, The Crowd, would react appropriately (the guy who always followed Stan Ross [who wears #20, by the way] in the order was named "Osbourne." Needless to say, it didn't take me too many faux AB's to realize that my destiny as an actor was to lead the crowd in a chant of "OZ-ZEEEE!!! OZ-ZEEEE!!! OZ-ZEEEE!!! OZ-

ZEEEE!!!", so if any such chant makes it into the movie, that was *my doing*, and I want royalties. *Where's my two dollars???*). Occasionally, Bernie Mac would fuck up and actually get to first base successfully, then stand there sheepishly, absorbing mild hecklement from the crowd but, for the most part, the filming was three straight hours of watching a guy in a Brewers uniform strike out: As such, the sad fact of the matter was that the filming was virtually identical to the whole 2002 season, 'cept I had better seats.

Originally appeared in issue #7, Fall 2003.

Hey, Talk to the Sock!

Steve Reynolds

The Red Sox Nation—the millions of Sox fans around the country so dubbed by their cable network NESN—rejoiced throughout the winter of 2004-2005 after the team broke their 86-year World Series drought. Much of that acclaim went to pitcher Curt Schilling. The outspoken right-hander had a radical procedure done on his right ankle to enable him to pitch the crucial Game 6 in the ALCS against the New York Yankees. But true Sox fans know that it wasn't Schilling's arm that did the most damage that night to the Yanks lineup—it was the bloody sock. Once A-Rod and those other corporate hacks saw blood on the field, they were struck with fear and lost the will to compete.

So the sock has earned its rightful place among baseball's elite—at the Baseball Hall of Fame. The sock spent quality time in Cooperstown before embarking on its second career as a celebrity endorser and as a cast member on the new version of *Laugh In*. Zisk had the chance to speak with the bloody sock just before it was to film a cameo role in the latest Bruce Willis action thriller, *I'm Just Here For My Paycheck*.

Zisk: So how did you land the role in this film?
Bloody Sock: Well, Bruce's people saw my work in this great Clint Eastwood film—

Zisk: You were in *Million Dollar Baby*?
BS: No, *Blood Work*.

Zisk: Oh, I didn't see that one.
BS: And they were impressed by the support I gave all the other actors, so they thought I'd fit in perfect for this scene where Bruce kicks in a door and hurts his ankle. You'll see me for a couple of minutes when his leg is bleeding while he's interrogating Colin Farrell's character.

Zisk: Sounds great. Getting back to baseball for a second, what do you say to people who don't believe that the sight of you on Curt Schilling's ankle intimidated the Yankee lineup?
BS: Well, those people just don't know how powerful the image of blood on the field can be. Baseball players aren't used to seeing blood, unless it's an umpire or a coach getting attacked by a Chicago White Sox

fan. Football players are used to it—heck, I started my career working for the Cincinnati Bengals' defensive line. So when I got the opportunity to switch sports in 2004, I knew that I could have an immediate impact. And who else could I work for but the Red Sox?

Zisk: Indeed. And do you feel slighted that Curt hasn't given you any credit for his pitching performance in that game?
BS: Yeah, it definitely hurt. But when he found out I was getting into the Hall of Fame before him, I know it pissed him off. I sent him a postcard from there that said, "The only way you'll make it in here is to buy a ticket."

Zisk: Ouch. So with your new-found celebrity, have you scored any endorsement deals?
BS: Of course. I've just signed on to be the print image for a new line of Fruit of the Loom products called Wounded Wool Socks. I'm also going to star in series of commercials for Lee jeans alongside their current mascot, Buddy Lee. They're going to call my character Blood E. Lee. Get it?

Zisk: Yes, very tasteful.
BS: I'm also in talks with Taco Bell to endorse their new Bloody Beef Burrito.

Zisk: Ugh. So, are there any pet projects that you intend to do, now that all this cash is rolling in?
BS: Yes. The whole sports and acting thing has been rewarding, but what I really want is to kick off a recording career. I just signed a three album deal with Bloodshot Records out of Chicago. My first release through them will be a reimagining of my favorite album of all time, The Rolling Stones' *Let It Bleed*.

Zisk: Um, won't that be kind of hard, considering you have no hands?
BS: No problem at all—I've got a stellar cast of musicians lined up, led by sax man Bleeding Gums Murphy. It will be so loud, it will make you ears bleed.

Originally appeared in issue #10, Spring 2005.

Zisk vs. ESPN

Mike Faloon

ESPN's Anthony Kazmierczak: Mike Faloon, please.

Zisk: I hate telemarketers! You're not a telemarketer are you?
AK: My name's Anthony Kazmierczak, I'm an associate producer with *Baseball Tonight*, and I'm . . .

Zisk: . . . calling to apologize for letting one of your ESPN.com goons steal our ideas? It's about time!
AK: I don't know what you're referring to.

Zisk: Come on. Jim Baker, *ESPN Insider*, January 13, 2004. He wrote about MEPs, "Most Entertaining Players," we introduced that idea back in 2002—*Zisk*, issue number five.
AK: I don't know what you're referring to, and with all due respect, a little gratitude would be nice. We only make one of these calls to fans a year. I'm calling . . .

Zisk: If you'd have called me a few years ago, you could have avoided hiring Rob Dibble.
AK: Hey, he's good. He played for a World Series winner. He's got personality, he calls them as he . . .

Zisk: Stop, please, before you compare him to Jim Rome. Isn't Dibble the wizard who said, "I'll run through the streets naked if Ichiro hits over .280?"
AK: Just like a Mets fan, living in the past. That quote's from 2001. It's ancient history, Swoboda. Let's cut to the chase: our coverage here in 2004. I've got a lunch with Musial at one.

Zisk: Seriously? Stan the Man? That's awesome!
AK: I know, Stan's a great guy.

Zisk: Where do you start with a guy like that? The '46 World Series? Winning three MVPs? His 3,000th hit?

AK: Actually, you act like you already know those answers, and you ask him about his last round at Pebble Beach or how his granddaughter's doing at CalTech.

Zisk: Curb your enthusiasm, right. I never remember that.
AK: That's why you're still in zines.

Zisk: And you're calling me because?
AK: Because that doesn't mean you're always wrong. Our numbers are down this month, and we hear you don't like our Ichiro coverage, just wondering if there's a connection. A little bit of market research.

Zisk: Your numbers should be down, your Ichiro coverage—or lack thereof—sucks. When I checked the scores this morning, on ESPN2—you know when you guys list the scores on the bottom of the screen?
AK: We call that a crawl.

Zisk: You showed the Mariners-Rangers score from the previous night. The Mariners won 16-6 and Ichiro got four hits and yet he didn't even get mentioned in your "crawl." But you did list Randy friggin' Winn. That's wrong, that's second-class treatment. And don't feed me the "small market" line either. Sure, Seattle's smaller than LA and New York, but it's not like you're waiting for the Pony Express to deliver news from that little remote outpost in Seattle. Just look at the guys Ichiro's going to pass in the coming weeks: Ty Cobb, Rogers Hornsby, Lefty O'Doul. Legends! Ichiro's putting up numbers nobody's approached in over seventy years, and the Devil Rays got more airtime for arriving late in New York for a meaningless series with the Yankees. The Devil Rays!
AK: Let's be honest. Ichiro . . .

Zisk: I'm not done yet. He's also got a shot at the record for most hits over a four-year span. Granted, that's more obscure, but it's no less impressive. And all I hear from ESPN is how Ichiro never walks, and how few RBIs he has, and his low slugging percentage. He's not there to slug the ball, he gets on base. And who's he going to drive in? The Mariners are awful. What more can you ask for than a guy, like Ichiro, who hits over .360 with runners in scoring position?
AK: Where'd you hear ESPN make those arguments?

Zisk: On ESPN radio.
AK: There's a reason those guys work in radio. Where was all your righteous fervor the last time Ichiro took a shot at the single season hit record, back in 2001? You come across like a stats geek. Let me guess,

you own a copy of Cat Stevens' *Numbers* album, right? His numerology record?

Zisk: Anthony, put the gloves back on. But just to be clear, that's the one with "Banapple Gas" on it, right?
AK: Just as I thought—just like I told the other producers—you've got nothing. Next, you're going to tell me to cut back on the amount of airtime *Baseball Tonight* gives to home runs.

Zisk: (Pause) Hear me out. All homers pretty much look the same. But, triples! It's all about triples! The throw from right to the cutoff man to third base, the slide, the tag! I've also got an idea for an hour-long special on why the pitching mound should be lowered. Originally, I envisioned it as a three-part series, but I'm pragmatic.
AK: Well, now . . .

Zisk: You know what I mean, right? And web gems, those are cool, but you should make each clip longer, show more of the set up leading to the great play. And you should lead with the Ichiro countdown. Don't wait until he's five hits from the record before you start cutting away for every one of his at-bats. Who cares about Bonds? It's just a matter of time before he passes Henry Aaron, he just has to stay alive to get his record—which is a mere thirty years old, I might add. Ichiro has severe limitations on his record, he's in a race against time!
AK: You know, you're making a lot of good points. We've got a couple guys leaving for Fox's Saturday game of the week—you're a teacher, maybe next summer, during your break, you'd like to come in and do some freelance work?

Zisk: Seriously?
AK: Hell no. Triples? Thanks for your time. (Click)

Originally appeared in issue #9, Fall 2004.

A Ray of Hope: The Devil Speaks Out

Steve Reynolds

The Tampa Bay Devil Rays finished in last place in the AL East in 2007. In 2008, the Tampa Bay Rays finished first in the AL East and made it to the World Series for the first time. Was it the development of the club's young starters? The emergence of Rookie of the Year candidate Evan Longoria? The wisdom of the wily veteran Cliff Floyd? Nope—it's because the franchise's deal with the Devil was finally over. Without "Devil" in their name (and the dark prince of all that is unholy messing up the works) Tampa Bay finally has a winner. To get more on this story, we tracked down the Devil at his vacation home in the Caribbean, where he was creating hurricanes to destroy lives in North America.

Zisk: So what do I call you? Satan? Beelzebub? Your holy darkness?

The Devil: You can call me Ron—but just don't call me late to dinner like my last wife, Anna Nicole Smith! Whoa, I thought things would be great when I brought her down to my pad, but she would not shut up! She was the eighth wife in a row I had to burn to a crisp.

Zisk: Well, Ron, after seeing that *South Park* movie, I thought you were gay.

The Devil: That was just a phase I went through. I was young, I needed the souls.

Zisk: Um, okay. So as I understand it, you originally made a deal with former Rays owner Vince Naimoli. He got an expansion franchise and you got a piece of the name.

The Devil: Well, the deal for the devil name was only for ten years because I wasn't sure how being associated with the game would impact my public image. I mean, this was right after the strike of 1994, and baseball's public image wasn't much better than mine. (Evil laugh) So I said we'd do a deal for a ten-year period only, and that we would revisit it during the 2007 season.

Zisk: Legend has it that when you make a deal for a soul, people usually get something great at first and then it comes back to bite them in the end. It seems to me with the Devil Rays that nothing good ever happened.

The Devil: Well, Naimoli said he wanted a competitive team quickly, and he got one. They did compete in games. That didn't mean they would actually win any of those games. You humans are always suckers. Well, except for that Daniel Webster guy. That case still chaps my ass.

Zisk: I guess it's easy to hold grudges when you're immortal. So now that the deal with the team expired—when Naimoli sold and the new ownership group removed your name from the team—do you have any regrets about causing all that misery? I mean, people did notice the team started playing better when your name was taken off the uniforms.

The Devil: Nah, I don't have any regrets. That deal got me great seats to see the Red Sox and the Yankees. Being the lord of all that is unholy doesn't get you great seats at Fenway without at least a grand to back it up.

Zisk: One last question while I have you on the phone—who did the worse job portraying you on the big screen—Al Pacino (*The Devil's Advocate*) or Elizabeth Hurley (*Bedazzled*)?

The Devil: Oh, Pacino, that's for certain. The day we signed that deal so he could be in *The Godfather* he said to me, "I like your style. I'm going to remember that if I ever play you in a movie." He got my hair all wrong.

Originally appeared in issue #17, Fall 2008.

Darryl, Off Broadway – An Interview with Chris Gethard

Mike Faloon

Like most baseball fans, we at *Zisk* are a refined lot. We never wear white after Labor Day, we tip 20%, and from time to time we check out the latest in off-Broadway productions. This past spring, at the always reliable Upright Citizen's Brigade Theatre in NYC, we saw Darryl Strawberry's one-man show, *Darryl*.

The show was brilliant—even with understudy Chris Gethard in the title role. Rather than rehash well-known events, *Darryl* tracks Strawberry's long, slow, painful fall from grace, showing us never-before-seen sides of the troubled ballplayer—how he was inspired by wheelchair basketball, how he patched things up with Keith Hernandez, how he found the cure for cancer, and how he reigned supreme over the pits of hell.

As it turns out, Strawberry was unavailable for an interview but his understudy, the aforementioned Chris Gethard, was willing to chat with *Zisk*, offering a behind-the-scenes look at *Darryl: Darryl Strawberry's One-Man Show*. (Interview by Mike Faloon)

Zisk: We're talking with actor Chris Gethard, understudy for Darryl Strawberry. How many weeks have you been his understudy?

Chris Gethard: The first draft of the play was written four years ago, and I was involved from the beginning, so I've known about this for four years, and I've been doing the show for three months; I've been his understudy for three months, and it's been a lot more work than I thought because he has not shown up a single time. As far as I know he has no idea that he has an understudy that's performing his show, which he may or may not know even exists, which probably explains why he hasn't shown up.

Zisk: Have you received any feedback from either the Mets or the Yankees?

CG: I have not yet heard anything, but I know that someone in the Mets organization knows about it only because someone who came to the show whose uncle worked in the Mets organization had told him about it. My great fear is that they're going to show up and sue me and/or the UCB Theatre for the existence of the show, but so far no luck on that. That would be the worst thing ever, but also the coolest thing ever.

Zisk: Were you there when Darryl wrote it, or did he feed you ideas and you wrote it? How did that work?

CG: He wrote the whole thing is what we pre-suppose, Darryl Strawberry sat down and wrote that whole thing. That's the in-character answer, that I didn't write a single word of the entire thing. Darryl Strawberry wrote the entire thing and just can't make the performances. In reality, I started writing it four years ago. But even in the premise of the show at the end of the show I like to thank him and say we're tinkering with this part or we're going to rewrite this bit so it'll be different next week. I do like to tell the world that Darryl Strawberry wrote this show.

Zisk: What sparked the idea?

CG: The show actually started with my brother. He went to LaSalle, a tiny liberal arts school where everybody knew everybody and he hung out with the punk rock kids and there was a large hippie contingent and in a very clichéd way they hated each other. These hippie kids would hold open mic poetry nights, and my brother and all his friends would go and disrupt them and try to ruin their poetry nights. Then my brother started signing up and giving monologues as Darryl Strawberry. I asked him if I could steal the premise, and I came up with the idea of being the understudy and added a lot more layers to it. I think there's one joke of my brother's, the one about Darryl Strawberry's great-great-grandfather inventing the strawberry.

Zisk: I love it when Darryl takes a bite of a strawberry and then reminds the audience, "Royalties, bitches!" My wife hasn't seen the show yet, but she loves that joke.

CG: We started getting written up and a rumor went around that Darryl Strawberry's actually doing a show and the first three times I did the show [the audience was] friends of mine, it was comedians, it was people who knew me. And then about a month in there were lots of people showing up fully decked out in Mets gear and showing up with things they wanted autographed. At first it was funny, but then to get on stage in front of those people was terrifying. There have been times when they announce that Darryl can't make it and there are resounding boos and I have to win them over, and that strawberry bit tends to get them, that is where I can feel people being like, Okay, we get it.

Zisk: When I saw the show, I found it interesting to scan the crowd to see which people were there because it was a comedy show and which people were there because they heard that Darryl Strawberry was appearing off-Broadway.

CG: Instead of house music I play a copy of the "Let's Go Mets" video that they put out in '86, and these guys, all across the room you could feel these Mets fans uniting, it was really kind of amazing. Backstage, I couldn't see them, but I could hear them. One guy would yell out something about Gary Carter, and then another guy on the opposite side of the audience would yell out a stat or another player's name, or Mookie Wilson would come up and everyone was like, 'Mookie!' or they mentioned Rusty Staub and it got a big cheer. That was one of the weeks where there was an 'ugghh' when they announced, 'His understudy Chris Gethard will be doing the show tonight,' but then two minutes into it those guys were laughing more than anybody. From the start, I was hoping this show would go beyond just the comedian scene. I got a big rush out of having the Mets fans show up and actually enjoy it because that's going to a totally different audience.

Zisk: Most of the show is fabricated. Are there any events that are actually from his life?

CG: The first time we did the show it was probably five minutes longer and that entire five minutes was true facts, things that actually happened, exposition about Darryl Strawberry's real life, his career, coming up in Crenshaw and being on the best high school team ever, a lot of stuff like that. And what we found was that the people who thought it was Darryl just wanted a comedy show after a certain point, once they got the premise they didn't care and it was amazing to me. The thing that shocked me the most was how little convincing I have to do. The very first video that plays in the show is Mike Wallace doing the intro to a *60 Minutes* piece and it's the exposition they did—he had an amazing career, then he got into drugs, cancer, beset by demons, and this and that. Once the audience saw that they didn't give a shit about anything else I had to say about Darryl Strawberry, so we trimmed stuff out, to the point where the entire show is a lie. Every week, people come up to me, even good friends of mine, and ask, How much of that is true? Did Darryl Strawberry really beat up a cop and knock out his horse? People think the most ludicrous things are true. I was a huge Andy Kaufman fan as a kid—and I would never compare myself to Andy Kaufman—but, wow, it's so much easier to trick people than I thought.

Zisk: Was that the idea from early on, to follow the arc of his career but plug in different events?

CG: My original idea when I sat down with my director, I was like, I have this idea I'm going to pretend to be Darryl Strawberry and I'll say that I'm his understudy and basically what I'm going to do is tell a story that everybody knows about him—like everybody knows that he and Doc Gooden were drug buddies—so I'll get up and reference something like that, something that actually happened, and then I'll follow it up by saying here's the stuff that didn't make the papers, the stuff that the Mets covered up. I started doing monologues at open mics around town and even then people didn't respond at all to the true stuff and the fake stuff they flipped out for. Everybody knows enough about him already, he's a character, especially in New York City. He's almost mythological at this point. I can say anything—anything's feasible—and if anything could be true, nothing has to be.

Zisk: Now that I think about it he was part of the '80s Mets and the '90s Yankees, the city's two biggest teams of the past twenty or twenty-five years.

CG: Yeah, I grew up in northern New Jersey which is one hundred percent under the wing of the New York media and I remember the '86 Mets. That team had hero status and he was one of the chosen few and every time he got arrested and every time he got kicked out of baseball you could feel it, the entire city would get back on his side. I remember so well when he came back in the minor leagues in the mid-1990s, Minnesota, I think.

Zisk: Right, he came back with one of the independent leagues.

CG: In New York, when that was on the news, that wasn't sports, that was anchor desk material. In this town, there's very little need for exposition. Anyone who's been here, even for five years, knows who he really is. It's almost like Mike Tyson, with very few alterations this could be the Mike Tyson story but I would never do that because I would have to impersonate his voice.

Zisk: And you'd have to commit to the face tattoo later in the show.

CG: That would be funny if I did his understudy and I came out with the fake face tattoo. There's your sequel. Yeah, those videos—the '86 Mets video and the *60 Minutes* piece—are priceless. You have Mike Wallace calling Strawberry a loser. My show kind of begins and ends with Darryl Strawberry saying, Leave me alone, every time I do anything it's on the news and that's not fair. Watching that video that was a point where I was like, this guy has had a rough life and we forget that. He's a freak show, and we tune in or read about him hoping he has another downfall so he can come back, but it is not an easy life. I'm sure all the scrutiny doesn't help. The only two guys in that video who stick by him are like these equipment managers from the Mets who never gave up on him. I feel bad for the guy in the sense that people make mistakes and people never ever let him live down his. I'm sure a large percentage of people have done things as bad or worse than Darryl Strawberry has but he will never be allowed to move on with his life.

Zisk: It would be funny if one of the anecdotes you made up came back to him, a person walking up to him and asking if he really punched out a horse.
CG: A girl came up to me and said her parents live next to him in Florida and she said she'd be sure to tell them about the show, and I was like, Please don't! I don't want to get sued. But my ultimate dream is for him to come see it and see what he thinks.

Zisk: It's like you fear the cliff as much as you want to go over it.
CG: The first time I did the show, someone made a reservation under the name Sid Fernandez to mess with me. I saw that on the list, and I freaked out. I would love for someone from that team to see it. It would be a complete disaster but it would be completely fascinating.

Zisk: Have you done anything to directly to draw the attention of the Mets?
CG: For the first two months, it was easy to get a crowd—the premise is good enough, people heard it was a pretty decent show, and it had a celebrity's name attached to it. As long as that was happening I was happy to get some press, but I didn't go to [the Mets] directly. I do think that if they know about it it will get shut down. I've been doing it for two and a half months and the crowds are starting to wane, so I'm starting to look for ways to get more attention for the show, to keep it alive. Part of that is seeing if I can get into some kind of trouble and parlaying that into crowds again. That will kill it faster but at least it will go out with a bang.

Zisk: At one point in the show you wear a Yankees jacket. Is that autographed?
CG: Yeah, that's why I wear a Yankees jacket and not a Mets jacket. I like that idea that he signed it and I'm wearing it in the show. In a sense, there is a little bit of him there, I'm bringing as much of him as I can to the stage. If I'm going to make fun of the guy, this is my attempt to honor him. Maybe that's too much of a stretch, too cheesy.

Zisk: You've got fifty tally marks in the "mock him" column and one tally mark in the "honor him" column, but it's there.
CG: Yeah, I don't think it balances it out at all.

Zisk: I also like the Dodgers jacket that you wear at the end.
CG: I found that on eBay. I would type in Darryl Strawberry, and I found that about a month before the show went up. When I opened the

box that it came in, I was laughing with tears in my eyes. The other thing I did was order thousands and thousands of Darryl Strawberry baseball cards and used those as flyers. I also got a copy of "Chocolate Strawberry," the rap song he put out, I got it on vinyl. I'm still looking for a copy of "Let's Get Mets-merized," which is a rap album that the entire '86 Mets put out. The best line is You all know me/I'm the baddest terror/They call me Rick Aguilera, it's all lines like that. Those guys were amazing. I'm sure readers of *Zisk* are going to hate this, but I grew up a Yankees fan, but doing this show has made me obsessed with those Mets teams of the past. Did you read the *Bad Guys* book (*The Bad Guys Won*, Jeff Pearlman)? It came out a year or two ago, and it was about how the 1986 Mets were collectively the worst group of human beings to spend any amount of time together. It's all the stories of all the things they did, the fights, coke parties, everything, all the arrests. They said in that book that, I guess, Mel Stottlemyre ruined Dwight Gooden by forcing him to learn a curveball that subsequently tinkered with his fastball mechanics. I did obsessive research, I became one hundred percent obsessed with the Mets, the hardness with which they attacked being rock stars.

Originally appeared in issue # 11, Fall 2005.

Tom Sawyer to Tom Glavine – An Interview with Rush's Geddy Lee

Steve Reynolds

We at *Zisk* have been Rush fans for a long time, and haven't been afraid to admit it. As a matter of fact, the first time I ever saw Rush was with Mike at the Broome County Civic Center in Binghamton, New York, many moons ago. And when I found out through my day job that singer-bassist Geddy Lee is a huge baseball fan, the band's coolness grew like Randy Johnson's ERA in the AL. When presented with the opportunity to speak with Geddy during the first week of April while he was promoting their fine new album *Snakes and Arrows*, it seemed too good to be true. And how could I not talk to a guy who placed a Warren Cromartie reference in the *Signals* inner sleeve? As I soon found out, the voice of Geddy Lee isn't that high, and he speaks like an ordinary guy that's just as obsessed with baseball (especially about fantasy leagues and his hometown Toronto Blue Jays) as we are.

Zisk: I gotta say, the beginning of the season is always an exciting time.
Geddy Lee: Oh yeah, totally.

Zisk: So what's your feeling going into this season? Do you have any sleeper teams or anything you think is going to be surprising in 2007?
GL: I think it's a pretty wide open race this year. I see real parity in a lot of divisions. Early in the off season, I felt the Phillies really had the edge, but if you really look at their bullpen there's a lot of question

marks there. And when you see the Mets and you look at their lineup, top to bottom, you think they're going to be really tough and it's going to be hard for them not to repeat. But their starting rotation, I think, has a lot of question marks, and their bullpen has a lot of question marks, too. So again, it's down to pitching, and I think the more teams you look at, the more you see that common thing, the question marks.

Zisk: Everyone's got holes.

GL: Everyone's got holes. I really like the Red Sox. If you look at the starting staff, you really gotta like their chances. Matzusaka is an incredible acquisition. I think he's going to shock a lot of people with how good he is. And I think it was very smart that they put Papelbon back to the closing role and solve that problem.

Zisk: He seems to thrive there. Games that I watched last year, he really seemed to thrive in that role of coming in and shutting someone down.

GL: I agree with that. He wanted to do that. He wanted to go back to closing. I think he knows why he wanted to do that. The AL East, I think, really favors the Red Sox, if I were to pick someone today, and that's strictly because of their starting staff. Beckett and Schilling, even though he got off to a shaky start the other day, Schilling is Schilling, man, and he will quit this "pitch to contact" nonsense and start striking guys out again as soon as he realizes that that's who he is. Don't pretend you're a control pitcher, just power pitch! I mean, he was one of the greatest power pitching control pitchers ever. But he's a fly ball pitcher, and I don't think you want a fly ball pitcher pitching to contact. In some of the other divisions, I think the AL Central is really kind of interesting. The Indians are really making a case for themselves, although they do have a questionable bullpen, as well.

Zisk: And even with the Joe Borowski signing, you never know what you're going to get with him.

GL: I mean he's good, but he's not one of those pencil-in perfect guys. I think he'll help them for sure, but getting to him is going to be a potential issue. And the White Sox have question marks about their rotation. I'm really puzzled about a couple of the trades they made. Getting rid of Brandon McCarthy, I'm not sure I like that. I think he could have done very well for them in that starting rotation. And I'm not sure the guys they picked up really will do well for them.

Zisk: And getting Gavin Floyd for Freddy Garcia . . .

GL: Yeah, I don't like that trade. Freddy was struggling last year, and he's a bit injured this year, so it remains to be seen if he can regain his status. But I like that trade for the Phillies. I think that was a brilliant pick up getting Freddy Garcia. I wish J.P. (Ricciardi) in Toronto would have been awake during that time period to pick that guy up because he's exactly what Toronto needs, a good solid number three starter.

Zisk: Especially after Ted Lilly getting that crazy contract from Chicago.
GL: Well, after the debacle of him and John Gibbons on the field last year, I think you had to know he was just using the Jays to get his price up. I was not surprised when he didn't resign. He's a good pitcher. I think he'll do really well for the Cubs. Again, an American League lefthander going to Wrigley Field, and that team's going to score a lot more runs this year, so I like him to win a few games over there. And I like the Cubs chances in that division, although it's a tough division this year.

Zisk: It's weird, this may be the first year in a long time that the central divisions are the most fascinating ones to watch.
GL: Yes, I agree with you.

Zisk: And what about the western divisions this year?
GL: Well, I think the Padres have gotten a lot better offensively. Having Kevin Kouzmanoff is going to help them. Marcus Giles should be, well, hopefully he'll be happier working with his brother there.

Zisk: And Adrian Gonzalez will have another year under his belt.
GL: Yeah, and Josh Bard is a surprisingly good hitting catcher, too. I think people will be surprised by him. My son grabbed him in our league, and I think that was a really smart move.

Zisk: Let's talk about your fantasy league. You're in a keeper league—how long have you been in this league?
GL: I was trying to think of when I actually joined up in this league, and I think it was around '92. I was in a league previous to that in Toronto. I partnered with a friend of mine, and that was right when Rotisserie first started, and that was, geez, quite a long time ago. And that was a four-by-four league. And I found it frustrating. I don't really like the four-by-four idea of winning categories. So our league is more complicated. It was originally part of the Bill James/Stats league that they ran. That's the league I joined when it was a Bill James league. And eventually, we kind of moved away from Bill James, found our own stats guy, and created our own league. It's just a private league that we run. But the lovely thing about having your own statistician and webmasters is that you can tweak the league every year. And every year we change

Steve Reynolds

the rules a little bit and every year we improvise and try to make it harder to win, but at the same time we create more parity.

Zisk: What did you tweak this year?

GL: The tweaks we made this year is that we went from ten teams to twelve teams. And we went from two divisions to three divisions. And we changed the playoff format, as well. Previous to this season, the DH was always kind of a nebulous position in our league. We made it an actual position. So if you're a guy who plays DH and first base, you'll come on our screen as DH/first base. We have very tough eligibility in our league, and I think that's one of the things that makes our league so great. You can't play three games at third base and call yourself a third baseman. You have to have a minimum of five games to qualify, and twenty-five percent of all your games have to be at that position or you lose that eligibility. And we have specific left field, center field, and right field, not just this nebulous outfield. So you have to create a team. We have fifteen hitters, we have ten pitchers—five of which have to be starting pitchers. And we have certain balance things. Like you cannot have more saves than wins. And that's a real key because that keeps you from just going out there and scoring five closers, like these four-by-four and five-by-five leagues. I mean, you have five closers? That's ridiculous. So it forces you to kind of assemble an actual team. And the same thing with our hitting. You cannot have more RBI than runs scored. So you keep that balance. That's a holdover from all the Bill James/Stats leagues. They do that and I think that's really smart. So it keeps you from stacking up on home run hitters and forgetting about guys that steal bases and score runs. Anyway, it's complicated, and we have points for defensive accomplishments.

Zisk: I kind of wish we had that in our league, some defensive category. I've picked up some guys and thought, if we had defensive stats, I'd really be doing well.

GL: Well, if you think about a real team—if you have a middle infielder that can hit, wow, what a bonus to your team, right? So we try to reflect that by counting those defensive stats. So that means that middle infielders that are home runs hitters and turn a lot of double plays have great value because you get double play points. So it's a fun league, we use catcher wins, catcher caught stealing statistics, outfield assists. And even if a pitcher or a first baseman initiates the double play, then he gets a double play point.

Zisk: This summer you're going back out on the road, so I have to ask this—how fixated on the league are you when you're on tour? Do you use all your downtime between shows to check on your team?

GL: Hey, man, in between sets.

Zisk: (Laughs) Really?
GL: Oh yeah, totally. I get off stage, have a long drink of water, and go straight to my computer and see who I've got going that night. (Laughs) It keeps me sane, or keeps me insane I should say.

Zisk: Have you ever gotten off stage, looked at your team, and said, Oh no, I have three pitchers going tonight and they've all given up like eighteen runs. Does that affect your mindset when you go back out?
GL: It makes me close the computer quickly and get back to work. (Laughs)

Zisk: The escape is over for the night then.
GL: That's right, it's like Ooooh, damn. As a Roto guy, you know that pain of your pitcher getting beat up.

Zisk: Yeah, I had Schilling on Monday, so I was feeling that pain.
GL: See, I had Schilling for years, and he was—year in and year out—the only pitcher I would keep. Because he was just dependable. Even though he was injury prone, he was so good and one of the elite guys. Last year, I finally let him go, and I should have kept him last year, that was a mistake. Last year, he had a great year. But I was worried about his health, and I had other guys to keep. This year, my son grabbed him on his team and he was in pain during Schilling's first start.

Zisk: Yes, it was very painful. Do you remember the first major league game you ever went to?
GL: I don't really remember, but I do remember the first minor league game I went to. It was at the old Toronto Maple Leafs Stadium. And that's when Toronto was the farm team of the Detroit Tigers. I was very young, and I remember going and loving the hell out of it. Taking the bus down to the stadium and watching the team come onto the field. The stadium was about a quarter-filled. It was just a typical minor league game. I think Sparky Anderson was playing on one of the teams, if memory serves, but I'm not one hundred percent sure. But I remember that day very vividly.

Zisk: Did you have a favorite player when you were first getting into baseball?
GL: Well, as a kid, I was enamored of the whole Mickey Mantle-Roger Maris era of the Yankees. They were high on my list to watch. Also the Detroit players, like Al Kaline and people like that. And of course you couldn't grow up in a Jewish household anywhere in North

America and not be a Sandy Koufax fan. Of course, Sandy was the man!

Zisk: Did you ever read the Jane Leavy biography?
GL: Oh yes, it was great.

Zisk: It's one of the best baseball books ever written.
GL: I agree.

Zisk: So, moving back to today's game, your hometown Toronto Blue Jays. They made it to second place last year moving ahead of the Red Sox. As a fan, is it frustrating to be up against these two behemoths that get all the media attention and spend all this money—even though your team has spent money to get back into the race? What is your mindset as a Blue Jays fan?
GL: Well, I think it's frustrating because you never have the budget that those other teams have. But at the same time, that's a challenge. Look at the Twins—to me they're a perfect example of Budget? What Budget? They're a small market team that always fields a great team. And they're an inspiration. I think there are a few teams that are like that. So that shouldn't necessarily be a limitation, it just means you gotta be smarter and you gotta be a horse trader. And I'm not sure that we have a horse trader running that team. There's a lot to like about the Blue Jays. I love Alex Rios, Vernon Wells. I miss Orlando Hudson in that lineup a lot because he's blossoming now and becoming one of the premiere second basemen in the National League. Doc Halladay is a pleasure to watch, what a great pitcher. A.J. Burnett I think is going to have a terrific year. He's healthy. I'm hoping this is the year—I drafted him. A.J., buddy, come on man, this is your year! (Laughs) But there's a lot of question marks at the bottom end of the rotation as have been well documented by people who are savvier than me. But you never know in the course of a season. They have some kids that I like. I like Casey Janssen, they're going to pitch him out of the bullpen for now. Maybe that's a great place for him. I think they've got a better bullpen than people realize, even though it's a young bullpen.

Zisk: The B.J. Ryan signing ended up being pretty good last year.
GL: Brilliant signing. I had absolutely no problem with that signing. That gave them security at the back end of the bullpen. And I think the right attitude is to not spend a lot of money on setup guys. The Orioles have spent a helluva lot of money this year on setup guys, and I don't know if that's a good place to put your money. If I'm a budget guy, I go cheap in the bullpen, especially with setup guys. I'd try to develop some young arms and try to grab some experienced veterans. You spend your money on your everyday guys.

Zisk: That's kind of what the Mets have done over the last two years. They let Chad Bradford go to the Orioles. They ended up getting Scott Schoeneweis, but that was because they wanted someone left handed.

GL: I think you gotta spend your money on starting guys and everyday guys. The Orioles to me are a sad example. They need a power hitting leftfielder, and why are they dicking around spending so much money on setup guys? Go get your leftfielder for crying out loud! Let Jay Gibbons DH every day because he's injury prone and he'd probably be a damn fine DH. And you picked up Aubrey Huff. Let him play first base. It amazes me that certain teams fail to recognize and address their weaknesses. The Expos were always like that. They had a hole at second base for years and years and years. And now, the Jays are becoming like that. They have this hole at shortstop and Royce Clayton is not the answer, I'm sorry. J.P., buddy, listen to me. (Laughs)

Zisk: Royce Clayton has never been the answer to any question. (Laughs)

GL: He's never been the answer for anybody. And that just makes them older, and I don't like that. So I find that shortstop is their real problem. And personally, as much respect as I have for Frank Thomas, and I do have a lot of respect for him, I would not have spent the money on Frank Thomas. I would have tried to sign somebody to play short like Julio Lugo. I mean, he's good enough for the Red Sox but he's not good enough for Toronto? I don't buy that. They don't really have an answer at short in the system either that I can see. So that would have made more sense than signing Frank, who is exactly the same kind of hitter as Troy Glaus. And having them back-to-back in the order makes me a bit nervous because they're both .250 hitters with tremendous power, and slow.

Zisk: Yeah, and last year might have been Frank's lightning in a bottle year.

GL: I think he's going to have a good year, if he's healthy. He hits well in that park. He could hit 35 home runs this year.

Zisk: If he makes 500 home runs, is he going to be a Hall of Famer?

GL: I think he's got a good shot at it, even though he had that nebulous period in the middle of his career. I guess it depends a lot on how he finishes.

Zisk: Last question—you shot an ad for ESPN's fantasy league with Peter Gammons and John Kruk, what was that like? And did you know Peter Gammons played guitar before that shoot?

GL: I didn't know that until I got there. I learned a lot about Peter. He's a terrific guy and incredibly knowledgeable about music. All day, he's just quoting Little Feat lyrics and just kind of jamming. That was a lot of fun for me, hanging out with some real baseball geeks, geeking out with them, as we're doing now. This was pretty much how that whole day went! (Laughs)

Originally appeared in issue #14, Spring 2007.

Grooving to Gorman Thomas – An Interview with The Minus 5's Scott McCaughey

Steve Reynolds and Mike Faloon

Young Fresh Fellows/Minus 5 frontman and R.E.M. sideman Scott McCaughey has been a favorite of *Zisk* since, well, as long as we can remember. The Seattle music scene mainstay gave great interviews to our sister publication *Go Metric* (most of which included some sort of baseball chatter that ended up on the cutting room floor). He was also one of our first subscribers, which helped with the mailing and printing costs we had back in the old days. So it just seemed like a matter of time before we would sit down with one of America's most criminally overlooked songwriters to talk about baseball, old-school Bay Area and Pacific Northwest style.

Steve Reynolds: So you were at the Juan Marichal game where he hit John Roseboro over the head with a bat.

Scott McCaughey: Let me think how old I was, ten or eleven? It was in August, season was pretty far along. The Giants and Dodgers, as I recall, were battling for the National League. Dodgers might have been a game up, but it was super tight. Koufax and Marichal were the starting pitchers. They were both in their prime. I think it was '65. It was the biggest match-up in the rivalry and my dad took me to the game. We lived in San Jose, it was like a fifty-mile drive. We had a bus, used Volkswagen bus. We got up there and frankly you didn't usually have to worry about getting tickets to a game at Candlestick. I went to so many games in the '60s and '70s when there were less than 2,000 people there. They had some really bad attendance years, but they were good then. McCovey, Mays, Jim Ray Hart, amazing team. So we got there and it was completely sold out, and my dad hadn't thought about it but he wasn't about to drive all the way there and be turned away. So he looked around; there were scalpers there. He ended up getting two tickets that were ten bucks each; they were dollar fifty seats. And my dad is not someone who parts with money willingly. He's an awesome guy, nothing bad to say about him, but he grew up in the Depression. He knows the value of a nickel. I know it was really, really hard for him to give that guy twenty dollars for two outfield seats but he did. We went in and it was total electricity. We weren't used to being there when it was sold out. The Dodgers got up pretty early on. We were in the centerfield bleachers. When the thing happened with Roseboro and Marichal I didn't know what happened. I saw Marichal swing at him with the bat but I had no idea why or where it came from. Then this huge melee happened. Everybody was going crazy. Then the next inning, I think, Mays hit a three-run homer off of Koufax that landed about ten feet away from us in the dead centerfield bleachers. They were ahead 4-2 in the ninth. I know Maury Wills got on base and they scored a run and at that point it was 4-3. Then the Giants had Masanori Murakami playing, he was the first Japanese player, and I think it was the first or second time he ever pitched. He came in and saved the game. Unbelievable game. Then we went out to the car and my dad had locked the keys in the car. So on top of spending all of this money he had to break the window to get into the van. Yeah, it's a really historic game but for me I just think so highly of my dad for that whole thing.

Steve: What would happen if that happened in a game today? What would the coverage be like?
Scott: Can you imagine? I remember when the *San Francisco Chronicle* had "The Sporting Green"—it's still called that but in those days it actually was green, the sports page was green—I was so excited to get that every day and I remember one day when the headline was like, 'Mays Gets $100,000 Contract.' It was either him or Marichal was the first player to get six figures.

Mike Faloon: We were also talking about sluggers with low batting averages. Guys like Richie Sexson whose batting averages are measured with the Kelvin scale but they hit 26 home runs so they keep hanging around. And that led us to the legendary Gorman Thomas.
Scott: Who was a hero for the Young Fresh Fellows in our formative years. We were crazy about him. When he came to the Mariners he was almost over the hill, but he hit like 32 homers and 90 RBIs, still throwing himself around in the outfield, which was great. There'd be articles on these guys (Mariners from the early '80s) Harold Reynolds and Alvin Davis, these guys won't even have a cup of coffee, they're having prayer meetings before games and he (Thomas) was like, "I can't get anybody to go out and have a beer with me. These guys won't even drink coffee!" Gorman Thomas is baseball. He's so great. Total all or nothing, home run/strike out kind of guy. Not to the degree of Dave Kingman, but along those lines. Gorman Thomas was actually a pretty great outfielder before he wrecked his throwing shoulder. He wasn't fast but he could get after balls. We heard that a couple months after he retired, or was forcibly retired, the police had to come to his house for some kind of domestic issue and he was sitting there in his underwear, drinking beer, eating

pizza. And we were like, "That's our Gorman!" The Fellows played in Milwaukee and the first time we went there we went to his bar—he and Pete Voukavich had a bar—we were hoping that one or the other of them might be there. Just the old time, beer drinking baseball players.

Steve: I hate to say it but I think David Wells is the last of that bunch.
Scott: I got to go to a Yankees playoff game a couple of years ago against the Twins and we sat in David Wells' seats. The guy who works for R.E.M., our security guy, Rangy, crazy, awesome guy from New Zealand . . .

Mike: I think you have to be crazy with a name like that.
Scott: It's short for orangutan. He got to be really good friends with David Wells and it was the first game of the Twins/Yankees series two or three years ago, so we went and watched the game like right behind the plate, six rows back. It was awesome. When they were lining up for the national anthem, Wells turned around and waved.

Mike: Did you guys used to do that a lot, coordinate Young Fresh Fellows shows with ballgames?
Scott: Yeah. Lots of time it was just by accident—we'd get our tour dates lined up, okay, we've got this day off, is there a game? After we had little bit of success with that, we started planning it a little more—it'd be really great to have this day off in Detroit. The first time I ever went to Wrigley Field, it was on a Young Fresh Fellows tour. It was a day game, and it poured for like two hours. We were in the bleachers and the game never even started. We had the best time with all these bleacher bums just getting hammered, smoking pot. It was awesome. I was like, I still haven't seen a game at Wrigley but I feel like I have. When I finally saw a game there, which was also on a Fellows tour, it was the second night game. One time in Boston, we went to Fenway, even though it was November, and we get there and the gates were open and we just walked in. Then this guy drove in and got out of his car and it was Tony Armas. We started talking to him and they took us out onto the field and (Popllama Records impresario and Egg Studios owner Conrad) Uno got some grass from the field. Weird stuff like that happens.

Steve: How about touring with R.E.M., are you able to work in games?
Scott: I do what I can. Couple years ago in Arlington, I wanted to go to a game and none of the other R.E.M. guys wanted to go. Mike Mills is the only one who ever would; Mills is a huge baseball fan. So it was me and a bunch of the guys from the crew, and we showed up and they gave us a luxury box. Fox Sports Southwest, or whatever it is there, interviewed me during the game. I was like the ugly imposter. There was

a rain delay. I was hyping our shows around Texas. The box was filled with cases and cases of beer, so I was hammered. I tried to hold it together. It was against the Mariners. It was a lot of fun. In fact, both games I've seen in Arlington were with the Mariners. The first one Jay Buhner hit a couple of home runs.

Steve: Back to the Gorman Thomas guys.
Scott: Exactly. Forty home runs in a good year and I'm going to kill myself trying to catch a home run. Made one of the greatest catches in Fenway, smashing into the right field wall, robbing a home run, and flipping over the fence.

Mike: Those Mariners teams of the '90s were a lot of fun.
Scott: Chris Fazio, another guy with a large ass. He pitched a no-hitter for the Mariners.

Mike: Another ass like a barn door, right? [*Editors' note: Before dinner we discussed the Ass like a barn door theory developed by* Zisk *contributor Joe Knox: the bigger the back side, the better the pitcher. A theory developed before the full onset of steroids and weight rooms.*]
Scott: We were lucky. One of the times R.E.M. was on Letterman, Cal Ripken was one of the guests. On Letterman they stick you up on the sixth floor, and there are two little dressing rooms. We had one and Cal Ripken had the other one, so Mills and I went and chatted with him for like a half an hour. It was great. He was like, Anytime you want to come to a game in Baltimore, here's my card. Call my manager and we'll set you up. If I had gone there in the next couple of months I would have done it, but not three years later. I was talking to him about how he murdered the Mariners in the Kingdome, so many huge games in the Kingdome, three home runs, eight RBIs.

Mike: Not a lot of tears shed the day they demolished the Kingdome.
Scott: No, but one thing that pissed me off was that they just finished paying $55 million fixing the roof. That was just pathetic. And Safeco Field got voted down twice by the taxpayers. I voted against it. I don't think people should have to pay for a millionaire's baseball stadium.

Steve: Wait, you're a musician that voted?
Scott: Yeah, right. I stuck to my moral grounds—I like baseball, but not everybody does. They voted it down twice, and then they said, Well, we're doing it anyway; we're taxing you anyway. The people have spoken and we have not listened.

Steve: What was the first game that you went to?

Scott: I count this because it was the first time I ever saw major league players. I lived in Tucson before I moved to California, the Bay area. I went to Hi Corbett Field, which I believe still gets used [*Editors' note: It's used by the Rockies today.*], and it was the Cleveland Indians spring training ballpark and they were playing the Giants. I got to see Mays and McCovey in '63. I think that was Jim Ray Hart's rookie year, and I was just in awe of seeing Mays and those guys. I was a Giants fan before we moved up there (the Bay area). I think it's been used up to recent years, which means it must be really, really funky. I drove by it a couple years ago, and it was still there.

Mike: Hi Corbett sounds like a character from an Erskine Caldwell story.

Scott: He was probably a friend of Birdie Tebbets. Anyway, I grew up going to Candlestick Park and that was not a paradise. My most vivid memory is of the top of my mouth being burned by the hot chocolate as we huddled under our blankets. Then you'd get that film on the top because it was so cold out and then you'd sip it and scald your mouth.

Steve: And that was in July.

Scott: Right. I went to a game there once (Candlestick) and in San Jose, which is forty or fifty miles south, it was like 103 degrees and I'm going, Okay, I've got to bring a coat because I'm going to Candlestick but it can't possibly be that cold. It was 58 when the game started and it got down to like 48. I went to so many games where there was nobody there. I went to A's games, too, but nobody went to those either. I went to World Series games that weren't sold out. I saw two games against Cincinnati, which was '72, and one against the Mets ('73). The game I went to against the Mets, was really awful because, well the A's won, but Mays was playing for the Mets and he made an error while he was in right field, I think, not even center. It was a single that got past him and went to the wall, and I was like cheering as the A's went around but I never wanted to see that. It was so sad. Really harsh.

Mike: I just finished a great biography on (former A's owner) Charles O. Finley.

Scott: I went to games where they had orange baseballs. When the umpire had to get new baseballs they had this trapdoor in the field and this rabbit—giant plastic rabbit—rose up on an elevator right by home plate and it had a little basket with balls in it and the umpire had to get the balls out of the basket of this rabbit—this giant rabbit—that came out from underneath the ground. Charles O. Finley was insane. MC Hammer was the batboy, but then for one season he was like the vice president or something. He was fourteen.

Steve: He would make calls down to (A's manager) Alvin Dark's office like, Why is this guy playing? MC Hammer telling Alvin Dark what to do.

Scott: No one knew who he was at the time, he was just this kid, but Finley was insane. So have you guys been to many parks?

Mike: I've been to a lot of minor league ballparks, especially when we lived in North Carolina. We saw the sprinklers turn on in the middle of a game in Greensboro.

Scott: I went to one in Lancaster, California, last summer. Diamondbacks rookie league or maybe Double A. It was free hot dog day and they were going, Remember, every Tuesday is Tumbleweed Day—if you bring a tumbleweed you get in free. That's the best promotion ever.

Originally appeared in issue #14, Spring 2007.

A Golden Voice for the Braves – An Interview with Emmylou Harris

Steve Reynolds

Emmylou Harris is best known for her haunting harmony vocals that have enriched albums for over three decades and her collaborations with the likes of the late country rock pioneer Gram Parsons, Dolly Parton, and Linda Ronstadt (on *Trio*), and most recently *All the Roadrunning*, a tremendous album recorded with former Dire Straits frontman Mark Knopfler. While Harris was doing a series of interviews promoting her latest solo disc *All I Intended to Be*, we chatted about her love of baseball and the Atlanta Braves.

Zisk: Do you think John Smoltz will come back next year for the Braves?

Emmylou Harris: Oh man. The guy is so determined to play. And certainly the fact that he can be a closer as well as a starter gives him more of an opportunity to come back.

Zisk: With all the promo duties of a new album and touring, have you been able to watch any games?

EH: I've gotten to watch a few games, but not as many as I'd have liked because for some reason they put all the Braves games on a channel I can't get. And then when I try to get it on my computer they think I can get it so they black it out. (Laughs) But there is XM radio, so I can listen to every single ballgame.

Zisk: I assume you'll have that on the bus, but you're probably on stage when the games are being played.

EH: True, but I also subscribe to MLB.TV for my computer so I can watch the games afterwards. Of course, when you've seen the score by then, who wants to watch a game unless their team has won? (Laughs) My brother used to do that. He went to Auburn when Alabama would be up on them every year. It was a very painful time to go to Auburn. And even now, for years, he would tape the Auburn-Alabama game and find out the score. And he would only watch the game if Auburn won.

Zisk: So how do you feel about this current Braves team?

EH: I think they've got some great young players. I love this guy Yunel Escobar. And Chipper Jones has had a great year. It's too bad we didn't have the pitching because we lost Smoltz and then Tom Glavine. Some of the young guys I don't know because I haven't seen them enough this season. It's baseball—you gotta take the knocks. We had some great years. But at a time like this you gotta stick with your team. Fortunately, I love baseball enough to where I can really enjoy watching a game and seeing the subtleties of the game. I thank God for baseball. That's how I chill out. I enjoy it.

Zisk: I obviously knew before coming in that you were a Braves fan, but I didn't find an explanation why. Is it that Atlanta is the closest city to Nashville that had a major league team?

EH: Well, there you were either a Cubs fan or a Braves fan because it was either TBS or WGN. And I didn't have enough soul to be a Cubs fan! (Laughs)

Originally appeared in issue #17, Fall 2008.

Take Me Out . . . To Baseball Songs – An Interview with Billy Bragg

Steve Reynolds

Woody Guthrie. The name of the legendary Dust Bowl balladeer and author of "This Land Is Your Land" is as much of a part of America as baseball itself. Who would've thought he would write about one of the game's greatest players, Joe DiMaggio?

The lyrics for "Joe DiMaggio Done It Again" were written in 1949 at Guthrie's Coney Island home, but the music for the song died with him in 1967. So in 1995, English singer-songwriter Billy Bragg was invited by Guthrie's daughter Nora to go through the Guthrie Archives in New York and to put music to some of these lyrics. Bragg brought in the Chicago area pop-roots band Wilco to work on these songs, and their recordings yielded two albums—1998's *Mermaid Avenue* and 2000's *Mermaid Avenue Volume II*. "Joe DiMaggio Done It Again" appears on *Volume II*, with music by Bragg and vocals by Wilco's Jeff Tweedy. I asked Bragg how an Englishman ended up writing music for a song about one of America's greatest athletes.

"One of the things that divides America from the rest of the world is sport. For instance, there are not many nations in the world where driving over small cars in a big car with very big wheels is seen as a sport. Some of the games that you do play that you've taken into your heart and made your own—most obviously what you refer to as football, and the cricket without a wicket game, baseball. Those of us in the rest of the world who play the one true football [soccer], we don't look at [your sports] dismissively, but we don't have much to talk about. So one of the things we do have to talk about is who invented this game. And as you all probably know, baseball was invented in England. There is a drawing from the year 1717 of four men standing on a diamond playing cricket with no wicket.

"So these kind of discussions seemed to bring out a residual patriotism in Wilco. (Laughs) I don't know why. And when it came to the crunch, they kind of formed an alliance and said, Bill, we don't think you know enough about baseball—which actually, I think they were saying, You don't *respect* baseball enough—to sing a song about Joltin' Joe. People would ask me, So do you know who Joe DiMaggio is? And I would say, Yeah, I've listened to Simon & Garfunkel. Of course I know who he is, give me a break. (Laughs) I mean, he's one of the most famous baseball players of all time, of course I know who he is! And so I said fine [you sing it]. They did it justice. I was very pleased with it.

"So when Nora came to listen to the tracks, we played it for her, and she said to Jeff, 'I thought that was one of Billy's song's, Joe DiMaggio.' Jeff laughed and said, 'Yeah, we didn't let him sing it because he doesn't know anything about baseball.' And Nora, completely straightfaced, said to Jeff, 'You think Woody knew anything about baseball?' And I was like, 'Yes!'"

Originally appeared in issue #3, Summer 2000.

My Life as a ~~Big League~~ ~~Minor League~~ ~~College Ball~~ College Summer Ball Announcer

Rev. Norb

August 1, 1973: A date that will live in infamy: my childhood's answer to December 7, 1941. The powers-that-be had decreed that anyone wishing to participate in the 1973 Little League season needed to be eight years of age on or before August 1, 1973. My eighth birthday? August 2, 1973. Despite impassioned entreaties by my father to the dolts at Park & Rec on my behalf, I was shunned; banished; cast out: I would not be allowed to start Little League that year. So crushed was my 7.99-year-old self by this practically arbitrary edict, that the next year—and all subsequent years—I flipped the bird back at the Allouez Park & Rec Department, refusing to play in their dumb ol' Little League, and thereby depriving the world of the services of surely the most spectacular five-tool player ever birthed on these shores. So, yes: I have never played baseball on any level, ever. Nor have I particularly wanted to: What's so great about stinky, medium-sized guys in dirty polyester? Conversely, however, it was easy for me to fall in love with the concept of the small-town sports announcer (or, more correctly—and somewhat ironically—the Hollywood archetype thereof): Harry Doyle from *Major League*, Jim Carr from *Slap Shot*, et al. Who doesn't love drunk guys in loud sport coats, swearing off-mic (and occasionally on-mic) about their team's ineptness, tasked with the seemingly Promethean chore of presenting the daily chaos, futility, and despair at their run-down stadiums as *some top-notch shit behind which you'll surely want to get, fans!* The job exudes a certain romance, like writing detective novels, or being a caterer for the mafia. Ergo, presented with the opportunity to spend the summer as the P.A. announcer for the Green Bay Bullfrogs—a six-year-old franchise in the Northwoods League, a summer collegiate league with teams in Wisconsin, Minnesota, Michigan, Iowa, and Ontario—it did not take me long to come to a decision on the matter: On the down side, the pay wasn't a hell of a lot, and the schedule would prevent me from teaching a summer class, which would have paid me triple the money per night. On the up side, who the fuck wants to be sitting in some goddamned tech school when they could be announcing fucking baseball outside?

Nobody, that's whom! My decision took all of about thirty seconds: *get me a hat, I'm in* (as to how I wound up with the job offer in the first place, apparently my brother—who, by virtue of not being born on August 2, played Little League all his life and is a big jock—knew the owner, and, rightly concluding this gig might have my name all over it, gave him my email. The owner then asked me if I had any "audio clips" of my "work." I sent him back a link to a YouTube video of me running around the track in a Grand Poobah hat and Madonna headset mic at the Indoor Sports Complex in Rockford, Illinois, introducing the Fox Cityz Foxz women's flat track roller derby team. Apparently that did the trick. Dress for success).

The Bullfrogs play at Joannes Stadium, across the street from my old high school on Green Bay's east side. The Jo was built in 1929; in 1935 it hosted an MLB exhibition game between the Pittsburgh Pirates and the St. Louis Browns. Rogers Hornsby played first base for the Pirates; Honus Wagner was their coach. In the '50s, it was the home to the Green Bay Blue Jays, a minor-league team in the Brooklyn Dodgers system (and launching point for 1960 NL Rookie of the Year Frank Howard, who eventually made his home in Green Bay), but when the Dodgers moved westward, so did the Blue Jays. In the '70s, it was home to the Green Bay Blue Ribbons, a Wisconsin State League wrecking crew idolized by myself and my brother (years later, I wound up buying a drumset from former Blue Ribbons pitcher Paul Wilmet, who pitched two-thirds of an inning with the Texas Rangers one September. Lifetime big league ERA: 15.23). The park was like a little Wrigley Field—wood, peeling white and green paint, more wood, and the ever-present trepidation that shit was going to collapse any second. In 1987, they "upgraded" Joannes by tearing out the wooden grandstand, the nightmarish pressbox accessible only by a rickety wooden walkway, the Flintstones-era scoreboard (scores were hand-hung between innings by Tim Thyrion, a kid with whom I went to junior high, and lived down the block from the stadium), the urinal system that consisted of a cement wall and a drain, and all the other marvels of 1929 technology—replacing them with a few rows of generic aluminum bleachers, a men's room with actual urinals, a scoreboard that used light bulbs, and not much else. The bastardized Joannes (seats about 2,000, I guess . . . I'm not really sure; we never had 2,000 people in it) became my home for the thirty-five home games of the Green Bay

Bullfrogs 2012 season; I suppose I should appreciate the fact that I didn't have to take my life into my hands every time I walked to the pressbox—the walkway to the old suspended pressbox was so life-threatening that my father prohibited us from setting foot on it, even when we'd won a door prize or something and actually needed to go there to claim it—but, all the same, for maximum small-town sports announcer charm, I think I'd rather be pissing on the wall and watching fat-ass Tim Thyrion hanging numerals in the outfield if it's all the same to the renovation gods.

In the grand fraternity of sports announcers, P.A. guy is low man on the totem pole. He's sub-Harry Doyle, sub-Jim Carr, sub-just-about-everybody. You'd need to contact Digger's Hotline before you actually *found* the P.A. guy on the totem pole. Pretty much the only people he outranks are the interns who run around throwing T-shirts into the crowd. Even the guys who do the commentary on the internet broadcasts of the Northwoods League games, with viewerships rarely threatening the triple-digit mark, are—by virtue of the fact that they travel with the team and do have some journalistic component to their tasks—accorded some modicum of respect. The P.A. guy is just some oaf who tries to talk in a race car announcer voice whilst reading promo spots for roofers and pizza joints. An hour before first pitch, I start reading announcements as the fans trickle in, whilst attempting to write out my rosters for the evening, based on the lineup cards which should already be in the pressbox, but never are. As with all other tasks in life, I find the four-color Bic© pen to be indispensible here: I scrawl "GREEN BAY BULLFROGS" in big block letters in green ink across the top of one side of a piece of paper, and our opponent's name in similarly-sized letters on the back (color-coded as best I can using my other options of red, blue or black ink). I use red ink to number the batting order down the left-hand side of each page, then make another column for positions, also using red ink, using a blue vertical line to separate the two. Since our league is summer ball for college guys, my next column is each player's school, year, and height, in blue ink. University of Texas Permian-Basin represent. To the right of that, I use red ink for jersey numbers, and, finally, black ink for player names, separating everything with blue ink lines because blue is clearly the most drably utilitarian color of the Bic© four-color pen. Fifteen minutes before the first pitch, I go into my various pregame spiels: Welcoming the fans, picking our Pepsi® Punch-Out Batters and Miller™ Beer Batters for the game, announcing our thrill-a-minute Pizza Ranch® game ball delivery and Meadows Conference Center Meeting of the Minds at home plate, chucking out some ceremonial first pitches, and introducing the teams and mascot and national anthem singer and what-not. Introducing the teams is probably the most exciting thing I do, so adjust your instrumentation accordingly.

After that, the job becomes a largely perfunctory series of announcements and sponsor reads. I introduce the first batter; if he hits a foul ball, I inform the crowd that if their kid twelve and under catches a foul ball tonight, they can take it in to Shear Sports for a free haircut. If he strikes out, I welcome him to the Tri-City Glass & Door K-Zone, but if he's the Pepsi® Punch-Out Batter and strikes out, I not only welcome him to the Tri-City Glass & Door K-Zone, but inform the locals that all fountain sody pop is one dollar off for the rest of the inning. If he's the Miller™ Beer Batter and strikes out, I inform all and sundry that it's half-price Miller Lite™ draft beer for the rest of the inning. If there's a particularly astounding play in the field by our guys, I deem it the Great Clips Great Play of the Night, as Great Clips is a proud sponsor of all Northwoods League teams. If our pitcher happens to strike out the side in order, I duly inform all fans in attendance that they've just won two free games of bowling at Ashwaubenon Bowling Center, in addition to welcoming the surely-receptive player to the Tri-City Glass & Door K-Zone and such. At the end of the half-inning, I draw the fans' attention to the (sadly Tim Thyrion-free) Nicolet National Bank Scoreboard, then introduce whatever wacky between-inning promotion we've got going on (the Fox Communities Credit Union Home Run Derby? The Sinclair Plumbing Toilet Catapult?), throwing it down to my on-field colleague for the particulars. I then repeat the process for our guys, except we don't have Pepsi® Punch-Out Batters nor Miller™ Beer Batters, we have the Kroc Cleanup Hitter. If we score a run, I announce that the runner is safe at home, courtesy of Advanced Roofing Specialists, keeping *you* safe at home. If we score during the Taco Bell® Fourth Meal Fourth Inning, I inform all lucky fans in section whatever that they've won a free taco (as well as being kept safe at home by Advanced Roofing Specialists, same as everybody else); and hopefully have enough time left to inform those selfsame fans that it's now the Budweiser® Thirst Inning, with all Budweiser products on sale for just two dollars. If there's a pitching change, I announce that the call to the bullpen has been made, brought to you by Cellcom, and then start exultantly shilling through my three pages of in-game sponsor reads, interspersed with birthday notifications, shout-outs, and other items of greatest importance. At the end of the game, I thank everybody for coming and inform them of the next game—then, after a concluding "ta ta!," sprint to the men's room, as my in-game windows of peeing opportunity are virtually non-existent. More shilling than thrilling, but, much like being a head-in-a-jar on *Futurama*, it's a life of quiet dignity.

Which brings me to the crux of my piece: After viewing an entire season's worth of Northwoods League baseball from a dozen rows behind home plate, the thing that made the greatest impression on me, the one item that I will take away from this season, above all else, the

Fan Interference

one question that still resounds in my beer-battered cranium, largely to the exclusion of all else, is this: Not to put too fine a point on it, but *what the fuck has happened to walk-up music these days*??? Do these people have *any clue whatsoever* as to what types of emotions a player's walkup music is supposed to elicit in fans? Now, shit, I realize that times change—that, in my mind, when I look out at these guys from the pressbox, in my head, they look like the 1976 Padres or somebody, but when I see them in person they look more like, I dunno, my paperboy or whomever—but, *goddammit*, their complete and utter *cluelessness* on what constitutes good walkup music is *so amazingly appalling* that it veritably beggars comprehension. This is not an annoying but ultimately meaningless generational squabble—like leaving those stupid fucking stickers on the brims of ballcaps (from whom have you kids been getting your fashion tips? *Minnie Pearl*?)—this is a *complete* and *utter breakdown in musical understanding*, not to mention a shocking display of unfamiliarity with the concept of "cool." I mean, what the fuck, man! John Rocker was a racist, homophobic toad, but at least he had the good sense to dash out of the bullpen to Twisted Sister, ya know? Kids today are striding to the plate to the most absolute puss teen-pop imaginable; malarkey bordering on madness! Therefore, for those of you brave enough to read further, might I present—with horror veritably curdling the cheese in my cheese curds—the walkup music from a representative night at the ballpark with the Bullfrogs. The names have been omitted to protect the innocent. Actually, myself.

1. LF: R. Kelly "Ignition"
One of the great advantages of being a punk rock margin-dweller is not knowing whom people like R. Kelly are. In point of fact, all I know about the guy is that he got in trouble for nailing underage girls, which seems more like a commentary on the shortcomings of management than anything else (I mean, doesn't he pay them to do shit like pay the underage girls off before people like me can find out about it? If not, my conception of the traditional artist-management relationship is sorely malformed). So, yes: We lead off with music by a guy whose output is so puss it makes "Boogie Oogie Oogie" by A Taste Of Honey sound like Motorhead by comparison.
Grade: C+, because, I mean, it could have been "I Believe I Can Fly."

2. CF: Brantley Gilbert "Kick It In The Sticks"
Some redneck thing about being in the land of barbed WAAR and moonshine whiskeh. The implied testosterone levels are decent for a walkup song, but being as how the kid is from Spokane and plays for Gonzaga—not exactly *Deliverance* country—I'm pretty sure the only reason this is our center fielder's walkup song is because his name is

"Billy," and the song makes mention of the term "hillbilly." *Yes, it's just that simple, folks.* The tragic thing is that his last name is "Moon," which clearly sets the table for the use of "Full Moon Turn My Head Around" by Off Broadway, "Moon Upstairs" by Mott the Hoople, "There's a Moon in the Sky (Called The Moon)" by the B-52's, "Mister Sun, Mister Moon" by Paul Revere & The Raiders. Even "Moon Over Marin" by the Dead Kennedys would at least have the time zone correct.

Grade: B-, because this is, at bare minimum, not the music of an overt sissy.

3. 1B: Carly Rae Jepsen "Call Me Maybe"

The first time I heard this song being used as our first baseman's walk-up music, the previous batter had been hit by a pitch, and I thought it was actually some kinda hit-by-pitch music. Like, you know, *"HEY! I just met you! Stop hitting me with pitches!"* This is a cute song and all, but anyone who can explain how a chirpy teen-pop song about a girl giving a guy her number equates to the type of anthem one would wish to hear as they purposefully stride to the plate as a soon-to-be-conqueror with intent to knock the ball to kingdom come, I'm all ears. *Call me maybe!*

Grade: D+

4. 2B: Akon "Keep Up"

The sentiment expressed—*"I'm a beast / I can go thirty days and nights without sleep"*—makes sense, but the part of the music that plays when the second baseman is actually walking to the plate is just the guy singing in his high, airy voice, over some really dorky one-handed '80s pomp-rock keyboards, drawing the bestialness very much into question. He sounds more like a dance student trying to find where his boyfriend hid his Ultravox cassette.

Grade: C+, although ghost points should be awarded for the editing job required to remove the phrase "my niggers" from just before the first line.

5. SS: Miley Cyrus "Party in the USA"

When I think of athletic warrior-kings, leaving it all out on the field in pitched combat, testing the bounds of their endurance, bound for glory, muscles rippling, tendons straining in the throes of the thrill of victory and the agony of defeat—obviously, my thoughts *always* go immediately to Hannah Montana. Yep. Pete Rose, Roger Clemens, Vince Lombardi, Hannah Montana. That's how the world works. The craziest thing was that this song had *multiple players* on our team requesting it as their walkup song. First one guy had it, then he left the team for a while and another guy had it (no use letting such a tailor-made carnivorous sports anthem go to waste!), then the first guy came back and wanted to reclaim

it, because "it says *'welcome back'* in it." Actually, the line is *"welcome to the land of in excess."* Or maybe it was "INXS," although I guess that'd be "Party In Australia" then.
Grade: D-

6. C: J Cole "Who Dat"
This actually makes sense, because the player's last name is "Hoo." What *doesn't* make sense is why Hoo is a catcher, not a first baseman.
Grade: A

7. DH: The Outfield "Your Love"
This song often wound up falling to the "new guy," who rarely had walkup music picked out; "Your Love" was—for, as always, whatever reason—the default walkup music for players who had no specific music of their own. I guess it's an adequate enough song, but I always thought it faded out at a curious time—right after the line *"you know I like my girls a little bit older."* One assumes this song was included for purposes of balancing out the R. Kelly number.
Grade: B-

8. 3B: Justin Bieber "Boyfriend"
What. The. Fuck. Seriously. Seriously. *What. The. Fuck.* I can't even write anything funny about this that would be funnier than what it already is. *What. The. Fuck. Beware, John Rocker and "I Wanna Rock!" Look to thy laurels, Mariano Rivera and "Enter Sandman!" Go jump in the lake, Trevor Hoffman and "Hell's Bells!" The sentiments expressed in "Boyfriend" by Justin Bieber will clearly put you all to rout*!!!
Grade: F. Seriously, dude. What the fuck.

9. RF: Jimi Hendrix: "All Along The Watchtower"
I like Bob Dylan, and I like Jimi Hendrix, but I don't particularly like either version of this song, and don't really see how it constitutes good walkup music. Wouldn't "Purple Haze" be a much more logical candidate, as far as Unimaginative Jimi Hendrix Songs To Use As One's Walkup Music go? A joker and a thief and plowman digging his herb? Geez, no wonder you're batting ninth.
Grade: B-, which should show you exactly how low the fucking bar is set for walkup music these days.

Quibbles aside, it was a swell summer gig. I hope to be back next season, and doubly hope that I will be allowed to pick out walkup music for each player on my birthday (August 2, 2013). I also hope that Robb Woodcock is in the lineup that day, as I've got "Cock on the Loose" by Antiseen already cued up in the pressbox on his behalf. Then again, having been robustly censured on my first day of work for beginning the Klement's Sausage Race with "ALL RIGHT FANS, LET'S GET THIS SAUSAGE PARTY STARTED!" perhaps that's more of a fantasy league item.

Originally appeared in issue #21, Fall 2012.

Top 10 Games I've Attended

Kevin Chanel

I love making lists. It all started with *The Book Of Lists* back in the mid-1970s. I was hooked. Anything listy and I get transfixed. It's like looking at box scores. My eyes get glassy, and the numbers just start to blend into each other. I can look at 200 pages of lists, be entertained the whole time, and later on not be able to tell you a word of what I was reading.

Over the years, the conversation has come up repeatedly concerning favorite or most memorable games attended. While some stand out like a biker at a box social, a few I had to sort out and research the dates. So here you go:

1) Expos vs. Padres. Jack Murphy Stadium. 6/3/95.

Simply amazing. Pedro Martinez threw nine perfect innings, only to have Bip Roberts break it up with a double in the 10th. Unfortunately, the Padres' Joey Hamilton pitched perhaps the only good game of his career, going nine and only giving up three hits and two walks. Montreal couldn't muster up even one run though, as there were two ungodly amazing double plays turned by a juiced-up Ken Caminiti and second baseman Jody Reed. When Pedro walked off the mound after the bottom of the ninth, the paltry crowd of 9,000-or-so gave him the standing "O." They did the same after manager Felipe Alou removed him from the game after Roberts' hit. Absolute finest pitching and defensive performance I've seen.

2) Pirates vs. Padres. San Diego Stadium. 6/12/70.

Dock Ellis' lysergic no-hitter. Supposedly—if you can believe my father—this is the first game I ever went to. I have no memory of it, as I was only five, and my mother shipped us off to the game with a cache of homemade burritos. Word has it he (Ellis, not my father) dosed up in L.A. with his girlfriend hours before the game, and was tripping balls by the time he hit the mound. The first pitch bounced ten feet in front of the plate. Ellis walked eight batters and hit at least one. "I was zeroed in on the (catcher's) glove, but I didn't hit the glove too much. I remember hitting a couple of batters and the bases were loaded two or three times."

3) Giants vs. Angels. World Series Game 4. Pac Bell Park. 10/23/02.

Rookie phenom Francisco Rodriguez gets tagged for a single by David Bell for the deciding run. My wife and I, after a week of trying to get tickets to the game, went online in the first inning of Game 1 and snagged three tickets for Games 4 and 5. Not only did we see the best game from the Giants standpoint, but we scalped the three tickets to the next game for a total of $750. We watched the game from the Acme Chophouse next door to the stadium, eating steaks and drinking expensive wine in front of a huge TV and a room full of fans.

4) Padres vs. Astros. San Diego Stadium. 9/24/71.

First game of double header. 2-1, Astros in 21 innings. Yup. Twenty-one innings . . . in the first game of a twin-bill. Pretty much everyone there just wanted this thing over with, including Astros' outfielder Jesus Alou, of the Flying Alou Brothers. Much to the crowd's appreciation, he stole home in the top of the twenty-first. Padres catcher and future father of an All-Star Fred Kendall dropped the throw to allow the run. My dad and I left at 12:30 a.m., during the third inning of the second game, because he had to work in the morning. Some loud hick behind us was yelling "Hey Jeee-zus" to Alou the whole game.

5) A's vs. Yankees. ALDS Game 3. Network Associates Coliseum. 10/13/01.

Yankees 1, A's 0. Around the Coliseum in Oakland you can still hear the echoing strains of "Slide, Jeremy, slide!" This was the play that made Derek Jeter's career. With the A's Jeremy Giambi ("the other Giambi") on first, Terence Long hit a sweet liner down the right field line, a sure double. Jeremy, running at full speed (somewhere between a snail and an anvil caught in an updraft), chugged it around third and was heading for home. Right-fielder Shane Spencer's throw missed the cut-off man, and Jeter was miraculously there to receive it, tagging the non-sliding Giambi at the plate. He never lived it down. A's pitcher Barry Zito hurled the game of his life, going eight innings and giving up only two hits.

Unfortunately, one of those was Jorge Posada's solo blast in the fifth, which was the deciding run. Devastated, the A's couldn't win the clinching game in their next two tries, bowing out in the first round.

6) Boise Hawks vs. Bellingham Mariners. Memorial Stadium. Boise, ID. Summer 1991.
Don't remember too much from this mid-summer scorcher except seeing some lady get totally creamed by a screaming liner to the stands about a row from my girlfriend and me. The poor woman never had a chance as the ball smacked her in the face at 125 mph, and was still moving pretty fast by the time it rolled our way. She had to be carried out on a stretcher. The Hawks also had this "Crazy George"-type fan guy with a trumpet or something that was terrorizing little kids, much to everyone's (except the kids', probably) delight. He was big, fat, drunk, and scary. The Hawks' manager was the legendary Orv Franchuk, and I believe the only guy from that team to make it to the bigs was current Cardinal Orlando Palmeiro.

7) A's vs. Devil Rays. Network Associates Coliseum. 5/26/02.
Bought ten tickets and forced a bunch of people to go with me to the game, just because it was my birthday. The night before, Dead Low Tide was in town, and we ended up closing the Eagle, a nearby bar. Rolled out drunk as skunks by 3:00, only to get up bright and early for Oakland tailgate-action. My many friends and I (and some others we ran into at the stadium bar) wound up closing *that* bar as well, an hour or so after the game was over. Closing two bars in less than 15 hours, a new indoor record!

8) Padres vs. Braves. NLCS, Game 3. Qualcomm Stadium. 10/10/98.
I was living in San Francisco by this time, and my pal Mario down in San Diego had procured tickets to the first of the playoff games in SD for this series. So, naturally, I made the nine-hour drive to see this game. The Pads had already taken two in Turner, so just two more wins and they are off to their first World Series since the dreaded 1984 series drubbing at the hands of one of the best teams in the history of baseball, the '84 Tigers. There were some great moments in this one: Sterling Hitchcock out-pitching Maddux in his prime, John Vander Wal throwing out Walt Weiss at the plate from left field . . . the list goes on. What I'll remember most was in the top of the eighth, bases loaded for Javy Lopez, and Bruce Bochy made the switch to bring in MLB's best closer, Trevor Hoffman, to finish up the inning. First, you heard the bells, then the slow, grinding guitar, then AC/DC's "Hell's Bells" kicked in and the crowd went totally apeshit. I had never seen 63,000 people waving a sea of white hankies in person, but this was just plain awesome. Hoffman

then struck out Lopez on three pitches and the whole place was thundering. He finished them off in the ninth; SD won one more and then got demolished by the Yankees in the Series. I hate the Yankees.

9) Padres vs. Reds. Jack Murphy Stadium. 7/25/90.
Unremarkable game, other than that this was *the* infamous game in which noted comedian and pariah Roseanne Barr bleated the national anthem before the game; a moronic stunt devised by a total moron—Padres owner and itinerant shithead Tom Werner—to promote one of his banal and unwatchable TV shows. When you read about this event in most recollections, they always paint the crowd as 100% anti-Roseanne, screaming boos and raspberries at her during and after her rendition. The truth is, since she had taken on a godlike status with the housewives of America, there was an overwhelming amount of families—if not only sets of mothers-with-children—in attendance. It's not an exaggeration to state that the crowd was split about 50/50. There were many cheers from indignant women, one of which sat in front of us, monitoring our section for anyone who would dare malign her hero during her big moment. After the "song," the mother of five was seen screaming hysterically at neighboring fans for their lack of support for Ms. Barr. Needless to say, the media coverage the next two days was blanket-like. Every news station led off with her performance, with one or more newscasters losing their positions for criticizing her openly.

10) Padres vs. Cubs. NLCS Game 5. Jack Murphy Stadium. 10/7/84.
My first experience at a post-season game. Brought an old, beat-up teddy bear on a homemade noose and sat directly above one of those loge-level mini scoreboards, swinging it among a packed Padres crowd, similarly armed as such. This was San Diego's first time in the postseason, and having lost the first two games, they surprised the country by coming back to win two with their backs firmly placed against the wall. No one expected the Padres to advance to the World Series in '84. Noted Chicago crotchety geezer Mike Royko summed up the entitled feeling of the Cubs faithful by decrying San Diegans as a bunch of unworthy, "quiche-eating" "lousy wimps." This is the first time I remember being kissed by older women I didn't know and being high-fived by total strangers, as a Tim "Parrothead" Flannery groundball through the legs of Leon "Bull" Durham sealed the victory for the heretofore laughingstock Padres. I do recall having watched only one or two of the World Series games the next week. The whole town knew their homies would be slaughtered by the far superior Tigers and they, in fact, were.

Originally appeared in issue #7, Fall 2003.

My 5 Most Miserable Experiences at the Ballpark

Jake Austen

I love going to games, and I've been blessed with a woman, and two children, that can take (and sometimes enjoy) three hours of professional crotch-scratching and sunflower-seed spitting. I've been to at least 20 games a year for almost 20 years, and I've seen some amazing things, including a three no-hitters (one a perfect game), a four-homer performance, and a ballplayer have an on-field seizure. But it hasn't always been as fun as these incidents. Here, in no particular order, are five ballpark memories that left me questioning my devotion to this particular church.

In 1993, the White Sox were in the ALCS. I was at Game 1, and Jack McDowell was pitching. I was in the outfield bleachers, which are aluminum bleacher benches with the seat numbers painted on. So when it's super-packed, and a lot of fat people come, you are squeezed in like sausages. Not only was the park extra-packed and uncomfortable (they sold copious amounts of standing-room tickets), it was also saturated with this feeling of joyless, dire importance, like this game really meant something and if we lost it was doom. Well, doom came quick, as our starting pitcher Jack McDowell, who is now a vanity recording artist (who is as good a singer as I imagine he would be an NBA starting guard) gave up about 87 runs before he got his first out. He was absolutely awful, which in itself would have made the game somewhat dreary, but the true ugliness was yet to come.

Sometime before the third inning, in an incident that was reminiscent of some Broadway musical where a spreading crowd on the street turns to each other and sings, "Have you heard the news, have you heard the news"—and also brought to mind the green plague cloud in the film *The Ten Commandments* that inspired Metallica's "Creeping Death"—a rumor organically, manically spread throughout the park that Michael Jordan, who had thrown out the first pitch, was quitting basketball. It felt totally fucking depressing and awful, and to gain that sad knowledge (without the future knowledge that he would be back to re-three-peat later) while watching your favorite team fold like a napkin in what was sure to be a humiliatingly short playoff series, was the definition of ballpark misery.

Jake Austen

    A few years ago, the White Sox started out hot (Kenny Lofton was getting several hits a game and stealing bases left and right before he cooled off) and I, and tens of thousands of other people, decided to take advantage of that evening's half price night and buy some "walk up" tickets just before the game started. The problem was that the Sox had just switched from Ticketmaster to TicketWeb, an online firm that actually did not know how to process 20,000 walk up tickets. So the slow-moving lines snailed along for over an hour and a half into the game, as we listened on the PA to a radio broadcast of Jack McDowell slaughtering the national anthem and Lofton continuing his hot streak against his former team, the Cleveland Indians. When the masses settled inside, upset at the indignities just endured, there was a weird mood in the air. The next two hours featured several dozen spontaneous brawls throughout the seating area, and I have never seen anything like it. Every ten minutes or so someone would start pounding someone either across the stadium or across the aisle. It actually started to become funny, but I literally saw blood streaming from at least eight heads that night. After the game, we actually saw two guys fist fighting as they walked down the walkway exiting the park! The next season would be the one where drunken fan William Ligue would storm the field and for no reason beat an elderly first base coach into deafness, helping the recently renamed US Cellular Field earn the nickname "The Cell," for all the fan arrests. But it was the Take Me Out To The Brawl Game Night that is more outstanding in my mind. A pathetic postscript occurred when I was making a rare (for me) defense of the Cubs at a party one night, expositing the theory that the comparisons of "long-suffering" Cubs fans to then-long suffering Red Sox fans was bogus because Red Sox fans, like heroin addicts, were joyless pits of nihilism, and that negativity was part of their collective character, while Cubs fans were more like lax reefer smokers, not particularly depressed about the losing and usually content to appreciate the beauty of the field while drinking their Buds. Upon mentioning Cubs fans drinking, a Cubbie booster/Ohio native mistook my story for a condemnation of Wrigley Field drunkenness and railed at me that White Sox games were the equivalent of spending a violent night in an overcrowded drunk tank. Because, of course, the only Sox game he'd ever attended was a recent one against his former favorite team, the Indians.

    I went to one game in Anaheim in 1992, and my journey behind the Orange Curtain was no treat. The first sign of trouble was an army of pre-eBay memorabilia prospectors who were handing neighborhood kids tickets so they could enter, exit, and reenter the park to receive and return with collectible Nolan Ryan Day giveaway souvenirs. I actually can't cite exactly why this experience was bad, but I just found that park dreary, and dreary in a soulless way (not richly dreary like the Cleveland

Indians cavernous old stadium or bizarrely dreary like the gray, concrete Kingdome when the smoke would settle after the absurd indoor fireworks). The actual game was okay (the always amusing Pasqual Perez had a bunch of strikeouts for the Yankees in the early innings), but something about that place just made me decide that the Angels are my all-time least favorite team.

Around 1988, or so, I officially experienced "Too Much Baseball" when the White Sox scheduled back-to-back doubleheaders against the Red Sox, and I attended all four games. Thirty-six innings in 30 hours is a bit of overkill, and the only thing I remember about the first day was playing "Exquisite Corpse" with my friends to kill time between the two games. Exquisite Corpse is the game where you fold a piece of paper into horizontal thirds and the first person draws a head then gives it to the second person who, without seeing the head, draws the torso. Then the third person, also clueless to the work of his/her predecessors, finishes it off by drawing the legs and feet. At that early stage in the two-day marathon, my crew was already demonstrating signs of mental fatigue, as evidenced by the fact that we each drew one-third of Andy the Clown, the White Sox elderly, moribund, semi-amateur mascot. But the real pathetic moment came during day two, game one, when my brother, our friend Eric, and I were sitting in the upper deck behind home plate. A foul ball rainbowed backwards and in slow motion it gently floated in front of our faces. So the trio of us, all 20-year-old, tall, athletic dudes who were actually wearing baseball mitts, reached out for the ball. Our three gloves then, still in super slowmo, converged each causing the neighboring glove to shut tight, resulting in the ball bouncing off our gloves and into the possession of an obviously more worthy recipient. Not only have I been to hundreds of games, but I've been to dozens of games where there were only hundreds of people in attendance, and I have never been graced with a game ball. And I never will because of that sorry display, which the baseball gods clearly watch over and over on a blooper reel along with Jose Canseco's noggin homer and that umpire being bitten on the finger by a cat.

I guess this next one isn't really at a ballgame, but it is at a park. I went down to Florida to see spring training in 1989, and stayed in a trailer park with my aunt, which was not a pleasant experience. She made me bathe with the door open, she turned off a Depaul NCAA tournament game because *Alf* was coming on, and she made fun of my handwriting. So I decided to just stay in Sarasota where the White Sox trained. I didn't have much money so instead of renting a room one night, I snuck into the Sox' old stadium (they had just moved into a new state-of-the-art place and abandoned the old park which was more like a high school ball field) and slept in the bullpen. The stadium was across the street from the police station, and while I had no fears of Florida vagrants, serial killers, alligators, or Katherine Harris-looking hookers, I was petrified of being hassled or arrested by the police in a city I was unfamiliar with. (I had been harassed by Chicago cops plenty of times and always assumed Southern law enforcement was worse than my hometown's notoriously corrupt men in blue.) I had the most tense, restless, one-eye-open sleep of my life, and certainly awoke more exhausted than when I laid down.

In conclusion, none of these seem truly miserable, so I guess going to the game is never really that bad. But if I ever attend a game where Michael Jordan retires, there are 20 fights, a collector offers to buy my souvenir, I drop a ball, and a cop prods me with a nightstick, I'm switching to the WNBA.

Originally appeared in issue #10, Spring 2005.

Ten Cultural Observations While Sitting in the Right Field Corner of the Tokyo Dome During a Yomiyuri Giants Game This Past July, Or Why Billy Beane Will Never Hire a Manager From the Japanese League

Jeff Boda

1) In America, we boo. And we love it, and don't deny it. From the boobirds in the supposedly cuddly Wrigley Field bleachers to hurling invectives (and a few fake needles in San Diego) at the top slugger in history, we love to hate in America. But in Japan, there is no booing. None. In the left field bleachers of the stadium sit the visiting fans, and the right field bleachers are reserved for the hardcore fans of the home team. In the top of the inning, the visitors cheer, and in the bottom of the inning, the right field bleachers cheer. And it's not just a few chants of "Let's go." It's organized flag waving, full brass bands, multiple percussionists, and about four thousand people clattering their plastic cow bells at once. Imagine European soccer, without the drunks and hooligans, with  4,000 towels creating a blur of team colors accompanied by chants urging on their team. But in the most culturally and racially homogenous country on earth, where fitting into the group is the most desirous attribute, there's no booing, because that would upset the dynamic. It's not oppressive, but uplifting, like being at a Polyphonic Spree or Flaming Lips concert. Advantage: Japan

2) The group matters, not the individual. Sacrificing for the group is glorious, and Japanese teams have fully drunk the Kool-Aid on this concept. Leadoff batter gets on during the first at-bat of the game? He's

bunted over, automatically, because the Japanese believe scoring the first run of the game also means delivering a psychological blow to the opponent. So, you give of yourself to help the team. I've seen teams ahead 2-0 in the top of the third, and the number-three batter—with a .335 BA, a .400 OBP and a slugging percentage of about .650—bunt over the leadoff batter. Now imagine Gary Sheffield, David Wright, or Derek Lee being asked to do the same, and doing it with nary a peep. Someday, Billy Beane and PECOTA and OPS fans are going to convince the Japanese that bunting really doesn't end up in more runs being scored overall. Until then, I'll be thankful I can watch Derek Lee swing away instead of bunt. Advantage: U.S.

3) Nationalism is a source of collective pride, in accomplishments that help boost the group, and not as a way of bonking you over the head and saying our country is better than yours. In Japan, there are stories every day in the papers about how Ichiro, the various Red Sox pitchers, and even Devil Rays third basemen do. Boston games are shown live in the middle of the night because the Japanese want to see how their players stack up against the best. In America, we've destroyed decades of tradition by starting to sing "God Bless America" during games because it makes us feel better to think the big cloud in the sky approves what we're doing. Advantage: Japan

4) In America, we like to celebrate our individuality, our entrepreneurship, and our freedom of thought and speech by joining together to sing the national anthem before games. In Japan, there's no national anthem sung before games. At Jingu Stadium, home of perpetual losers the Yakult Bay Swallows, there are synchronized cheerleaders on the field to get people to join together to sing "Old Man Baseball," with the immortal line, *"now, yes do my best."* So while the team may suck for decades on end, at least we're all in this together. Japan wins points for consistency and cool songs, but tradition counts for something, too. Advantage: Tie

5) In the States, bigger is better. Who do we love: Jamie Moyer or Randy Johnson? Brandon Webb or Curt Schilling? We love the overt displays of success, be they the Hummer or the 14-strikeout game. It's no fun to see someone record a 2-1 game with the winning pitcher getting 21 groundouts. But in Japan, the pitchers don't throw anywhere nearly as fast; most top out in the high 80s. But fastballs are few and far between; about 80% or more of the pitches are junk the likes of which you've never seen before. (Ever played RBI Baseball for the original Nintendo in the '80s and wonder why they let you curve a ball in three different directions? Well, that's because that's what they grew up watching.) It's

a land of subtlety—there are dozens and dozens of protocols for bowing—and of craftsmanship, where it's better to be the best instead of the biggest. (Honda and Toyota vs. Ford and GM through the decades.) And that's extended to the diamond. Pregame warmups center around turning double plays, hitting your cutoff man and bunting the man over, not mashing it out of the park. Advantage: Japan

6) In Japan, as in much of Asia, there still is an embedded respect for the elderly. So much that Respect for the Aged Day is a national holiday on the third Monday in September. That flows over onto the ball diamond; the coaches come in and spend a few minutes watching the relief pitchers warm up and make sure he's doing okay before he pitches to the first batter. The managers are quoted most often in the next day's paper, not the players. In the States, we beat up near-octogenarian Don Zimmer and throw him to the ground during playoff games. But then again, our rebellion against those older than us helped us create punk rock, rockabilly, and grunge. Advantage: U.S.

7) In Asia, including Japan, there's less of a rush in everything, mostly because of the group dynamic that permeates everything. Road rage is the rare exception, not the rule; when you're in a car and signal to change lanes, the other driver slows down to let you in instead of speeding up so he can flip you off as he speeds by. It's better for the group to work as a whole, even if it takes a little more time, than for things to be disruptive but time-saving. There's no such thing as a two-man conference on the mound in Japan between the pitcher and catcher; everyone in the infield joins. It takes about 40 seconds, not 20, to establish the next pitch and convey it because you need to figure out how to outwit the batter with junk instead of blowing them away with a fastball. That said, imagine a land where every game is like Steve Trachsel pitching against Steve Trachsel, with Steve Trachsel relieving, then closing. That's Japan. Advantage: U.S.

8) The best way to learn about a country is through its food. America's the great melting pot, and not just socially. We take in everything, no questions asked. We may bitch about it for a while (first the Germans, then the Irish, then the Italians, and now the Mexicans) but eventually they all get absorbed into our whole. We accept outsiders, and eventually the original cultural identity is absorbed into the whole. And that blends into the food, too. Anyone who has eaten in Italy or Spain or France and compares those dining experiences to their counterparts in the U.S. will see what dissolution does. We've blanded everything down so everyone fits in; why eat diced wild boar at an Italian restaurant when there is spaghetti with red sauce? Why have tripe when we can have chicken

breast? Japan takes in bits of other cultures, but stands firm in its love of its own. There are plenty of non-Japanese restaurants in the Tokyo area, but their influence hasn't seeped into their food, which they love for good reason. In America, you go to a ballpark in Chicago and there are hot dogs (German), pizza (Italian), fries (Belgian or French), soft tacos (Mexican), and Budweiser. We've based our food on our interpretations of the original, but made them worse. In Japan, you go to a stall and order curry rice bowls, sushi, the best pork cutlets on earth and edamame (instead of peanuts) and the best macrobrewed beer on earth. (For the record, you can get a hot dog at the Tokyo Dome. And truth be told, it's better than what I've had at ballparks in America, because Japan is a country of craftsmen who refuse to do anything poorly.) Plus, in Japan, you don't throw your garbage and edamame pods on the ground. You save them and take to the recycling bin, in the spirit of fitting in with the group. Advantage: Japan.

9) Japan, for all its group dynamics, still has an incredible amount of repression going on, a lot of it sexual. You walk into a 7-Eleven and there are porn mangas right by the checkout. There are kiosks near train stations that sell cards with numbers of teenage girls any older man can call and talk to. And it's not uncommon for a 40-something to help "support" a teenage girl, who needs to have the latest fashion and trend, right then. The pervs aren't hidden like in America; it's right in the open. And who are the vendors selling beer and whisky in the aisles at the Tokyo Dome? Incredibly cute young women, most in their late teens, I would guess, wearing short skirts or shorts, as part of their uniform advertising the beer they sell. Japan knows sex and youth sell and embraces the fact, unlike America, which sells sex and youth but then denies it. That said, it's more fun buying beer in Japan. You know which beer each girl sells because it says on her uniform, instead of someone yelling out what beer they're selling at the top of their lungs. They wear backpacks filled with just-tapped beer, so each cup you order is poured fresh just for you. And service is with a

smile. The single beer fan in me says that cute young women in short skirts pouring fresh Kirin beats loud-mouthed, greasy mullets selling tepid Bud Light any day, even if the liberal in me says that's sexist. So be it. Advantage: Japan.

10) In Hong Kong, my current hometown, there's a phrase called FILTH. It's short for Failed In London, Try Hong (Kong). If you can't succeed in the west, either professionally or romantically, try Asia. It's where you go to cash in if you don't have the chops to make it back home. That's what the Japanese League is for baseball. There's a reason Tuffy Rhodes didn't succeed in the majors, even if he did tie the all-time record for homers in Japan. In Yokohama, Matt White might get known for his pitching skills with the Baystars instead of owning land in Massachusetts worth billions because of the quarry-able stone underneath. America still is the land of opportunity, and that's why you see a one-way flow of talent; they call it the big leagues for a reason. Advantage: U.S.

Originally appeared in issue #15, Fall 2007.

Burning Down the House: Why Camden Yards Stinks

Bob Mason

Before I begin, I should issue a warning that many of you will find this article offensive and inflammatory. To the casual fan, what I am about to say will elicit disbelief and angry replies: in baseball circles it will be considered a heresy for which there can be no forgiveness. So in the interest of preserving the harmony and goodwill that the 1998 season brought to baseball fandom across this great land of ours, I implore you to move on to the next article, forget you even started reading this. At the very least, small children, the elderly, or those with heart conditions should stop reading right now so they can enjoy the rest of their day in blissful ignorance. What could I possibly have to say that is so horrible, you ask? Okay brave guy, but remember, you asked for it.

Camden Yards stinks.

Now before you grab your torches and pitchforks, hear me out. I know you're thinking, "But Camden Yards is the Mecca of baseball. It saved us from bland, cookie-cutter fields of the '70s like Riverfront, Three Rivers, and Veterans Stadium. It served as the inspiration for new fields in Cleveland, Texas, and numerous other cities looking to cash in on the retro stadium craze. It helped save the game of baseball itself." To which I reply, have you been there?

Now I readily concede the ballpark is aesthetically pleasing, hearkening the collective baseball unconscious back to such quirky fields as the Polo Grounds, Ebbets Field, and Crosely Field that prospered during the heyday of the game. The asymmetry of the field's dimensions, the high wall in right field, and, of course, the brick warehouse combine to make Camden Yards immediately recognizable to even the novice fan. But the atmosphere at the park owes much more to the garish era of Charles Finley, exploding scoreboards and the Chicago White Sox wearing short pants than it does to Joe DiMaggio, weekday afternoon doubleheaders, and the pastoral simplicity it tries so hard to evoke.

My problem with the field has nothing to do with the top-heavy name "Oriole Park at Camden Yards" that was foisted upon it by a bureaucracy of suits and beancounters (though in all my years living in Maryland, I never heard one person refer to it as such except the men who target Peter Angelos's derriere with a daily barrage of pursed lips). My distaste

Fan Interference

is in no way connected with my strong dislike for the Orioles themselves, even though I admit they are one of the few teams in the major leagues I actually root against. No, the reason behind my feelings is simply this: a game at Camden Yards is nearly unwatchable.

Upon entering, the park seems pleasant enough as you stroll down Eutaw Street past the warehouse, mingling with a crowd of seemingly excited fans and wide-eyed kids. You take your seat anywhere in the park (I prefer the bleachers) and find that you have a great view of the field. Hey, you think, there isn't a bad seat in the house. It might have taken ninety years, but someone finally figured out how to build a stadium without placing seats behind huge pillars or facing them away from the action so you have to suffer with a sore neck for the next week just to see the game. You kick back and sip your drink, looking at the split level bullpens or scoreboard on the right wall, and prepare yourself for what will most assuredly be a great baseball experience, regardless if your team wins or loses. And then the game starts.

The first sign that something might be horribly wrong occurs as soon as the Orioles take the field. The public address system drowns out the cheering of the hometown crowd with a song that surely must be the bastard child of the Spice Girls and Up With People. Imagine, if you will, that the people who think the Super Bowl halftime show entertains football fans wrote a song for baseball...them multiply it by a factor of three.

Okay, you suspect that had to be an aberration as you settle down to an evening of the greatest game around with a group of fellow diehard fans. But as the top of the first progresses you notice no one seems to be paying much attention to the game. It's not that they're chatting or hurrying off to the snack stand to buy nachos dripping in vulcanized cheese, they're just kind of sitting there, unsure of where to put their eyes. When the Orioles finally take their turn at bat a brief crackle of energy swirls throughout the stadium, but after the first pitch to the leadoff hitter, the crowd settles back into indifference.

With two outs, an Oriole hitter smacks a double into the right field corner. Surely this will energize the crowd, they were simply waiting for a reason to get excited. After a momentary smattering of applause, though, they again fall silent. Then a funny thing happens. Every scoreboard around the stadium orders the crowd to "Make Noise" in bold flashing letters and music pipes out at them in rhythmic pulses, prodding everyone to clap in time. Suddenly, the stadium is alive in a cheering, clapping frenzy. But as quickly as it started, it stops: the scoreboard has stopped telling them what to do.

This pattern holds throughout the rest of the game. The crowd sits silently on their hands until the all-knowing scoreboard tells them it's time to cheer their team. I'm sure it's this way at many ballparks, but it is so bad at Camden Yards that when the Orioles were losing 8-1, I saw a two out, bases empty walk to Rafael Palmiero cheered as if he just hit a game-winning grand slam.

How can this be? Baltimore has a reputation for being a smart baseball town. Their advertising campaign goes so far as to label it "Baseball City, U.S.A." To earn that sobriquet their fans must be at least as savvy as those of New York, Boston, Philadelphia, and St. Louis. Well, guess what? The main basis for calling Baltimore "Baseball City, U.S.A." comes from the fact that George Herman Ruth was born there. Outside the stadium they even have a statue of The Babe instead of immortal Orioles stars Brooks Robinson, Frank Robinson, or Jim Palmer. The official press release promoting Camden Yards states that it is located "only two blocks from the birthplace of baseball's most legendary hero." Never mind that Babe Ruth never played a day in an Oriole uniform. The Orioles didn't even exist when he died in 1948—they were still the St. Louis Browns. Based on this way of thinking, Tupelo, Mississippi, must be Music City, U.S.A., because Elvis Presley was born there.

All of sudden, the robotic nature of the crowd ceases to become your primary source of annoyance because the wind blowing off the harbor has changed direction and you find yourself choking in a cloud of smoke. Unfortunately, the smoke isn't from a raging inferno that will cause a premature end to the contest and force evacuation of the stadium. No, the pungent, stinging stench of burning flesh that surrounds you comes from Boog's Barbecue, a pit of flaming cadavers in right center field run by the former Oriole slugger and the man voted Most Likely to Have Triple Bypass Surgery, Boog Powell.

You don't mind being blinded by the smoke that much because it means you can't see the baseball cap shell game currently taking place on the Jumbotron scoreboard. If you haven't had the misfortune to see it, the shell game is a computer-generated version of Three Card Monte. A small ball is placed under one of three identical baseball caps, which are then quickly shuffled around in a manner that's supposed to make you lose track of the cap that holds the ball. The object of the game is to then guess which cap will have the ball under it. What you'd think would be a minor between-inning diversion garners fan attention and excitement that shames all on-field action short of a home run.

Luckily for the Orioles and their fans, though, there is no shortage of the long ball. Gopher balls fly out of Camden Yards as such a rate that American League President Gene Budig must have Carpal Tunnel Syndrome from signing so many baseballs. Even with expansion-thinned pitching and beefed-up hitters, baseballs leave the Yard at an alarming rate. Combine minimal foul ground with seven foot high outfield fences everywhere but in right, where it rises to 25 feet, and you have a formula for a ton of taters. Cal Ripken, Jr. once hit a towering pop fly down the left field line that the human defensive lapse, Gregg Jefferies, allowed to bounce off the top of the wall for a grand slam, 333 feet away from and seven feet above home plate.

The ironically named "power alleys" just add to the pitchers' nightmares. To poke one out in left center you have to hit a ball of 364 feet, to right center a monumental 373 feet. These cozy dimensions lead to more routine pop flies going the distance and more pitchers watching their ERAs skyrocket after throwing good pitches than any place other than a backyard Wiffle Ball game. And before you argue that a hitter could swat a homer down the lines of the Polo Grounds on an "excuse me" swing, at least that ballpark expanded enough so that the center field fence was in another time zone. In Camden Yards, the center field fence stands 400 feet from home plate, nowhere near far enough to punish hitters for other cozy dimensions.

Don't believe that Camden Yards is the home of the cheap round tripper? Then let's take a look at the curious case of Mike Bordick. Without a doubt, Mr. Bordick is an above-average, dependable player that every team without a Garciaparra, Rodriguez, Jeter, or Larkin would love to have at shortstop. But a home run threat? Coming into the 1998 season, Bordick had 28 home runs in 3,152 at bats, with his career high being eight in 1995 while playing in Oakland's admittedly cavernous Coliseum. This averages out to one home run every 112.5 at bats. But lo and behold, last year with the Orioles Bordick smacked 13 home runs in 465 at bats, or one every 35.8 at bats, an increase of over 300%.

Did Bordick bulk up a lá Mark McGwire over the off-season? No. Did major league pitching get worse? Actually, by a lot of statistics it was healthier than it had been in the last few years. So if it's not the batter and it's not the pitcher, and the inane "rabbit ball" theory is discounted, the only other factor that can be taken in account is the ballpark. And Mike Bordick plays half his games at Camden Yards. Draw your own conclusion.

Don't get me wrong. I like a good slugfest as much as the next guy. I just don't want to see a pitcher bust a batter inside with a high blazing fastball and then have to dodge bat fragments as the ball soars over his outfielder's head. New Oriole Albert Belle must be salivating when he thinks of playing 81 games at Camden Yards.

Though all the above reasons make watching a game at Camden Yards nearly unbearable, they pale in comparison to the abomination that greets you during the seventh-inning stretch. As you rise from your seat to prepare for the final two and a half innings, the PA system squawks to life and "Thank God I'm a Country Boy" attacks you before you even have a chance to scream. Let me repeat this as a public service: DURING THE SEVENTH-INNING STRETCH AT CAMDEN YARDS, THEY PLAY "THANK GOD I'M A COUNTRY BOY."

Bob Mason

After that aural lobotomy there aren't many surprises left in the late innings. Another '70s leftover, the giant, cartoon bird that wanders the ballpark as the Orioles official mascot, tries to maintain fan interest when the commands of the scoreboard start to lose their appeal. First, he leads the crowd in a rousing spelling of the team name. Then he shows what a unique talent Jim Carrey truly is by waving his buttocks at opposing players. As entertaining as all this sounds, it has the shelf life of a Guns n' Roses album. For my money, the only team mascot worth his salt is the Phillie Phanatic, and that's only because he looks like my Uncle Ed.

Of course the diehard fans of "Baseball City, U.S.A." leave in the 8th to beat traffic, no matter how tight the contest (I'm going to start doing this at other events I pay lots of money to attend, getting up and walking out before the last act of a play or movie or last course of a meal). But at this point you're glad they're gone; it'll make it easier for you to leave when the actual final out is recorded.

After the game as you walk out the gate and the stadium lights go dark, you find yourself yearning for the nostalgic romance of Fenway Park, the cheering throngs of Busch Stadium, or the flat-out best ballpark in the majors at Chavez Ravine in Los Angeles. But another more surprising feeling also takes hold of you as Camden Yards fades to oblivion in your rearview mirror, you find yourself actually missing the excessive heydays of the '70s. At least in the days of Day-Glo baseballs and White Sox pajama uniforms they were trying to sell you on the circus atmosphere at the ballpark. At Camden Yards they promise you Mays, Gehrig, and the Big Train, but what they deliver is the baseball equivalent of a Kiss concert.

Originally appeared in issue #1, Spring 1999.

Goodbye to Stadiums

Shea Stadium – Mike Faloon

Shea Stadium isn't the best baseball stadium in New York City. It's not even second best, trailing the more aesthetically pleasing parks in the Bronx and Coney Island. But Shea is my favorite.

Shea's shortcomings are numerous and obvious. The stadium is located in Flushing. It's far removed from any sense of neighborhood. For those taking the subway there's nothing to do in the area before or after games.

Hopefully, the last game I saw at Shea will fade from memory, but I'm still going to miss the place, even more than I'm going to miss Yankee Stadium.

Despite a rather pronounced disliking for the Bronx Bombers I never turned down a trip to Yankee Stadium. The narrow hallways. The low ceilings. Monument Park. I'm far too much of a baseball sentimentalist to resist. The last time I went to Yankee Stadium my wife and I lucked into box seats. Walking to the elevators, we passed Rudy Giuliani. Later, we passed George Steinbrenner in the hallway. We also witnessed this exchange.

Thirty-something Yankees fan getting into elevator, to 10-year-old wearing a Mets cap: Hey, Mets fan, good luck!

Other thirty-something Yankees fan getting into elevator, to same kid: (Bends over, gets eye to eye with the kid, points to Yankees insignia on his cap) Don't worry about luck, kid!

That's the thing about the Yankees, and Yankee Stadium, the aura and brushes with fame can't mask the nastiness. Shea doesn't bother trying.

The last game I saw at Shea was a forgettable late-August blowout against the Astros. My brother and I made a day trip out of it. On our way to Flushing, we had lunch at Virgil's Barbeque. We stopped for a beer at Jimmy's. After the game we hit a midnight movie in Times Square. There wasn't a moment all day when we forgot that we were in New York City. That's why I always loved a game at Shea. No matter how good or bad the game I was watching—even that 1993 game lost when a ground ball squirted past an out-of-position Joe Orsulak—I was always getting a thoroughly warts-and-all NYC experience.

When you looked past the outfield fence you got an eyeful of the

Queens skyline—expressways, parking garages, car repair shops. And when you closed your eyes, the sounds of the game were periodically drown out by air traffic from nearby LaGuardia Airport. All of those things will be there to greet the completed Citi Field, which is going to look great, no doubt. But when I look at Citi Field, I get a sense that its designers, consciously or otherwise, don't care if I'm aware of New York when I'm there. It's newer and shinier and it's the model that will get better mileage, but it'll always lack Shea's scratch and dent charm.

Shea Stadium – Steve Reynolds

As unenthused as I was about the 2008 Mets (which I hated until Willie Randolph got the ax, so maybe I just didn't like the former Yankee?), I was very excited for my last trip to Shea Stadium on July 26 that season. This was no ordinary trip, as I was joining about 35 other people on a cruise from the East side of Manhattan up the East River to the stadium. We were all gathered together to celebrate our friend Jonah's birthday. But it was much more than a birthday celebration—it was a life celebration. Three months earlier we found out that Jonah had melanoma that had spread to one of his lymph nodes. And while my circle of friends (and Jonah himself) were optimistic that everything would turn out for the best, it was apparent to me that we all had seeds of doubt. As someone who has lost two family members to cancer and has friends who have lost spouses and others to this tenacious disease, I know I couldn't help but dwell on the negative.

Fortunately, things went well with Jonah's surgery and his radiation treatments. As a matter of fact, Jonah's last day of radiation was two days before the cruise, the game, and his birthday. So that ride to Shea was perhaps the most joyful I've ever experienced going to a Mets game. People hugging each other, drinking really overpriced "cheap" beer as if it were water, and waving to people on the shores of the river—it was quite a party. The game almost seemed secondary compared to the fun we had on the way. And it was for almost everyone, as I was the only person left at the end of five hours and 14 innings when the Mets finally lost. I'll admit to being disgruntled by yet another loss as I walked down the numerous ramps from the upper deck. Once I got to the ground, I paused, turned around and looked at Shea one more time. And I thought to myself, "Yeah, this place has always been a dump. Bring on fewer seats, higher prices, and gourmet food at Citi Field!"

Candlestick Park – Ken Derr

The last time I went to Candlestick Park, I was drunk before noon. It was teacher cut day and we were wearing party hats. It was also the last time

I tailgated at a Giants game, because the temple of AT&T does not allow such vulgarity. You also don't see fans in the new joint like the one who sat behind us that day, the only man in the bowl more hammered than we were. "Let's go, Johnny Bench. Come on, Johnny, ya punk." We were playing the Braves in 1999, but no matter—we loved this dude, for his public behavior was worse than ours, and our next-day guilt would surely be attenuated. Visiting the Stick was like making the pilgrimage to Mecca, if you believed in the trinity of wind and cold and intoxication. I saw the face of Johnny LeMaster in a Carnation Chocolate Malt, and it's still sitting in my basement freezer. I'm still waiting for the right eBay moment to dump that one. I can't remember a single detail of that last game. We got plastered, sunburned, and embarrassingly confessional, and I've been in counseling for years trying to erase the image of that science teacher and the attendance secretary with the asymmetrical bootie. I think we drove home, but that image is lost in unnavigable psychic caverns. The only thing I can recall is that the Giants were good then. Russ Ortiz and Robb Nen and Bill Mueller weren't that great in our eyes and hearts during those years, but boy are their replacements stinking up the laundry. I can't say the same thing about the new place, because it is gorgeous. But I do miss the loudmouths, and I've yet to hear the name Johnny Bench uttered in the palace Peter built.

Connie Mack Stadium – John Shiffert

Although I saw Game 2 of the 1980 World Series at the Vet, Connie Mack Stadium (formerly Shibe Park) is still my favorite stadium among the two former stadia wherein the Phillies have performed.

My last game there was the last Opening Day at Connie Mack Stadium—April 7, 1970. The Phillies had a new manager (Frank Lucchesi) and a much-heralded new rookie double play combination, shortstop Larry Bowa and second baseman Denny Doyle. This was my senior year at Germantown Friends School, and since the senior class was not required to attend classes (we were all working on senior projects), I was free to go the game with my grandfather, the one and only Ralph M. Shiffert—an old catcher and A's fan from way back in the Eddie Plank/Stuffy McInnis days.

Since he had recently retired from the Philadelphia Electric Company after 50 years, he still had an "in" with Peco, and we parked over at his old substation on Hunting Park Avenue (as everyone in Philly knows, Hunting Park spelled backwards in Krap Gnitnuh—say it out loud a few dozen times), by that other famous Philadelphia landmark, the Tasty Baking Company. This was much preferable to trying to park near 21st and Lehigh, where the neighborhood kids, undaunted by the specter of the Vet raising in South Philly, were still playing the old "watch your car for a dollar, mister" game. So, we walked about a half mile to the old ballpark.

There was quite a buzz that day, mostly about the new skipper, who was, among other things, the first Phillies manager since Gene Mauch with any kind of personality. Indeed, Lucchesi had a lot of personality, but not many players. (The Phillies would finish the season 73-88.) As it would turn out over time, Bowa would live up to his billing. No, that's not right. He lived over his billing—there were serious questions on April 7, 1970, as to whether or not he'd hit his weight (155 lbs). He could field, and run like the wind, but he looked like a Little Leaguer in the field, and the Cubs, the opponent that day, played him at Little League depth. Nonetheless, Lawrence Robert Bowa would go on to play in 2,246 more major league games, to accumulate 2,191 hits, help lead the team to the 1980 World Series title, become manager of the Phillies, win the Manager of the Year Award in 2001, and become one of Philadelphia's favorite adopted sons.

This first game wasn't particularly edifying for Bowa. He popped to shortstop batting leadoff for the Phillies in the first, and ended up going 0-3 with a walk, although he was flawless in six chances in the field. Although Doyle had three hits, and one of the Phillies two RBIs in the game, his career would be a lot less noteworthy, just 944 games in eight years.

In the other dugout were three genuine Hall of Famers, another should-be Hall of Famer, and former Phillie favorite, Johnny Callison. Nonetheless, despite the presence of Callison, Ernie Banks, Billy Williams, and Ron Santo on the field and Ferguson Jenkins (another former Phillie) on the mound, the home team won their last opener at the park they had occupied since 1938 (and which had opened 61 years before). Chris Short, coming off back surgery, and pitching one of his last great games as a Phillie, shut out the Cubs on five hits and the Phillies won, 2-0, scoring single runs in the third (on a triple by Doyle) and seventh (on a double by Don Money).

Although neither Stuffy McInnis, nor Eddie Plank, nor Dick Allen (my personal childhood favorite) made an appearance, granddad and I went home happy.

Memorial Stadium, Shea Stadium, Candlestick Park – Frank D'Urso

Luckily, as a Red Sox fan, we have owners who understand the importance of history and consistency. Hopefully, I'll never have to have a last memory of Fenway Park and I'm able to have my ashes spread across left field so I never have to leave. But here are my last times at other, less fortunate ballparks.

Memorial Stadium
It was the Orioles last season before moving downtown to the Fenway-inspired Camden Yards. I had attended a few games at Memorial Stadium, was particularly impressed with the suburban neighborhood that surrounded this great old bowl of a park. This last trip was special, with my now ex-in-laws, we watched as Harmon Killebrew was honored for hitting the longest home run in Memorial Stadium history. I remember the big sporty jacket Harmon wore that day, impressed that that much fabric could drape a man of his stature. A living idol of mine ever since the *Boston Globe* Sunday comics page had a series of full page posters of major league stars. Appropriately, it was a Twins versus Orioles matchup. I forget who won.

Shea Stadium
We got box seats through my friend's company. I had the balls to wear my #14 Jim Rice Red Sox jersey and was impressed that there were other members of Red Sox nation in the stadium. I disliked the way they chained off the empty seats in front of us. What a waste. The upper level was so far away and so vertical I had nightmares just looking up at it. (Not to mention the skeevies I felt looking down at first base.)

Candlestick Park
This time, I got tickets through my job. We had two extra and tried to give them away (wanting to avoid the land sharks known as ticket scalpers). People avoided me though. (Did I look that shady?) I resorted to shouting out "I've got two free tickets to the first person who can tell me the Giants original team name."

People just looked at me.

"Okay, where did the Giants first come from?" The answer I was looking for was Troy Haymakers, but would have accepted New York.

People were a bit bemused, so I said, "Who can tell me who wore number twenty-four?"

To which, of course, the nearest teenager/college kid replied, "Willie Mays."

I handed him the two $45 tickets and said thank you. I don't think anyone believed that I was actually giving away any tickets, let alone (what were then) expensive tickets.

MacArthur Stadium – Mark Hughson

My final game at the MacArthur Stadium (home of the Syracuse Chiefs of the International League) in the summer of 1996 had three unforgettable moments. I had been away at college for two years and hadn't been keeping up with the local media hoopla surrounding the decision to "sell out," close the park, and move the team down the street. When I arrived at the park and saw the back of a T-shirt that read "Last Crack At Big Mac," I finally recognized that there are season-ticket-holding baseball lovers here that lived and died by the local farm team. It was the first time it dawned on me that 62 years of history was soon to become a parking lot. Depressing.

The second moment happened halfway through the game when two old dudes turned around and told me to shut up and watch the game or they'd call security on me and have me removed. I guess they had grown tired of my incessant yelling, cheering, and (justified) umpire booing. My brother and his girlfriend were with me and naturally did not rise to my defense, so I stayed quiet. Upsetting.

The storybook ending is close at hand, though. In the final inning, we were down by three with the bases loaded. There was still an outside chance and the crowd did indeed grasp there was a sliver of hope. As the outs tallied up and the baserunners stayed put, we started to lose our grip. I mean yeah, it could happen but it probably wouldn't. But it might. The only chance we had to win the game right there and then was a grand slam by the catcher. The pitcher slung one over and the catcher sent it to deep center right. It towered (crowd rises). It carried (crowd buzzes). It went out (crowd erupts)! We did it! *Fireworks*! *Amazing*! Great game.

Arlington Stadium – Kip Yates

I remember the last game I ever attended at the old Arlington Stadium. It was a converted minor league ballpark and had undergone several renovations, including a grandstand behind home plate. It was a hole though. It was one of the many charmless cookie cutter ballparks from the '60s. Think the Vet without the attitude. Shea without the airplanes. The Astrodome without the aura. It was the place I witnessed my first ballgame. It was the place where as a kid George Brett made a gesture to get my attention just so he could return the wave I gave him from the stands. I grew up an Astros fan but since I lived in Arlington, had to watch the fruitless Rangers. Their seasons usually went like this. Play like gang busters in April and May, cool off in June as the weather became warmer, cling to first or second come All-Star time, and then fall dramatically during the sweltering second half. I think the Rangers finished second once or twice while I was growing up.

Arlington Stadium does have its limited place in baseball history. It was the birthplace of nachos at the ballpark. They didn't just give you some tortilla chips and then slip some melted cheese into a tiny cup attached to the plate. No, they smothered your nachos with cheese. Want beef with that? You got it. Jalapenos? Well help yourself; they're by the condiments. Ah, good times! My dad could take the four of us to game, sit behind home plate (the screened part, not the nose bleeds), buy beer, nachos, and peanuts and a souvenir batting helmet for $60. I spent nearly $100 recently at Shea for two tickets and a bobble head.

I witnessed good games and bad games at Arlington. One of my favorite memories was the opening four days of the 1980 season. It snowed in Arlington in April and they still played. Not only that, they played a doubleheader. However, the Rangers opened their season 4-0 by sweeping the Yankees. I was at all four. I still wish I had my "Beat the Yankees" hankie that they gave away before one of the games. I have other memories beside Brett waving to me and beating the snot out of the Yankees. I remember going with my parents and showing up at the ballpark before the gates opened. Two hours before the gates opened, in fact. My brother, Kyle, and I still laugh that we would show up outside the right field fence at 4:00 for a 7:30 game. My mom's rationale was we have to get there before the crowds. Sure, Mom, but do we have to get there before the visiting team? Anyway, we would show up and be bored out of our minds for two hours until the excitement of the staff removing the chains from the locks. Then it was go time. We were off to the races. We always ran to get seats on the first row of general admission section and watch not only the Rangers take batting practice but the visiting team, as well. It was not all bad, though. I usually came home with some pitcher's autograph. I would toss them my ball while they warmed up, doing calisthenics in the outfield. I met Jim Kern, Steve Comer, Danny Darwin, Goose Gossage, Jon Matlack, Gaylord Perry, Fergie Jenkins—all players who stopped sucking when they wore another uniform. My brother worked the grounds crew during the summer of '81 (the hot one). He brought me Al Oliver's hat, Jim Sundberg's broken bat. One of my favorite stories that Kyle tells is the time he met Mickey Rivers. He told Mickey that he wore number 17, played outfield, batted leadoff to which Mickey scoffed, "Yeah, but you ain't black." Touché!

I attended my last game at Arlington Stadium during the summer of '89, five years before they would open The Ballpark at Arlington. I went to see the Rangers play the Mariners with my then girlfriend now wife, Jamie. I don't even remember a kid named Ken Griffey, Jr. manning the outfield. What I remember best was witnessing the only triple play I have seen in my life. Steve Bueschele hit a hard grounder to Dave Valle at third and before I knew it, the promising inning was over and the Rangers trudged on to another loss.

I finally witnessed my first game at the new ballpark this summer—a loss to the hated Yankees. The more things change, the more they stay the same.

Goodbye to Stadiums

Comiskey Park – Jake Austen

In 2000, for some reason, I attended the last game at Tigers Stadium, and it was a spectacular production, with a melodramatic, sentimental post-game ceremony that involved a seemingly unending parade of Tigers legends running, doddering, and being wheeled onto the field to take their historic positions for the final time. I was glad to be there, but it meant little to me as I never had particularly strong feelings for the Tigers. Once, when I was sitting in the Comiskey Park bleachers between a group of Michigan Girl Scouts who were holding up Kirk Gibson signs and a group of "Gibby's" buddies, I witnessed the then-future hobbling home run hero make obscene gestures at his friends, somehow not noticing the proximity of eight-year-old girls, but that is something that shaped my opinion of Gibby rather than of the Tigers. I admire a quote by Tigers skipper Jim Leyland about Magglio Ordonez' long curly locks that went something like, "He's a grown man, I'm not going to tell him he has to cut his hair. But it looks terrible." Still, that didn't make me a Tigers fan. And I didn't even become a Tigers hater after attending a new Comiskey Park game earlier in Detroit's historic 2000 season, in which the White Sox and Tigers had a series of brawls, the longest of which was an almost fifteen-minute sprawling melee that involved dozens of players wandering around the field like two armies in field combat, occasionally exploding into genuinely bloody fisticuffs. At one point, Magglio, then a young White Sox, actually used a karate kick on someone. This led to the biggest mass suspension in MLB history and was a highlight of the tenth season of new Comiskey Park.

Oh yeah, that's what I was writing about. My original point was that the final game in Detroit was a spectacular production, especially compared to the low-key affair I attended on September 30, 1990. At the time the 80-year-old Comiskey was the oldest park in baseball and was in the shadow of the soon-to-be newest park, a blue spaceship-looking monstrosity that, despite having less seats, towered over the old whitewashed brick stadium due to the extra level of luxury boxes and an elevated playing field necessitated by a space-age drainage system designed to allow safe ballplaying an hour after a monsoon. Anyhow, my brother, father, friend Marcus, one of my teachers, and I were among 42,849 attending the swansong of the "Baseball Palace of the World." The Sox had already diminished the occasion by selling it as a two-part finale, billing Saturday's game as "closing night" and ending it with spectacular fireworks. The only ceremonies I recall for the last game were the players throwing some balls into the stands and attendees receiving 8.5" x 11" certificates to frame your historic ticket that looked like something you got for participating in a day-camp Olympics.

The game itself was kind of perfect. It was a 2-1 victory over Seattle (there seemed to be more 2-1 losses or wins than any other score in Sox history). In our one scoring inning, the best Sox triples hitter of my lifetime, Lance Johnson, was driven in by a solid single by the best pure hitter of my lifetime, Frank Thomas, who came home bizarrely enough on a triple by lumbering, pot-smoking power hitter Dan Pasqua. This seemed fitting, considering that Sox fans expect to witness strange events more than they expect to see great baseball.

The most memorable part of the day came in the morning when I called up my visiting art school teacher, Richard Merkin, to wake him up for the delicious pregame brunch my mom prepared. Merkin, a well known painter (he's in the *Sgt. Pepper's* album cover montage), was staying in a downtown private club where he was surprised by the call, stumbled out of bed, and broke his nose. He arrived at our home with a bulbous crooked honker and some distressed under-eye blood vessels, forever convincing my mom that he was a W.C. Fields-esque damaged drunk. But besides that footnote, it was just a cool last game, totally appropriate for a team whose fans understand that they are rooting for the second team in the second city, a team that plays for working class dudes, broad-shouldered broads, shirtless teens getting high in the upper deck, and for pockets of whatever ethnicity is populating the Southside each decade. We are not supposed to have the national spotlight or the fanciest anything. The fact that our shiny new park, with instantly cracking concrete walkways and perilously steep upper decks, was a disaster seemed appropriate. It was quickly made obsolete by Baltimore's retro park, marking new Comiskey as the last terrible ballpark, and only an expensive re-retro-ization a decade and a half later (they removed the UFO façade and added old time wrought iron awnings) has made it a decent digs for the first Chicago team to win a twenty-first century World Series.

But there actually was one perfect "ceremony" to end the final game at the grand old, beautifully crumbling park. As we were leaving, Nancy Faust, the ageless veteran ballpark organist, the woman who introduced rock music to baseball parks and whose musical puns ("In-A-Gadda-Da-Vida" for Pete Incaviglia) put Chris Berman to shame, played us out with a song she introduced to professional sports. As fans wandered down the dank walkways out of Comiskey one final time her organ gently wept "Na Na Na Na – Na Na Na Na – Hey Hey Hey Goodbye!"

Originally appeared in issue #17, Fall 2008.

In the Pink

Dr. Nancy Golden

If not for the pink T-shirts, it might have been a perfect day.

The players were likely still sleeping off last night's rain-delayed game against the Braves when I showed up at RFK Stadium in D.C. that September morning. That's okay, because I came prepared to swing for the seats and take grounders at short—Felipe Lopez would only get in my way.

Ha! If only I had that much confidence going into the day. The truth was, despite the fact that the Nationals billed the day as a "Baseball 101 Clinic for Women," I was still worried that my desire to run around a major league ball field and meet some coaches might be hampered by my lack of certain skills that seemed helpful to the game. Namely: hitting, throwing, and catching. While I have a solid knowledge and appreciation of the game as a fan, the Nats' previous events designed to increase female attendance, mainly Ladies' Night happy hours, required only skills that I had long ago mastered—drinking beer and flagging down waiters carrying hors d'oeuvres. And now my dirty secret was about to be revealed: an avid fan of baseball, my mastery of its play is just about on par with George W. Bush's mastery of words containing three or more syllables. And while in reality I knew deep down that it didn't matter if third base coach Tim Tolman found out that I had a weak arm, I couldn't help but worry: What if I couldn't even hit the cut-off man?

Waiting outside the stadium at 8:30 a.m. for everyone to arrive, my co-clinician Kelly and I were assigned to groups and awarded our swag. Some of the freebies were standard fare: a Nats cooler, school supplies, a scorebook, etc. Others were decidedly girly: a pack of baseball cards featuring Nats players and their mothers, and a T-shirt in the girliest of all girl colors, pink (which will so perfectly match the pink baseball cap from that last Ladies' Night gathering dust in my closet). At least the wedding planners weren't sponsors this time around.

But who had time to gripe when we suddenly found ourselves led through the stands and down into the dugout? We took advantage of the requisite photo ops—sitting on the bench, leaning up against the railing, etc.—before our coaches arrived to teach us some baseball. On hand this morning were all of the Nats actual coaches. And even though they were up just as late as the players last night, each one of them acted like there was nowhere in the whole world he'd rather be than back here on the field that morning. Then again, it was just them and 75 enthusiastic baseball-lovin' chicks—maybe they actually spoke the truth on this one. Okay, so far all I'd had to do was smile, pose, and clap. It was time to get to business.

After a team stretch and warm-up in the infield, we broke into our groups and headed off to our mentors. My opening set of drills was at first, where coach Jerry Morales went over signs with us, fielded questions about a dubious call from last night's game, and taught us how to run with men on base. Morales was such a good coach that I swear I felt myself swell with pride as he praised me for a particularly well-executed banana turn around the bag. Next, over at third base, Tolman taught us how to get in front of the ball, and then hit grounders for us to field and throw back to the catcher. And here's where any fears of my dead arm dissipated because women—contrary to what you've seen on *Gossip Girl* and *America's Next Top Model*—are uber-supportive of one another in situations like this. My groupies clapped for every throw of mine that eventually trickled back to the plate like I was throwing out the tying run of some future World Series the Nationals might make it to when I'm too old to remember any of this. I even took extra grounders just to get the praise and wondered how it would feel to really make a play and have 40,000 fans cheering for me instead of ten.

Feeling more confident now, I followed my group into the clubhouse to the domain of bench coach Pat Corrales. Stepping through stagnant puddles of water and ducking crumbling concrete, I envisioned this being a good spot for a donation jar for the new stadium, its $611 million price tag a bit of a sore subject for the city. Following a brief lesson on form and execution, I entered the indoor batting cage to take my licks. Swing and a miss! Did I mention that the ball was on a tee? That's okay, because the real victory was that I was no longer afraid to swing for the seats. With a little personal coaching from batting practice pitcher Jose Martinez, I made good contact on my next few attempts and scored a double with two RBIs in my head.

Our last lesson was in the bullpen. After catching the view from that really tall bench, we all gripped practice balls as demonstrated by bullpen coach Rick Aponte and threw off the mound until the lunch bell rang. And that was it. I'd made it through my clinic without embarrassment, not because I didn't suck, but because it was readily apparent that nobody cared that I sucked. Thank you, women. And while we're speaking of women, let me make it abundantly clear that the piss-poor baseball skills described herein belong to me alone and are not some kind of general indictment against female athleticism. Most of the women present knew exactly what they were doing. I just happened to grow up playing sports that have no relevance to real life. (Pick-up game of field hockey anyone? Great, just let me grab my kilt!)

As we enjoyed our post-clinic lunch with Don Sutton and MASN broadcasters Bob Carpenter and Debbi Taylor, I couldn't help but think how much I loved major league baseball's attempt to pander to women for their attendance. (Please, don't tell them they had me at "Strike One.") Sure, sometimes you have to put up with pink T-shirts (c'mon folks, the team color is clearly *red*), handouts defining terms like "pop-up," and swag from perfume dealers and nail studios, but I've also enjoyed all-you-can-drink happy hours with the cost of my ticket, appearances by players about to take the field, memorabilia giveaways with excellent odds, and now, baseball lessons from major league coaches, and lunch with a Hall of Famer. And all because I have boobs! I used to feel funny about attending the Nationals' women-only events (what if the tables were turned?), but I've learned to relax and enjoy the benefits. I figure after so many years waiting on those really long lines for the bathroom, I must deserve some kind of payback.

I wasn't able to stay for the game that night, but ending my baseball activities that day on Don Sutton's stand-up routine and some autographed balls swiped from the bullpen was a nice way to go. I'll see you back here for the next event. And yes, you tricky bastards, I'll bring my girlfriends.

Originally appeared in issue #16, Spring 2008.

My Big League Tryout

Matt Braun

It was a warm summer day in 1993, and there I stood, on the turf of a Little League field somewhere in the Pacific Northwest. I was there, as were fifty or so other young men, to win a spot on the roster of the hapless Seattle Mariners. Sure, I'd probably have to put in a year or two in the minors, learn to hit the curve and whatnot. But soon, there I'd stand, on that vaunted piece of artificial turf once patrolled by the likes of Gold Glover Harold Reynolds and the fleet footed Julio Cruz. I would be a Rich Amaral for the new millennium because I, dear reader, was at a major league tryout.

It was an open tryout and anyone who chose to attend was free to do so. The first step was for the Mariners' scouts to separate us into four groups: pitchers, catchers, infielders, and outfielders. I went with the infielders. We were all given cards to fill out with important data like our height, weight, what hand we threw with, and whether we batted righty or lefty. The scouts explained that we'd be rated in several categories on a scale of two to eight as we performed various drills throughout the day. These numbers, we were told, would indicate our potential to perform on the major league level. Four was considered average. The name Pat Tabler wasn't mentioned but I thought of him nonetheless. It was never explained why they didn't use a scale of one to ten, though I suspect it was a tool to save face on the part of scouts. If they projected a player as a ten in any category and he failed to perform up to expectations (Gregg Jefferies) it would be a huge disappointment and probably land the scouts in some hot water. An eight, on the other hand, doesn't sound nearly as impressive.

The first exercise was a 50-yard dash. They had us run two at a time as two scouts used stop watches to measure our efforts. I was never much of a speed merchant on the base paths but I fared better than I had anticipated.

The fielding drill followed. The infielders were divided into two groups: first basemen and everyone else. The first basemen were a sorry lot. Some of them weren't even left-handed and certainly none of them were any sort of Cecil Fielder/Mark McGwire type. Anyway, the rest of the infielders set up at the shortstop position, and each hopeful fielded two grounders and threw over to the sad squad of first basemen. I fielded both my chances cleanly, though the second was rather weakly hit and perhaps I should have charged that one a little more. Still, I had fared better than many. No doubt I'd be signing a minor league contract by the end of the day.

Finally came the hitting. At last, my true chance to shine. This is where we'd separate the wheat from the chaff. I'd spent plenty of time frequenting batting cages that summer as there was precious little else to do in that small town. I was ready. Unfortunately, while the pitches were hardly overpowering, they were all high fastballs, a pitch I've never hit well. I hit a lot of foul balls and pop-ups with the occasional soft grounder mixed in. Still, I felt on the Kingdome's turf those grounders would translate into hard doubles down the line.

Alas, dear reader, it was not to be. Twos across the board was my fate that afternoon. Could it be that I'd been lying to myself all these years? That the majors were not within my reach? No. It's the scouts that were bad, not me. Besides there was no drill to measure the intangibles. No drill to measure heart, drive, or hustle. I'll show them all. One day.

Originally appeared in issue #2, Fall 1999.

1876 Barnstorming Tour

Kip Yates

This summer, my vintage baseball team, the New York Mutuals, traveled to the Mississippi River playing other vintage baseball teams from around the country. Our barnstorming tour had been in the works for several years. At first a casual suggestion, that suggestion became a plan, and that plan became a reality. In the past year, we decided that if we were going to pull this off, we were going to have to seize the day. We are not getting any younger, and with each year that we let pass without bringing this much-talked about plan into action, the further the reality of it ever happening seemed. Last summer, we grabbed the proverbial bull by the horns and said, "Now or never!" We knew it would be costly, and we knew that getting the entire team on the road for almost two weeks was next to impossible. But we had a dream and the desire to make it happen. After all, an opportunity like this comes once in a lifetime. Twice, if you are truly lucky! We planned for a full year and as the day of our departure crept up, everything miraculously came together, thanks to the tireless planning of Big Bat, the New York Mutuals' fearless leader. I decided to keep a running journal of the trip. I knew that in my elder years, when the base swiping and showing my "Ginger," as my nickname attested, had stopped, I would want to look back on my summer of Aught Two and reflect on that glorious trip that nine teammates and I shared.

Saturday, June 29 – I arrived at Old Bethpage Village Restoration a little before 7:00 a.m. for the first leg of our trip to Philadelphia. On the chartered bus that I dubbed Bertha, we were restless all morning but eventually settled down for a midmorning nap. We would need to conserve our energy. We had just embarked on an eight-city, nine-day barnstorming tour that would take us from Boston to Hannibal, Missouri, and back to New York. There were only ten of us so no one could afford to get hurt, or the bus driver would be suiting up, and if you saw our bus driver, you would know that we didn't want that to happen. I lounged in the back with the youngsters: Kid Speed, one of the best leadoff hitters I have ever been privileged to play with; our captain, Squid; and our team physician-clown-dynamo, Express. The older guys on the team, Big Bat, Rabbit, and Scoops, stayed up front, afraid to lie down for fear that they would never get up again. Sully, Magnet, and Big Dog watched movies at the front of the bus with Harry, the great grandson of Dick Higham, an original New York Mutual.

We arrived at the park in Philly and taped our fingers, got into uniform, mentally prepared for the game. John Fogerty's "Centerfield" blared from the speakers. We left the bus to warm up, stretch, and physically prepare for our game. We played a round of magic circle to get the crowd excited and waited for our opponent, the Elizabeth Resolutes, to arrive. We had lost to the Resolutes only a month earlier, and we were not prepared to go down again. The last time we played, we let up in the middle innings, and they clawed back into the game before we knew it and took the lead for good in the top of the ninth. There would be no letting up today. We won 26-11. Kid Speed stole home and the Express hit one of his legendary long shots. I scored two runs. We celebrated our fiftieth victory as a team with a couple bottles of bubbly and set out for Boston, where we would stay the night.

Arriving in Boston was a godsend, for that meant that a shower was imminent. We had a long day behind us, and all I wanted to do was sleep.

Sunday, June 30 – I awoke early the next morning and boarded Bertha the bus for the trip to the Boston Commons, where we would play *Zisk*'s very own Frank D'Urso and his merry band of Bostonians (and Minnesotans), the SABR Nine. Almost everyone on our team was interviewed by Boston Fox news. It was here that I began to get comfortable with my clichés, as Crash Davis once advised. In my interview, I mentioned that while I played ball, I imagined thousands of ghosts of years past watching me play the game to make sure that I played the game the way it was supposed to be played: hard, fast, and like a gentleman. Reporters eat that up. That's my story and I'm sticking to it. The game almost never occurred. Right before our first pitch, a Boston constable in turn of the century uniform rode up on his horse and threatened to arrest Squid if we played ball on a Sunday. He explained that it was against the law and after some haggling and much laughter shared by all, he sang our national anthem and shouted, "Play ball." The game was special in that Sully played all nine positions. The game got out of hand early. At last count, the score was Mutuals 37, the Sab's 5.

After the game, we all posed for pictures, said our huzzahs, and I became acquainted with Mr. D'Urso. We signed each other's copies of

Zisk and had a couple of photos taken. The Mutuals went to Cheers for a celebratory beer and then boarded Bertha for Akron, Ohio. Unfortunately, Bertha's air conditioning broke down en route, and we spent our last day with her, as a replacement bus awaited.

Monday, July 1 – After a nondescript stopover in Scranton, Pennsylvania, we arrived at our hotel in Akron long enough to unpack and rest a bit. Our game against the Blackstockings that evening was a hot one. Between the Blackstockings and the brutal Ohio humidity the Mutuals had our stiffest test yet. We took the field first and found ourselves behind for the first time all trip. Going into our frame, Akron led 1-0. It wouldn't last. We hung ten on them in the first inning and then spent the remainder of the game holding off their spirited attempts at a come back. Before we settled down defensively, the score was 16-9. That was as close as they would get. We put forth our best effort and came out ahead 20-11. Express hit a home run, which was tough to do over a hundred years ago and equally tough today. Big Bat legged out a couple of doubles. Sully and Rabbit played a stellar third and left respectively, and Big Dog was an exemplary backstop, despite a hamstring irritation. I made a timely catch in centerfield and Scoops hurled a solid game. The Akron squad thanked us for a fine game and fed us before sending us on our way. I had a date with the hotel hot tub after dinner.

Tuesday, July 2 – We awoke the next morning in great spirits. We had the day off. It was a travel day and we were headed for the Windy City. We watched Game 6 of the 1986 World Series. I still cannot believe what transpired that evening at Shea Stadium. As exiting as it was on the bus, one would have thought that the game was happening live. Some guys went sightseeing, and Express, Big Dog, and I had a relaxed dinner at Carmines.

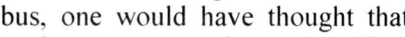

Wednesday, July 3 – We rode to Rockford to take on a fairly new squad to vintage baseball, the Midway Maulers. The name sounded softball, but they were far from it. They gave us a good match though the 37-9 score was not an indication. I scored six times. We just kept getting on base. Big Dog and the Magnet were hurt. After some negotiation, it was agreed that they could play the field but would not be required to bat. We had seven in the order and it seemed as though every time we scored and grabbed a cup of water, it was time for us to grab a bat and go again. We were moving around the bases with such rapidity. There was a house in left field with new windows that had the Express's name all over it. Alas, though he had plenty of opportunities to sail one of his trademark long balls into the house, Mighty E failed, breaking the hearts of women and children everywhere who had gathered to watch the Mighty Express fulfill his own prophecy.

Thursday, July 4 – We arrived at the village in Cincinnati to play the legendary Redstockings. That squad plays a spirited game of ball. We played with their ball, which is much heavier than the ball we are accustomed to, so our "power" game was taken away. Even so, Express still managed to hit four ground rule doubles into the forest beyond the outfield and, as a hurler, kept the ball in the infield. The most unorthodox play of the tour came from Magnet. He was playing third and snagged a ball on the sprawl. Without missing a beat, he relayed the throw to Express who finished the 5-1-3 play to Big Bat at first. Imagine our surprise when he started another 5-1-3 play later in the game! Sully made the defensive play of the game when he snagged a line drive over second base and doubled the runner for an unassisted double play. Scoops also connected with Big Dog for an outfield assist at the plate. We won 17-4.

Later that evening, we watched the Ohio River Fireworks show and some went out for a night on the town while others, myself included, went back to the hotel for some rest. I started to feel the rigors of the trip that day and was pulled in the eighth inning for an aching knee I suffered while scoring the previous inning.

Friday, July 5 – We toured the Louisville Slugger Museum & Factory before our game against the Indianapolis Blues. If there was a game for me to have my best day at the plate, this was not it, as absolutely no spectators made it out to the semi-pro ballpark in Louisville to watch some team from New York play some team from Indiana. It was as if no one cared, except us. I hit two doubles and scored four runs. It was one of the quickest games we played. It was over before we knew it. We remained undefeated, winning 16-3.

I will never forget the ride from Louisville to Hannibal to play our final two games of the trip. I had fallen asleep listening to my headphones and was awakened by Squid with the news that Ted Williams had passed earlier that day. I thought it was ironic. I read Teddy Ballgame's *The Science of Hitting* all off-season to improve my hitting skills, and after my second double in that day's game, I gave a silent nod of thanks to the Splendid Splinter while standing on second. We arrived early in the morning, and I watched the tributes on SportsCenter until my eyes weighed heavily and I put the day's events behind me.

Saturday, July 6 – We arrived at Clemens Field in the morning and the weather was already atrociously hot. We had a doubleheader and we were all praying for a quick and merciful end to the both games. We knew that if we struck hard and often, both games would be no contest and we would go home undefeated. The games coincided with the Tom

Sawyer Days festival and featured our best crowd yet, over five hundred people. We played by the 1860's rules of our hosts, the Washington Eagles. We were familiar with these rules; however, other rules were introduced that I could not quite fathom. We could not slide, could not steal, could only lead a couple of steps, the infielders could only play a couple of steps off the bag, and the ball we were playing with was hard as a rock. However, since it was a sunny day, the Eagles team captain proclaimed that we could wear sunglasses if we wanted. Go figure! We abided our host's rules and disposed of them 13-3.

Scoops, the Mutual hurler, started the second game of our doubleheader against the Decatur Ground Squirrels and was perfect through three. However, he lost his bid for perfection in the fourth when the Ground Squirrel batter put a knock just inside the left field foul line that Rabbit was unable to get to because the rules forbade any outfield maneuvering save for in and out. Again, as in previous Mutual victories, everyone contributed to the 14-2 victory.

We did it. We went 8-0 on the trip. We weren't completely surprised but with this game we knew anything could happen. We were exuberant over our accomplishment and thankful that we didn't sustain any major injuries. We went out for a celebratory meal and then started our long journey to Columbus, Ohio where we would stay the night before heading home.

The trip was sometimes tough but ultimately a blast. The games, the bus rides, the camaraderie! To this day, if I listen closely, I can still hear our laughter. I will never forget this trip for I have many fond memories. Huzzah, Mutuals! Huzzah!

Originally appeared in issue #6, Fall 2002.

Part IX: Baseball Warps the Mind — Oddities of the Game

I'm Peter Pan, I'm the King of England, I Have High Cheekbones: The Wit, Wisdom, and Facial Hair of Keith Hernandez

Steve Reynolds

I first joined the ranks of the iPhone cult in the winter of 2009, and one of the immediate impacts it made upon my life is that I started writing down my plans (personal and workwise). No longer would I forget when I had tickets for a concert or when I might have a gig with my band or when I had an interview coming up at work. I couldn't let any crucial event go by without it being digitally noted. So with this in mind, you can see how I found myself one morning in September 2012, hastily typing "11:45 – go to SNY.TV to watch 'stache shaving."

Yes, one of the things I *had* to remember to do on my computer was to visit a regional sport network's website so I could watch someone gain a clear upper lip. It would be well within reason if you thought, "Gosh, he's insane. And probably the IT department at his office should monitor what goes on with his computer." You'd be right. Yet, I think that anecdote neatly sums up just how essential Keith Hernandez has become to Mets and broadcasting fans over the past six years.

Let's head back to 2006 for a moment—that season was perhaps the best one for the Mets since 1983. Oh, I don't mean in the standings or player statistics—it's because it was the first time since the 1984 season that Fran Healy wasn't calling the team's games. When the Mets partnered up with some cable giants to start Sportsnet New York, they chose to not bring Healy on board, going with amazing radio man Gary Cohen for play-by-play.

(Pardon me, I must pause to yell in joy for the 1,210th time since *that* decision.)

Healy was one of the most incompetent "homers" in all of broadcasting (only that idiot Hawk Harrelson who openly roots for, I mean calls, White Sox games was worse) and every word out of his mouth was an obvious description of what fans had just seen—or was a shill for fans to come out to Shea for some stupid reason. SNY played the first post-9/11 game at Shea as one of the "Mets Classics" their first year on the air, and hearing Healy's voice almost ruined the emotion of that incredible game.

SNY reached back to the Mets 1986 roster for their analysts, grabbing Ron Darling from the Washington Nationals and keeping Keith Hernandez, the lone MSG and Fox Sports New York holdover. I expected Darling to be rather subpar because of what I heard from him during the 2005 season. But he surprised me by providing easy to understand analysis when it comes to why pitchers do what they do, coming up with a good joke or two once in a while, sharing great memories about the '80s Mets teams and, on selected weekend games, being the best announcer to interact with Ralph Kiner in many years. (How good Kiner has sounded the past half a decade, even in the 2012 season as he approached 90, is probably worth its own article. Time and time again, I've been amazed by how he'll make an insightful comment and then follow it up with a crack that causes Cohen and Darling to laugh for minutes.)

Hernandez had certainly taken flack from *Zisk* during his stint as a part-time Met broadcaster. Allow me to quote my *Zisk* co-editor Mike Faloon from a blog entry dated April 27, 2005:

> *"It was difficult to ignore [my dog's] begging for a walk—and try to convince myself that the game was more important—with the Mets getting spanked. MSG announcer Keith Hernandez didn't help my cause:*
>
> Ted Robinson: This night in 1988, Keith Hernandez hit a grand slam in Atlanta. He drove in seven runs for the Mets that game.
>
> Keith Hernandez: I also got divorced that day. Let me tell you, I was out late that night. HA!
>
> *Which reminds me of another Hernandez gem, this one from the night before. Bottom of the fourth, Mets down 1-0 . . .*
>
> Fran Healy: He's been terrific!
> Keith Hernandez: Who?
> Fran Healy: (The Mets') Chris Woodward.
> Keith Hernandez: I wasn't paying attention.
>
> *Error #1: Daydreaming on the job. Error #2: Telling everyone about error #1 just in case they missed it.*

Steve Reynolds

> *I think it's about time MSG sprung for one of those seven-second delay modules, one of those devices that allows the guys producing the game to hear everything a few seconds before the TV audience does. I'd take awkward silences over Keith."*

Needless to say, my vitriol for Hernandez was along the same lines, and I dreaded how far he was going to take down Cohen. Then on the way to broadcasting disaster, something amazing happened: Hernandez went crazy. Not in the insane asylum or serial killer or Gnarls Barkley kind of way—I mean that good, loopy kind of crazy that makes you laugh over and over again. Perhaps his open disdain for Fran Healy (which Hernandez held in check about as well as I did) sublimated his desire to make wacky comments. Or perhaps there's just something about the chemistry between the trio (now billed by fans as GKR) that has brought the entertainer out in Hernandez.

Even when the Mets have been awful (and that's been a great deal of the time since Gary, Keith, and Ron started in 2006), the banter of this trio is worth checking out nightly. I started writing down what crazy things Hernandez would refer to during games. Here are 10 of my favorite topics Hernandez has covered on air:

- He couldn't drink Kahlua again after spending on spring training with Ron Hunt.
- He prefers Eddie Vedder's solo catalog to his work with Pearl Jam.
- He's a fan of the Orson Welles classic *Touch of Evil* (which he talked about because Marlins pitcher Jason Vargas was working mop up duty, and Welles' character was named Detective Vargas).
- He can make an entire Tootsie Pop (his favorite candy) last four to five innings.
- He doesn't like to feel his own age. During a blowout, Cohen mentioned the AARP, and Hernandez mentioned he could never join them. Cohen then said Hernandez was still a kid. Keith responded with, "I'm like Peter Pan, a kid at heart."
- He knows his WWII history, as he once described a shift employed while Carlos Delgado was up as big enough to drive a whole Panzer division through.
- He isn't a fan of the Ask the Booth feature. One question posed by a fan asked if Jose Reyes could hit 30 triples. He suggested that if that happened, "I'm the future King of England."
- He thinks pretty highly of his appearance. During one day game, the Marlins players had their eyeblack drawn down the side of their cheeks. He explained that he couldn't do that because he has high cheekbones.

- He doesn't know his diseases. After a shot of Mike Pelfrey rolling the mouthguard around in his mouth, Cohen explained that Pelfrey had it for TMJ, which is the shorthand for the disease that causes difficulty with the joint that holds the jaw together. Hernandez suggested (and I don't think he was joking) that he thought TMJ was a banned substance.
- He knows his literature. During one lengthy game, Cohen suggested that it was longer than *Beowulf*. The quick-witted Hernandez responded, "Grendel, please come down and devour this field."

Hernandez keeps delivering even when he's not speaking. I did indeed watch when he had his graying, iconic moustache shaved off in the name of charity on September 27, 2012. I can't imagine doing the same thing for any other athlete-turned-broadcaster. Well, maybe if Tim McCarver shaved his head.

New essay written for Fan Interference. *Contains material from issue #13, Fall 2006 and issue #15, Fall 2007.*

Four Fans, One Shirt – An Interview with Marco Reosti

Mike Faloon

Last summer, while traveling through Detroit, I encountered the four-man shirt. Four Tigers fans who attend games wearing one, four-necked T-shirt. Such unbridled foolishness raises fandom to an art form. It also piqued my curiosity, so I tracked down Marco Reosti, one of the shirt's regular occupants. Marco and I talked about the upcoming season and, of course, the shirt.

Zisk: Let's start with the origins of the four-man shirt.

Marco Reosti: My friend Cooper Holewski's uncle is a barfly, and the bar he hangs out at got all this promotional merchandise from a tequila company. Boxes of it. And the guy who runs the bar didn't really want it so he gave it to Cooper's uncle, who's the barfly, and he didn't want it either so he gave it to Cooper. About a year and a half ago, we were rooting through this box of merchandise and what really stood out was this ridiculous looking four-man shirt. We would take it to parties and stuff, just to be idiots. For the last opening day (at Tiger Stadium, '99) we decided we weren't just going to bring signs like we had done in the past. We decided to bring the four-person shirt, turn it inside out, and paint "Tigers in the 9-9" on it. We were going to go to all these games anyway and we just kept taking it.

Zisk: Just to back up a step, it's actually described as a four-man shirt?

MR: There's actually a tag on it that says "4-in-1" or "4-necker" and it has this ridiculous bull on the front and the tequila logo. It's really odd.

Zisk: "Tigers in the 9-9." Did you really think the Tigers had it last year?

MR: We really did. I didn't think they were going to win the World Series, but I thought they were going to go to the playoffs. I really thought they were going to be a wildcard team, I bought into it.

Zisk: How did other fans react to the four-man shirt?

MR: Most fans think it's hilarious. They'll cheer when they see us walking in with it or they're just weirded out and leave us alone.

Fan Interference

Zisk: At what point do you put the shirt on?
MR: Usually once we get down near the stadium.

Zisk: So the two guys in the middle have to walk with their hands at their sides?
MR: Pretty much and the other guys only have one arm that they can use.

Zisk: Do you rotate to decide who gets those outside spots?
MR: Keegan Mahoney, if anybody had to be the leader, it'd be him. He's the biggest Tigers fan. He keeps the shirt at his house. He always gets the right sleeve. But the rest are rotated.

Zisk: Do the guys on the outside help out the guys in the middle with drinks and what not?
MR: We're lenient on the drinks, you can keep them under the shirt.

Zisk: Have you received any feedback from the Tigers?
MR: We went down to Guest Services one time, which is where the Tigers had their lost and found, and they gave us some promotional posters. We didn't get any real feedback until about a month ago at Tigers Fest 2000. We were walking around the convention in the shirt, and the team's CEO, John McHale, and Randy Smith, the GM, both came up to us and said how they always saw us at the games. We also got feedback from the guy who does the play-by-play, Josh Lewin. He came up to us and he was really nice. His color commentator is Kirk Gibson. They are always having their crews find us (in the stands) and putting us on TV. They work for Fox Sports Detroit. They do about ninety-five percent of the games, and if we're there we'll get on for a few seconds, they'll brush by us and say, "they're here again." The local UPN affiliate does Friday night games and they've shown us a couple of times, too. That's really cool because that's Al Kaline. To have Al Kaline point us out and talk about us is really big.

Zisk: You seem optimistic about the coming year. What's got you feeling this way?
MR: With Gonzalez, Tony Clark, and Dean Palmer there's a lot of power in the middle of the lineup. Luis Polonia, Damion Easley, and Deivi Cruz are good players, and if guys like Easley and Bobby Higinson have seasons like they've had in the past, I think they can challenge in the Central and definitely challenge for the wild card.

Zisk: How many games did you go to with the shirt last year?
MR: With the shirt, about twenty. I made it to thirty-two games but we

don't take the shirt all the time. Sometimes you just want to relax and watch some baseball and sometimes you want to get really into it and the best way is to bring the shirt.

Zisk: Are you guys wearing regular shirts under there? I can't tell from the photo.
MR: Yeah, definitely, we all have shirts under there.

Zisk: Will there be another shirt for this year?
MR: Actually for the last game ever at Tiger Stadium—by that point they had been eliminated from the playoffs—we repainted the shirt, "Tigers in the 0-0."

Zisk: So the original shirt was updated. Are there any reserve shirts?
MR: Yes, we do have another one but we take care of the shirt. We use washable paints. During last year's All-Star break, we washed the shirt and repainted it. We make sure we don't stretch it too much, we don't rip it. We're very careful around the shirt. Someone was saying we just wear the shirt to get on TV. I started to think about that and I don't think it's true. What I was thinking is that it's hard to stick with a losing team and Detroit fans are really bad about bandwagoning, like with the Red Wings. We want to be recognized as people who are fans now so when the Tigers do start getting good, next year or two years down the road, we can say we were there in '97, when they were horrible, or '98 or '99. We want to be recognized as guys who are there thirty games a year for a team that was sub-.500 for the whole season.

Originally appeared in issue #3, Summer 2000.

Baseball Truly Is a Religion

John Shiffert

It would be hard to find a less-ordinary player than Masumi Kuwata, even though he's on an exceedingly ordinary team, the Pittsburgh Pirates. It's not that there still aren't many Japanese-born pitchers in the bigs. It's not that 39-year-old major league rookies are exceedingly rare (although they are). It's not that he's a 5' 8" (i.e., short) righthanded pitcher, although they are almost as rare as 39-year-old rookies. And it's certainly not his record [as of press time], a very ordinary 0-1, 6.60 ERA, even though, outside of a terrible outing on July 2 against the Brewers (two-thirds of an inning, seven runs allowed) he's pitched pretty well (four earned runs in 14 1/3 innings.) No, what makes Masumi Kuwata extra-ordinary, or at least unusual, is something else. As Clayton Trapp has pointed out, "Masumi's apparently an adherent to Perfect Liberty Kyodan, a/k/a, the Japanese Golf Religion" or PL or PLK.

The what? Now, it's well-known that a lot of players are golf addicts. They have been back to at least Ty Cobb's era. (He called it "Pasture Pool." On the other hand, Rogers Hornsby refused to play, supposedly saying, "When I hit a ball I want someone else to chase it.") And it's also well-known that golf is a veritable religion among many, be they baseball players, baseball fans, or anyone else. But the Japanese Golf Religion? Yes indeed, grasshopper. You just need Mr. Trapp to enlighten you, from an article he authored that appeared in the magazine *Fringe Golf* about seven years ago. Trapp prefaces his thoughts by adding, "PLK views strike me as quite benevolent, actually." Here's his story for all you non-golfers:

> "Religions throughout the world have attached a special significance to cats, snakes, and wine. It should surprise no one that a religion now attaches a special significance to golf.
>
> "Perfect Liberty Kyodan (Kyodan is Japanese for 'Church') is the religion in question. Perfect Liberty (PL) is so enamored with the sport that the religion's international headquarters, its Holy Land, is surrounded by three golf courses.
>
> "In fact, opponents malevolently branded PL 'the golf religion.' To their consternation PL embraced the moniker for several reasons: it creates interest in the religion, the more

interest the more members; and the members love golf.

"PL membership numbers several million worldwide. Members worship in more than 500 churches located on every continent but Africa. Besides Japan, where one out of every 44 citizens is a member, PL has gained significant popularity in California and South America (particularly Brazil and Argentina).

"Founded in 1924, PL was persecuted sporadically for the next 25 years. One respite from persecution came when General MacArthur liberated PL leadership and members from prison. He was substantially less concerned about PL's denial of the 'divine absolutism' of Japan's rulers than were…the divine rulers who then replaced the PL leadership in confinement.

"OK. PL is a legitimate religion; it's paid its dues. What's up with the golf business?

"'Our Second Founder, the late Reverend Tokuchika Miki picked golf as a method of spiritual teaching,' explains Tatsumi Yano, a PL Minister in New York, adding that 'PL is a practical religion, and we focus on how to live life happily and meaningfully rather than talking about previous or next lives, or 'What is God?' issues.'

"The core teaching of PL is that 'Life is Art.' Golf is an art of special esteem, and self-expression through golf is wildly popular among PL members.

"'Golf is very good training for us in learning how to control our emotions, change our points of view, and accept various daily situations positively while making our best efforts at each moment,' Yano says.

"Several PL churches feature rooftop driving ranges so that members can practice self-expression as the spirit moves them. 'Man suffers if he fails to express himself' is a basic belief of PL, and one that you might keep handy next time your wife questions your golfing priorities.

"The caricature of PL as the 'golf religion,' if taken seriously, detracts from what its adherents consider important. PL is a religion of serenity and humility. The interlocking concepts of five-irons and spiritual liberation can be attractive, but the real goal of PL is to make one's life art."

While life may or may not be art, or golf, it would seem reasonable to classify Kuwata's beliefs under the "Unusual" heading . . . putting him on a firm footing with other major leaguers who also had unusual beliefs, some of which could be termed "superstitious," some of which were just idiosyncratic, some of which may have gone against commonly-accepted conventions. For instance, how do you feel about vegetarians? Unusual? Maybe. Well, Henry Aaron is one. Along another tact, it should be noted that the 50 or so Mormons who have played major league baseball were all born well after the LDS Church's doctrine of plural marriage was withdrawn in 1890, so there haven't been any doctrinal polygamists in baseball. And, Pedro Cerrano, the Cleveland Indians Cuban voodoo adherent from the movie *Major League* was, after all, a fictional character.

Of more recent and realistic (well, sort of) vintage, recall two pitchers, Scott Erickson and Turk Wendell. Erickson caused a stir back in 1991 by winning 20 games for the Twins in his first full season. Although he didn't win the Cy Young Award that year (he was second to Roger Clemens), he did win an award from Kiwi Shoe Polish for totally covering his spikes with black shoe polish before each game. Seems as if he didn't want any identifying marks showing on his footwear. (I should know about that award, since I'm the one that gave it to him when I was doing PR for Kiwi Brands.) Wendell came up with the Cubs a couple of years later, already somewhat renown for his personality quirks, which included chewing licorice all the time, brushing his teeth between innings, and always jumping over the baselines.

While these oddities may be dismissed by some because they involve pitchers, what are we to make of Reds outfielder Ryan Freel? An August 2006 story in *The Dayton Daily News* reported that Freel talks to an imaginary voice in his head named Farney. Freel apparently told the *Daily News* that everyone thinks he talks to himself, so he tells them he's talking to Farney. As in, "Hey, Farney, I don't know if that was you who really caught that ball, but that was pretty good if it was."

For that matter, what are we to make of Carl Everett, who insists that dinosaurs didn't exist, because they're not in the Bible?

Talking heads, dinosaurs, and brushing teeth aside, superstition has been a part of baseball from the nineteenth century to the twenty-first century. A hundred or so years ago, these beliefs tended to focus on things like hairpins or a truckload of barrels or hunchbacks—all of which were said to bring either good luck or good hitting. In fact, the Giants and Athletics, among others, had hunchbacked batboys/mascots for luck. More recently, individual players, like Erickson, have been known for their specific unusual beliefs. For example, most current fans will remember that Wade Boggs obsessively used to eat chicken as his pregame meal. There might also be some older fans who remember Babe Phelps, a catcher just before World War II. A devoted hypochondriac, Babe would stay up all night checking his heartbeat. You see, Babe was convinced that he had heart problems and that while your heart could miss three beats in a row without dire consequences, if it missed four straight beats call the undertaker. So Babe stayed up, counting his heartbeats. Going back a good bit farther, and similarly obsessive, was one of the great hitters of the old American Association, Pete Browning. The Gladiator, as Browning was known, not only never got rid of a bat, but he kept them all in his house—and he named them all as well. This may or may not have had anything to do with Browning also being nicknamed the Louisville Slugger, but he apparently not only remembered the names of all his bats, but how many hits he had with them as well. And, when he felt a bat's hits had all been used up, he retired it.

As interesting as these idiosyncrasies might be, Boggs, Phelps, Browning, or pretty much anyone else couldn't hold a candle to a couple of early twentieth century managers, George Stallings and John McGraw. Although this was, as Charles Alexander has noted, "a period in which almost all ballplayers had some kind of superstition," Stallings was a piece of work. A Southern Gentleman off the field and raging maniac on the field, he was profoundly superstitious—he absolutely hated to have any peanut shells or scraps of paper around his team's bench and would fly into a rage at the presence of either type of detritus. Even better, he would freeze in whatever position he happened to be in if his team mounted a rally. One story, perhaps apocryphal, has it that once he was leaning over to pick up something—probably a piece of paper— when the Braves broke out in a flurry of hits. By the time the rally was over, he couldn't move and had to be carried from the bench. It should be noted that Stallings managed in street clothes, so he had to stay in the dugout. One can only imagine the sort of stories that might be if he coached on the baselines.

And yet, Stallings wasn't in the same league as John McGraw. In addition to employing the hunchbacked Eddie Morrow, he designed the Giants' uniforms on whim and superstition. After his 1905 team took four out of five games from the Athletics in the World Series, McGraw was convinced that the special all-black uniforms he had dressed his team in held some kind of special post-season magic, despite the fact that the Giants had previously worn all-black uniforms some 20 years before, without any magic results. So, when the Giants next faced the Athletics in the fall—in 1911—he dressed them in all-black once again. However, Home Run Baker, Jack Coombs, and the $100,000 Infield weren't impressed and took the series in six games. Undeterred, McGraw continued to mess with the J'ints unis almost every year, once going so far as to use violet as the trim color, because he liked New York University.

Even his uniform frolics couldn't compare to McGraw's relationship with Charles Victor (or Victory) Faust—one of the strangest tales in baseball history. Various versions of the Victory Faust story abound, including those told by Noel Hynd, Alexander, and Fred Snodgrass in *The Glory of Their Times*. Although they all differ somewhat in detail, the essential story is the same. That is, McGraw received a telegram from Faust during the 1911 season, wherein he offered Little Napoleon his services for the pennant drive, having been told by a fortune teller that he (Faust) would lead the Giants to the World Series. Mac didn't think much of it until Faust, a 30-year-old Kansan with minimal, if any, athletic ability, showed up in St. Louis in late July and asked for a tryout. Despite finding out that Faust indeed had minimal, if any, athletic ability, McGraw kept him on after the Giants beat the Cardinals that day. One thing lead to another, and Faust stayed with the Giants as a good luck charm for most of the rest of the year, either helping out the batboy or warming up in expectation that he'd actually get into a game. And, what do you know, McGraw actually did put him in two games after the Giants clinched the pennant. In both cases, the opposing team went along with the gag, deliberately making three outs and even letting him tour around the bases after he was hit by a pitch while batting.

However, neither Faust's magic nor the black uniforms helped McGraw much against the Athletics in the 1911 World Series, so Mac tried to lose him before the 1912 season started. It didn't matter, since Faust, although certainly a few bricks shy a load, knew where the Polo Grounds were located and still believed that he was destined to lead the Giants to victory. McGraw finally relented in that he let Faust stay on the bench in street clothes and, wouldn't you know it, the Giants won the pennant again. This time, though, Faust decided to skip the World Series, believing his imaginary sweetheart, Lulu, had summoned him home. And the Giants lost the 1912 World Series, as well. By this time, though, Faust was mentally unstable enough that his brother had him committed to an insane asylum, where he eventually died in June 1915.

Thus ended the strange tale of Victory Faust. A strange story indeed, but no stranger than a story behind a real baseball player, James "Deacon" White. In the list of "Unusual Beliefs in Baseball," even John McGraw's belief in Victory Faust can't top Deacon White. An historic figure of the nineteenth century, White started playing early enough to have faced the 1869 Cincinnati Red Stockings. He then played on three of Harry Wright's champion Boston Red Stockings teams, plus the Chicago White Stocking team that won the first National League pennant. One of the first major supporters of players' rights, his career continued all the way through to the Players League in 1890. One of the three or four great catchers of the nineteenth century (he also played third base, though not especially well), White totaled 2,066 hits and an Adjusted OPS of 126 while racking up 28 points on the Black Ink Test, leading his league in batting, slugging, OPS, hits, total bases, triples and RBIs at various times. For a catcher, that's Hall of Fame quality hitting.

In addition, he was, by all accounts, an exemplary fellow. A religious, non-smoking, non-drinking, non-card-playing, sober and serious individual, he was indeed a deacon, although he also looked like a deacon, with a long face, walrus mustache and a solemn expression (at least he had one in his pictures). Bill James named him "The Most Admirable Superstar of the 1870s" in *The Historical Baseball Abstract*.

There was just one little thing about Deacon White—he thought the Earth was flat. It's a story apparently first told in the twentieth century by Lee Allen in *The National League Story* in 1961 and later picked up by Hynd in *The Giants of the Polo Grounds*. And, not only was White convinced the Earth was flat, but he tried to convince his teammates, as well, pointing out that, if a pop fly came back down to the same spot, well the Earth couldn't very well be a spinning globe, could it? Reportedly, he did convince one teammate, but, sadly, he failed to prove his theory any further than that. Oh well, at least he's a hero to the Flat Earth Society.

Originally appeared in issue #15, Fall 2007.

INTERVIEWS WITH PLAYERS

Semi-Amazing Deeds By Minor Legends of Amateur Baseball – An Interview with Oliver Hughson

Mark Hughson

My grandfather, Oliver Hughson, really likes baseball. He grew up playing it, he grew old playing it, and now that he's really old, all he does is watch it and talk about it. I love my grandpa. Back before baseball was organized, categorized, commercialized, and more or less "-ized" up the yang, Grandpa Hughson (though he wasn't called "Grandpa" back them) played for many a team in many a league in Central New York. Here's an excerpt from an interview done in the spring of '02. (*Note: To me, this transcription sounds as normal as anything, but if you can't quite follow it, just pretend an old grandpa-like guy is speaking and once in a while nod your head like you understand.*)

Zisk: When did you first start playing baseball?
Oliver Hughson: Oh, I started way back when I was a kid. (Laughs)

Zisk: I remember you told me you and the gang would take up a collection to buy a baseball, and then just challenge another team.
OH: Oh, we did that at first, I guess. Euclid had a team down there, and we got a team here in Clay, and then we went to play against them, and the winner would keep the baseball. We beat them 36-2. Then I played with a gang from both Baldwinsville and Euclid, back behind the hotel there was a baseball field, we played there for a long time. One [of] my friends at the time played for the East Syracuse Benedicts. He says to

me, We're playing over at Griffin's Field, why not come and watch us? It was on a Sunday, so after we ate dinner, Ernie (*Author Note: My great uncle*), went over to watch 'em. We sat there in the stands, and Aubrey Brown, third baseman, one of the fellas I used to play with, he waved at me and told me to come on down. So I came on down. He wanted to know if I wanted to meet George. Well, George Lawbick was the manager of the Benedicts. So I went down to meet him and he says Hughson, didn't you used to play against East Syracuse once? I says, Yeah I played against East Syracuse once. And George says, You beat us too I remember. You playin' any ball? I said no. He says, You wanna? I says, Sure would. 'Cause that was right at the end of the war when the teams were all broken up, you know. Two or three of our members got killed in France. So I went to Tuesday's game and sat on the bench, which is what I expected to do anyway. Thursday night they had a game in the city. Grayden Brown was a good batter, but he liked to clown around and talk a lot. He was in the warm-up circle, you know 'cause he was the next batter. And he turned around to holler at some guy on the bench and the bat slipped out of the hands of the batter and got him right on the elbow. Boy, he turned white as your shirt in no time! George turns around and looks at me and says, Get in Grayden's place quick! So I grabbed a bat, got limbered up, but darn if the pitcher didn't hang one over the plate, I drove it right out through for a double. Next game, down in New Woodstock I think, I got another double the first time up, so, I played regular from then on. (Laughs)

   Zisk: That's the way it seems to go.
   OH: We played in the New York State League. We were on top in the Central Division. So we got to go to Cooperstown and play in the Hall of Fame game. Right at the end of the war, around 1946, I think it was, the major league teams weren't allowed to make any unscheduled stops. So the committee down there took the top four teams in the State League, one from each division, and brought 'em in for a doubleheader. We played all over in the state. We played three games a week, right through to October, and we lost two games all year. We won the state championship. We got down to the southern tier area, we won the game Smitty pitched—boy he was a crackerjack of a pitcher, too! He used to pitch for the Chicago White Sox. Our shortstop used to play for the Detroit Tigers. The catcher and the first baseman were on the Army team at one time. So we had quite a team. So anyway, we got down there and won the state championship. Right after we got their last guy out, their manager rushed right over to George and challenged us to another game. He said I'll get a bunch of guys together, and we'll come up and beat you damn Benedicts! So we agreed to one more game, right in the end of October. They brought in guys from four or five different teams, thought

Fan Interference

they handpicked 'em sure to beat us—they came up on Saturday. Smitty couldn't pitch cause he just pitched on Thursday, so I pitched that game, and we beat 'em 4-0. I shut 'em out. (Laughs) We never heard any more from 'em. (Laughs)

Zisk: Tell me about your strikeout "record."

OH: (*Goes into detail about having a cyst removed*) I was in my forties about this time, almost done playing. They had what they called the Northern League, all the teams north of Syracuse. A team wanted me to manage them, I told them I'd come over and manage and play, thinking I'd go back to the State League when the cyst thing was better. Well, after a few weeks of monkeyin' around with them I said to heck with it, and stayed in the Northern League. So we went and played Caughdenoy, and I pitched the last two innings. Struck out six right in a row. That ended that. Next game was Cicero, and I pitched the last two innings of that game, struck out six right in a row. Next game was against North Syracuse, and I got in there and got the first two on strikes. So I had fourteen consecutive strikeouts. (Laughs)

We talked a bit more about the father-son games, how his knee got tore up on a play at home. Grandma brought in some lemonade. Yes, indeed, things are good, and so is baseball.

Originally appeared in issue #6, Fall 2002.

They Shot the Wrong McKinley – An Interview with Bill Monbouquette

Mike Faloon

Former pitcher and coach Bill Monbouquette accomplished a lot during his decades in the big leagues—a no-hitter, a 20-win season, and three trips to the All-Star game—but they pale compared to his ability to tell a story. When my brother and I attended the Syracuse Chiefs' Hot Stove Dinner this past winter, Monbouquette, who played with the Red Sox, Tigers, Yankees, and Giants over the course of an 11-year career (1958-1968), stole the show. His stories were funny and warm and well-rehearsed. It reminded me of the Don Rickles documentary *Mr. Warmth*. Rickles probably hasn't changed his act in years and why should he? It radiates heartfelt enjoyment. There's no fatigue, no cynicism, and no need for new material. Likewise for Monbouquette. Talking to fans was a pleasure not an obligation. *Zisk* caught up with Bill Monbouquette in February.

Zisk: I really enjoyed your stories from the Hot Stove League dinner in Syracuse, and one player who seemed to have a big impact on you, a former teammate, was Ted Williams. You went fishing with Ted Williams.

Bill Monbouquette: Yeah, I was up in New Brunswick. I stayed two or three days at his camp. We had breakfast every morning, and he'd get up at the crack of dawn and he would be yelling toot ta toot toot toot like he had a trumpet. He was a very early riser. I don't know how many guys have ever fished with him. That's Atlantic salmon, where his place is. When I was playing with him in the clubhouse he had a fly rod and a rumble lure and he'd say, Open that back pocket of yours, and about twenty-thirty feet away flip it right in there like it was nothing. This guy was not only a great player, the best hitter I ever saw, this guy was a great fisherman, fly fisherman, especially. I'm not the only guy that's ever said that. It was a pleasure to play with him. He was a boyhood idol and still today he is my idol. I was fortunate to play with him for '58, '59, and '60. I was there the last day he hit his home run. During the course of the game, he'd hit three other balls that the wind held back and you get to thinking, If only Ted could do this. There I was right in the bullpen, and we knew he wasn't going to New York to finish the season, and he ends up hitting this screamer into the bullpen—nothing was going to hold this ball back. I had a chance to catch it, and I was in such awe. When it hit the back of that bullpen, it made one hell of a loud noise and that was it. That was the end of his career. We all wish we could go out like that. Unfortunately, it doesn't happen. Only to the great ones, and he sure as hell was.

Zisk: And it was through Ted that you met John Glenn.
BM: Yes, I did. We met him, I'm trying to think if it was 1959 or '60, I'm not sure. It was in Washington, and when he said, I want you to meet the next man going to the moon, we all looked at each other and said, What the hell is he smoking? What was going on? Going to the moon? It just didn't sound right back in those days. It was quite a thrill. When we had the memorial services at Fenway [for Ted] I got to talking to John and I asked him what kind of pilot Ted was and he said he was the best pilot he's ever known. And [Ted's] a guy that never went to college. My oldest son is a pilot for American Airlines and all the calculus and all that math they had to take in college. But here he did it, and I don't think they had calculus in high school back in those days. Wonderful eyesight. Naturally great instincts, and I guess it's hard to teach instincts. We started talking about him, how he handled the plane, and then when he crash landed his jet where he had been shot when he was in Korea and [John] said to me, Boy he can run. I said, I don't think so. I mean, for three years I've never known him to have any speed. Anyway, he says when Ted landed that plane and he got the hell out of there you should have seen how quick he was. There are a million stories about Ted Williams.

Zisk: Another great story is your no-hitter against the White Sox.
BM: Oh yeah, of course Ted wasn't there on that one. This was 1962, and I hadn't won a game in a long time and we were flying over that day. We did a lot of that. You flew into the city and you played that day, sometimes in the afternoon, sometimes at night. I was sitting on the plane doing the crossword puzzle, struggling like hell with that and one of the stewardesses sat down and said, How are you doing?, and I said, I'm struggling with this puzzle. She goes, What position do you play, how you doing there? And I say, Pitcher and I'm struggling like hell with that one, too. She got up and said, You'll pitch a no-hitter tonight. The umpire that game was a guy named Bill McKinley and we go into the ninth inning and I'm winning 1-0 and I get the first two guys. I struck out Sherm Lollar and Nellie Fox was on deck. He was pinch hitting and he's got this big smile and I don't want to look at him because I don't want to lose my concentration, that's what he was trying to do. And [Fox] hit this weak ground ball to [Frank] Malzone who threw him out. Apparcio, I got

two quick strikes, and then I threw him a slider maybe a foot and a half off the plate, and I thought he swung and the umpire, McKinley called it, No, he didn't swing and as the ball was coming back to me from the catcher I heard somebody yell from the stands, They shot the wrong McKinley! Oh my god, I had to walk around off the mound. The next pitch I threw him another slider and he swung and missed and let me tell you something don't let anybody tell you that white people can't jump because I was way up off the ground. That was probably my greatest thrill. Winning twenty games was wonderful but nothing can beat that. I had a shot at two, three more. I had a one-hitter in Boston and a one-hitter in Minnesota, which I lost. You win some and you lose some.

Zisk: That was a good stretch for you. You went to the All-Star game three times in four years.
BM: Yeah, well, I didn't pitch very well in the game in Kansas City in '60. I gave up three home runs. Mays led off the game. I sidearmed him and he bailed out and hit the ball down the right field line and it went for a triple. Banks hit a home run off of me and Crandall hit a home run. That's why I tell kids I'm an authority on home runs. I gave up 221 of them. I think that allows me to be an authority. One of the nicest things that ever happened to me, in the '60 All-Star game, we played two [games] back then, we would try to raise more money for the [players'] pension and we played in Kansas City in that game that I pitched in. I was the loser. Then right after the game, we flew back to New York and had a day off and played the next day. We were sitting on the runway. It was hot. It was 120 at game time at the park, and it was down in the hold which made it much hotter. We were sitting there. I can't recall what was wrong—a strike?—but there was a long delay, a couple of hours, and Mantle comes up to me—I was with the Red Sox—he says, I can't hit you. I know what you're going to throw me. I know where you're going to throw it and I can't hit it and I can't lay off of it. You know, sometimes when they try to con you? Like Rocky Calavito used to say, Hey, how's your family? Anyway, we get to New York, and I was sitting in the lobby and it was around five o'clock and wondering what I was going to do. Stan Musial and four or five other guys come walking through the lobby and he says, What are you doing? I said, Just hanging around. He said, Have you eaten yet? I said, No. C'mon, you're going with us. You can't ask for a nicer thing to happen to you, to have Stan Musial ask you to go to dinner. Couldn't ask for a nicer guy. I got to know him through Mickey Mantle's Make a Wish Golf Tournament. What a wonderful guy. Always had time for the people. I like that in a player. You always have to give back. That seems to be a thing of the past. There are certain people that do it. I like the way David Ortiz is with the fans.

Zisk: You'd mentioned Willie Mays. You later played with the Giants. Did you get to know guys like Juan Marichal and Gaylord Perry and Mays?

BM: Oh yeah. One time, I was coaching for the Blue Jays in St. Caterine's, Ontario, in the New York-Penn League and some of our kids were running around and we had to bail them out of jail, so I took my pitching staff over to the bullpen, and I started saying, Ted Williams. Carl Yastremski. Al Kaline. Whitey Ford. Willie Mays. Willie McCovey. Juan Marichal and Gaylord Perry. Do you know who those guys are? A couple of the guys said, Who are they? I said, They're all Hall of Famers and they didn't act like you idiots. That put their heads down real quick. I got to know Gaylord pretty well. I knew Willie when I was in charge of minor league pitching for the Mets. Willie was working for the Mets. I loved Willie, really a great guy. The greatest all-around player for me was Willie Mays. One time, he hit a home run against me in spring training in Scottsdale. I had just knocked him down real good and I hung him a curveball and Yaz was in left field and he hit the ball so far and so hard and Yaz never made an attempt to go for it. It was 360 down the line in Scottsdale. Yaz just put his head down. In a kidding way, when the inning was over, I said, Hey, don't show me up, make an attempt for the ball. He said, That's over the swimming pool. There was a parking lot and then there was a swimming pool. Oh, it was a 500-foot shot. Then he hit one off of me over in Phoenix. It was a line drive. It was almost up on to the road and it hit the embankment out there and bounced all the way back to second base. What the hell's the difference if it's 500 feet or 320 feet, you know?

Zisk: You were with the Yankees in '67 and '68 and I noticed that a lot of future managers and coaches—you, Bobby Cox, Dick Howser, Mel Stottlemyre—on those teams, which Ralph Houk managed. Is there any connection between the way he treated players and the fact that so many of them went on to be managers and coaches?

BM: I'm sure everybody learned from him. He was a player's manager. He stuck up for the players. If there was a brawl on the field, he was the first guy there. We all know his service background. He was a major. He was easy to talk to. I was Billy Martin's coach; he wasn't very easy to talk to. If you're a guy's coach and you can't talk to the manager, it makes it tough. I loved [Houk].

Zisk: You also worked for the Mets when Doc Gooden came up.

BM: When he was in the minor leagues, I was there. In the Instructional League, all I ever said to Doc was, Don't let anybody fool with your delivery. There are pitching coaches that are happy to change deliveries. It's hard to change someone who's been throwing a certain way all his life. You can make a couple of adjustments here and there. I know guys who have said, It's time to change the delivery. What the hell? If it ain't broke, don't fix it. One thing you don't hear pitching coaches say any more, like the old timers you used to say: Get after him. The hitter knows when you're not challenging him or getting after him. I remember Ted used to say, Well he's going to do this and on this count he's going to do that, he's going to pussyfoot and not give me anything to hit. That was his memory. I can remember as an 18-year-old kid sitting on the bench hearing Ted say, C'mon, we've got to get this club. It was at Fenway, you know. I had just signed. You got to get these guys here because we're going to Cleveland and we're going in to face the Nasty Boys: Feller. Wynn. Lemon. Garcia. Narleski. Mossi. It might have been the greatest pitching staff of all time. And everybody would say, Yeah, sure, you really have trouble with those guys. He'd be talking about hitting and everything else. As an 18-year-old kid what the hell do you know about hitting? I said to myself, did I make a mistake here in signing or what? That was a great experience to be around him, to listen to him talk. He'd talk about meeting Babe Ruth, and he did introduce me to Ty Cobb in Scottsdale, Arizona. That was probably '60 or '61 or so and he was wheeling Ty around in a wheelchair and I had just pitched nine innings against the Dodgers and got beat 1-0 or 2-1. John Roseboro hit a home run off me in the ninth inning and [Ty] said, I like the way you pitch, son, get right after 'em. How can you not remember that? Of course, I said, Thank you, sir.

Zisk: One last thing: I see that when you were with the Tigers in '66 you stole a base.
BM: Did I have one or two?

Zisk: According to what I found you had one.
BM: That was against Kansas City.

Zisk: You have a pretty good memory of your pitching side, do you remember your stolen base?
BM: I guess I was with the Tigers when I stole that. That was in Kansas City. I remember the throw was high and Bert Campaneris tried to hit me on the top of the head. And I gave him a little shove. The game has been great to me.

Originally appeared in Issue #16, Spring 2008.

Don't Step in the Bucket – An Interview with Richie Zisk

Mike Faloon

When I was first getting into baseball, Richie Zisk was coming off the best year of his career: 30 HR, 101 RBI, and a .290 batting average (for the '77 White Sox). For me, his name has been synonymous with that era ever since. It is only appropriate that *Zisk*'s first interview be conducted with our namesake. Now the hitting coach for the Daytona Cubs, Richie was kind enough to take time out from his off-season schedule.

Zisk: Pitchers and catchers are reporting in about a month and I'm wondering if you're done with the off-season mode and getting ready for the upcoming year. When does that transition start for you?
Richie Zisk: Well, I think as an ex-player and having been involved in the game of baseball for thirty-some years, there really is no off-season. It kind of stays with you twelve months a year.

Zisk: What do you do during the off-season?
RZ: I do as little as possible.

Zisk: Will you be returning to Daytona this year?
RZ: Yeah, as a matter of fact, I just talked to the farm director, and I'm going to go back to Daytona for the fifth year. I'll be with the Cubs in the Florida State League.

Zisk: You guys had a good hitting team last year. You led the league in team hitting.
RZ: Yeah, we hit the ball okay. You know, when you leave spring training there are certain expectations. Last year, we felt we'd have good pitching and mediocre hitting, and it worked out the other way. We wound up hitting and didn't pitch quite as well. But every year, you get dealt another hand out of the deck. Sometimes, there are repeat players at that level, but most of the time, they move on to bigger and better things.

Zisk: Any particular prospects you might be working with this year?
RZ: I'm hoping to see our number one draft choice somewhere along the line, [Corey] Patterson, who has gotten rave reviews from everyone

that's watched him as an amateur. Our front office people are just tickled pink with the fact that we've got a kid who looks like he has a chance to be an impact player a little on down the road.

Zisk: Being in Daytona Beach and working with young guys, does that combination make it more challenging for you?
RZ: I tell them in spring training to get their clubbing out of the way early. The Florida State League is a very competitive league, a very good league. We've had quite a few guys make the jump from that league who are now playing big league baseball. The weather has a large impact on the players. The heat and humidity will take it out of you if you don't take care of yourself. I don't expect them to be choirboys but you've really got to learn how to budget yourself, pick the appropriate moments to have a good time or your production will really fall off the second half of the year. I've watched it for five years now and I know it's true.

Zisk: The Cubs had such a great year in '98, making the playoffs, Sosa, Kerry Wood, does that success at the major league level radiate throughout the farm system?
RZ: It doesn't have a direct impact. But you know it's always nice to come to the ballpark and there's a buzz going on about a number of things happening at the big league level, especially when they're all positive. We've been through some tough times before where you come to the ballpark and think, well, what's going on today? I can think of a couple years ago they lost, what was it, fourteen in a row to start the season off. There was talk of the big league club in the ballpark, but not always in positive terms. So last year was tremendous. Not only the fact that we had some players do very, very well, with Sosa obviously as the example, but the ball club put itself in the position to win a division. They eventually got into the playoffs via the wildcard and it promotes a great interest because these are the guys that our minor leaguers see when they go to spring training. They attend some of the big league games. They know them personally, they can relate to them and here they are on TV playing for a world championship.

Zisk: What was it like for you making the transition from being a player to being a coach?
RZ: After I got out of ball, I went back and finished my education and was going to pursue a career in radio and television. I did some spring training games down in the Pompano area when the Yankees were here, and also the Rangers. And I found out that I would rather have the uniform on. I enjoy working with the younger people. I have something to offer. Those who listen get better and they keep me going, they keep me young. I'm going to be 50 years old. I certainly don't feel it, I'm sure

I look it. But the younger guys keep me hopping and keep my energy level up. Also, being on the field keeps me close to the game that I played for so many years and love.

Zisk: You went to Seton Hall originally, right out of high school. Where did you finish up?
RZ: I wound up getting a degree from Barry University in Miami.

Zisk: You're a New York native, as well, right?
RZ: I was born in Brooklyn. Grew up in Greenpoint, lived on Long Island until high school years, and wound up going to Northern New Jersey to play high school ball.

Zisk: When you were growing up, was their one particular team that you followed?
RZ: I remember being taken to the Polo Grounds. I remember Yankee Stadium. I do not remember Ebbets Field though my Dad did say that he did take me there as well. Of course, when I was growing up the Yankees were the powerful team. Then I got caught up in the Met mania that took place when New York got another National League team after the two other clubs left for the West Coast. So I enjoyed watching the Mets grow from the horrible team that lost 100-some games to the '69 Miracle Mets.

Zisk: Who are celebrating their 30th anniversary, which is making big waves here in New York. So from college, you came up through the Pirates system.
RZ: Actually, I was going to go to Seton Hall University on a baseball scholarship and was drafted by the Pirates in the third round of the '67 draft. They offered me enough money, plus schooling, to make it worthwhile for me not to play college ball. I signed professionally out of high school and made my way up through the ranks that way. I worked my way up playing at the rookie level through A ball, Double A, Triple A, and then to the big leagues.

Zisk: And you came up with one of the best teams of the era, those Pirate clubs of the early '70s.
RZ: It was a offensively orientated organization. I learned a lot but it also cost me at least a year in the big leagues. I put up numbers my first year at Triple A that, in today's terms, would guarantee me a job at the big league level the next year, and I had to go back to Triple A and do it again. And it was through no fault of my own. I mean, Clemente was in right, Matty Alou was in center, they had Willie Stargell in left and they had a young guy named Al Oliver coming up. There really was no place to go and at that time there was no free agency, you were bound to a club

for a lifetime. So I spent at least a year, possibly a year and a half, more in the minor leagues than I should have, being with Pittsburgh.

Zisk: That was a team that didn't just last for one year, but won the division five out of six years. Do you keep in touch with any of those guys?
RZ: No, I don't keep in contact with them. I do bump into them occasionally in my travels, but I've kind of gone my own way. I don't do any old-timers games. I don't go back for any reunions. Once I realized that I had lost my skills on the field as a player, I would never go back and play in an old-timers game and not be able to perform the way I used to be able to. I just felt, and I do feel, that I love baseball and I love competing and I was pretty good at it but once my physical skills left me, and I wasn't able to perform at that level anymore, I didn't want to do it anymore. It's like golf. I play golf now but once my skills leave me, I won't play golf anymore for the enjoyment of it. I'm too competitive. So, the same thing with baseball.

Zisk: Was it surprising to you when you were traded to the White Sox?
RZ: No, there was no surprise. I had talked with the general manager that year and we discussed things and he brought in the gentlemen from Oakland, Chuck Tanner. I had a couple of conversations with Tanner on the phone and at the winter meetings there was a big trade made. I was traded for [Goose] Gossage and [Rich] Forster.

Zisk: Yeah, the White Sox gave up half of their bullpen for you.
RZ: Yeah, and each of them went on to do very, very well. I like to think it helped everybody out.

Zisk: And you go to the White Sox in '77 and have a bang up year. We were talking earlier about why the magazine is called *Zisk*. I first started following baseball around '77, '78 and I grew up in an area without a major league team in the days before cable TV, so everything I knew about baseball came from the backs of baseball cards. You were one of those guys who put up the magic numbers: 30 home runs, 100 RBIs. That put you on a level with very few others and that's one reason your last name, to me, encapsulates so much of what was going on at that time.
RZ: I think, more importantly, I've appeared in the *New York Times* crossword puzzle twice. I'm probably more famous for that then I am on the back of my baseball card. It just shows you how times have changed. Those numbers would barely get you off the bench today. I mean, guys are knocking in 160 runs. We had somebody hit 70, somebody hit 66 home runs. When I played, 30 was the landmark you shot for.

Zisk: I think there were close to forty guys who had 100 RBIs last year.

RZ: Numbers have changed and the game has changed. It's tough to compare apples to oranges but you know, when I played I did fairly well.

Zisk: Also, '77, as far as I understand it, there weren't high expectations for the White Sox but you guys managed to have a really good year. You put up 90 wins.

RZ: I think the White Sox had lost over 100 games the year before and they were the doormat of the American League. Veeck made some trades and there were no expectations coming in, but, for whatever reason, we had a great chemistry on the ball club. Guys had great offensive years. Soderholm put up some good numbers. Oscar Gamble put up some good numbers. Ralph Garr put up some good numbers. We were able to score runs and we were an exciting ball club to watch. Had we had a little more help in the bullpen toward the end of August, September we might have been a little more into it. We won 90 games, but I think Kansas City ending up winning something like 24 out of 27. They got real hot, and we didn't have enough left in our gas tank. I think we played .500 in August and September but that really wasn't good enough because Kansas City got so hot.

Zisk: They won over 100 games that year, that was a great Royals team. Was '77 the year of the infamous Disco Night at Comiskey Park?

RZ: No, I missed that. I think that was before me. We had the one game with the shorts, but there was no disco. I missed that, thank goodness.

Zisk: What was it like being a player on a Bill Veeck team? You were only there one year, did you get a chance to know him?

RZ: His philosophy was a lot like his son's, Mike, who is now with the Tampa Bay Devil Rays. When I read stuff that Mike has written in the paper, it sounds like his father talking. Bill Veeck couldn't guarantee you a win at the ballpark but he could guarantee you a good time. So there was always something going on to create fan interest, to make you want to come back again even though, perhaps, the ball club didn't play too well.

Zisk: I don't know how things are where you are, but that's an approach that's used by a lot of minor league teams these days.

RZ: Well, the owner in Daytona Beach doesn't really adhere to that philosophy, really, nor does the Florida State League. It's a notoriously bad league for attendance. The ballparks are beautiful, for the most part they are major league facilities but it's hot and humid, the attendance isn't there for whatever reason. The Fort Meyers Miracle, they draw.

Brevard County, the Marlins, will draw. And the Tampa Bay Yankees will draw. But really there aren't many promotions involved with each operation. They'll have special weekends where they are giving away T-shirts or helmets or fireworks (nights), but not on a daily basis.

Zisk: Going back to the transition of going from the Pirates to the White Sox, was that a big change in terms of changing leagues, that National League to American League change?
RZ: I didn't think so. To me, baseball is baseball. I had some new pitchers to learn. They had to learn me. Same rules for each league, same baseball.

Zisk: Well, there is one difference between the two leagues and that would be the DH. Was it with the Rangers that you first started to do some DH-ing?
RZ: Yeah, I've had three more knee operations since I left the game. I've got a really bad left knee, going to have to have it replaced. Toward the late '70s, early '80s, I wasn't able to play in the field. I could still hit, but couldn't really run the way I'd like to. I was relegated to DH, so that prolonged my career several more years.

Zisk: The knee injuries are what forced you to retire, is that correct?
RZ: Right, I stopped playing when I was 35. And it was really a matter of the doctor saying, look, if you want to walk when you're 40, I can't let you on the field anymore. Basically, it was the orthopedic physician for Seattle who said, You're a liability, you're a risk. We can't put you out there anymore. I really wasn't prepared for that. It's a sobering thought when, all of a sudden, everything you've done for twenty-five, twenty-six years comes to an abrupt halt.

Zisk: Was it hard making the adjustment to being a DH?
RZ: There's a little bit of mental adjustment that has to take place. It's almost like pinch-hitting four times. I used to go back into locker room, watch the television, stretch, exercise bike, whatever was available to keep the juices flowing, so it didn't become like four pinch-hit appearances.

Zisk: After your big year with the White Sox came a huge contract with the Rangers. Were there a lot of teams bidding for you at the time? That's early free agency and owners were going crazy.
RZ: It was early in free agency and it was untested waters, but I had several ball clubs who made substantial offers. At that point I thought Texas was a ball club that I was going to help. They looked they were a hitter or two away. That's why I decided to sign with Texas.

Zisk: It seemed like they had several "just a few pieces short" years during the '70s.

RZ: Right, one piece of the puzzle that didn't fit. You know, Al Oliver came over. Buddy Bell was playing third base. We had a good ball club. Jim Sundberg was catching. Hargrove was at first. We had a very, very solid team and for whatever reason, the pieces kind of fit together but not as tightly as you'd have liked.

Zisk: Do you look at free agency differently now, as a coach, then you did when you were a player?

RZ: No, the premise of free agency hasn't changed just the amount of zeroes after the dollar sign. That's the biggest thing that's taken place. I can remember my first or second year with Pittsburgh, I had an agent named Jerry Kapstein. I remember him talking about cable television. He was saying, Wait until cable television kicks in, you won't believe what's going to happen. I didn't realize it was going to have this kind of impact on, not only baseball, but all professional sports. Salaries are unbelievable.

Zisk: After Texas, you went to Seattle, which was a big trade.

RZ: Yeah, there were ten players involved, I couldn't name all of them.

Zisk: Between those four teams [Pittsburgh, Chicago, Texas, Seattle], you played in four different regions and saw four different ways in which towns appreciate their teams. Was there one of the four that really stood out?

RZ: We lived in a nice area in Pittsburgh and made some great friends that we still keep in touch with today, off the field. Chicago was exciting; it's a great town. We enjoyed our time in Texas. And we enjoyed our time in the Pacific Northwest. It was a good education for me and my family to have an opportunity, a great opportunity, to live all over this country of ours and see how life goes on elsewhere.

Zisk: Have you thought of maybe trying something in Southern California, just to fill in the map?

RZ: No, I'll stay away from California.

Zisk: Is one of the appeals of being in Daytona the fact that it's close to your home?

RZ: Right. I've had lengthy discussions with the farm director and there hasn't been a real active drive to get me to move but they keep asking me, you know, would I like to go somewhere else, would I like to go to a higher level. With the fact that I'm pretty close to home and I really feel I work well with younger people, and as long as I feel I can keep those lines of communication with the younger people open, and I'm still able to have a real positive impact on a lot of the hitters, I don't mind staying at this level. I really don't. I'll know when it's time to move on, like I told you with the golf and the baseball. I'll see for myself, I'll know when it's over.

Zisk: Have you considered managing?
RZ: I have absolutely no aspirations to manage.

Zisk: I've heard many people say that they are two completely different disciplines.
RZ: Absolutely. And you can to talk to any manager, at any level, and they'll tell you the easiest part of the day is when that first pitch is thrown and the game's being played. It's the hours leading up to the game and then the hours following the game that become problematic.

Zisk: The preparation and the review?
RZ: Well, I'm talking about the outside agencies. The media, you know, you've got worries with the front office, you've got player troubles you have to deal with, perhaps. You've got to deal with so much off-the-field activity before and after the game, that the game is kind of a relief. That's the easy part, running the game, putting the hit and run on, the bunt, and, you know, pitching out. That's the easy part. Any manager will tell you that. It's the peripheral stuff that would drive me absolutely crazy.

Zisk: As a hitting coach, do you use a lot of technology? I know a lot of guys are really into watching videotapes of their at-bats, to the extent where some hitters are watching their at-bats in between innings.
RZ: Unfortunately, at the level we're at, we're not that sophisticated. If I can get the camera battery charged and I can find a pitcher who isn't doing anything then I'll put him in the stands. No, seriously, I do tape the hitters and then make use of the tape to show them their pluses and their minuses. If you've ever watched yourself on tape do something athletically, you know that real and feel are two different things. So what you're feeling is probably not what you're actually doing. You have to show them right from wrong, and have them associate the good things with the feel so they can repeat that over and over. Hitting is like building a pyramid. There are a lot of blocks that have to be laid on the bottom, to build a real solid foundation. But the higher you go in ball, the less blocks there are to put on the top of this pyramid. So, at least by the time you're out of Double A and into Triple A, your mechanics should be down to the point where you're don't have to worry about them. Now

you're just worrying about the guy on the mound, what kind of stuff he's got, what patterns he's falling into, game situations. You see hitters struggle, especially at the big league level when they get into a bad habit with their mechanics. And usually what happens in a slump is it starts out mental and becomes physical. You'll go through a period where you don't get any hits but hit the ball on the button a couple of times and all of a sudden, well, What am I doing wrong? Well, you're not doing anything wrong, okay, you just haven't caught a break here or there and before you've know it, you've changed something and now you've screwed up your mechanics to the point where you've got a mental problem and now you've got a physical problem, too. What I try to do at the lower levels is build this solid foundation of the physical skills and try to get them perfected so when they leave me they've got a good grasp of the physical tools and also the mental part of it, too. Because you shouldn't have to worry about the physical stuff, the higher you go. It should be ingrained and locked in at that point in time.

Zisk: Because at that point you have to put some work into trying to figure out what's coming at you from the mound?
RZ: Absolutely, somewhere along the line, you've got to worry about hitting the baseball instead of pulling your head or stepping in the bucket.

Zisk: Speaking of what's coming at you from the pitcher's mound, were there any pitchers that you hit really well? A guy whose stuff you saw really well and you just owned him?
RZ: I don't think I could ever come out and say it. I had good success against different pitchers. I can tell you that I didn't mind the guys who threw it real hard. I thought it was a great challenge. I batted against some of the best: Gibson and Seaver, Carlton and Guidry, Righetti and Gossage, and I don't want to leave out anybody but against the guys who threw hard, I really seemed to be able to turn it up a notch and compete pretty well against them. But as far as owning a guy, no, I don't think a hitter ever owns a pitcher when consider we're only successful a third of the time. There was a guy in Little League that I hit pretty well. No, seriously, some guys you have better success against and other guys you don't. I can tell you two guys I used to screw myself into the ground against, one was Don Sutton and the other was Andy Messersmith. To me, Andy Messersmith had the best stuff of any right-handed pitcher I've ever seen. He was a great athlete, he was also a pretty good hitter. He pitched for the Dodgers, he pitched for the Braves, pitched for the Angels. When you keep your little books on pitchers, you note what's their best pitch, what's their second best pitch, what's their third best pitch. When we talked about Messersmith, he had four number one

pitches. He had a great fastball, a great curveball, an outstanding slider, and maybe his best pitch was his change up. If I'm batting against a guy who's a fastball/curve and I'm making a guess, I've got a one in two chance of guessing right. Now here's a guy who, in his prime, could get all four of his pitches across the plate so now I'm guessing and I've got a one in four chance of being right. So, Sutton and Messersmith, I had problems with.

Zisk: And you faced those guys in the '74 NLCS, right?
RZ: Right, Messersmith and Sutton in '74 against the Dodgers and it was '75 against Cincinnati.

Zisk: You hit really well in series [3 for 10 and 5 for 10, respectively].
RZ: Yeah, I did okay. I seemed to do well in playoffs and All-Star games, and that sort of thing.

Zisk: Which years did you go to the All-Star game?
RZ: '77, '78.

Zisk: Did you feel like the extra pressure helped you step up your game a notch?
RZ: You know what, I'll tell you what really helped me, it hurt me in one way, we talked about me having to spend an extra year in the minor leagues, but coming up from an offensively orientated organization where, when I was in the lineup in Pittsburgh, I was in the lineup with seven or eight good hitters. And I knew that if I didn't do it, well, Hebner behind me or Parker behind me was going to knock the run in. So you didn't place that great pressure on yourself, I have to get this run home, it's up to me. You went up there with attitude, I'm going to do the best I can but not screw myself into the ground and worry about not knocking a run in because I know I've got a good hitter behind me. And in some respects that helped a lot because when I had a Dave Parker, let's say, hitting behind me, I knew they probably didn't want to pitch to Parker so they were going to try to do something with me. So if they came at me, and challenged me, it might have helped me a little bit, too.

Zisk: And did that alter things for you during the end of your time with the Rangers and more so with the Mariners, when you didn't have as many good hitters in the lineup with you?
RZ: I was always in the middle somewhere. I was either three, four, or five, whatever team I played on. Once the DH came into effect, it changed the game a little bit, but it's tough to be a number eight hitter with the pitcher hitting behind you. You don't get a lot. I guess Tony LaRussa's now changing the landscape by batting the pitcher eighth.

Zisk: I have not heard an explanation of that that makes sense to me.

RZ: You'd have to ask Tony about that but all I know is if you're batting before the pitcher, chances are they're going to do their best to keep the ball away from you, unless they really have to pitch to you.

Zisk: Yeah, here in New York, our number eight hitter is Rey Ordonez, and he's convinced he's a doubles hitter. He's a wild swinger, he walks about 15-20 times a year.

RZ: I can name you two guys I played with, who were offensive players, who had the same approach; and they are Manny Sanguillen and Rennie Stennett. If they could reach it, they were going to swing at it. You're not going to strike me out, you're not going to walk me, I'm going to hit the ball hard somewhere.

Zisk: A real live or die approach with the bat.
RZ: Yeah, exactly.

Zisk: Well, that's it for my questions. Thanks very much for your time.
RZ: Okay, I hope I was helpful. Good luck with the publication.

Originally appeared in issue #1, Spring 1999.

About the Contributors

Jake Austen is a writer, puppeteer, cartoonist, and White Sox fan. He is the editor of *Roctober* magazine, co-producer of the cable access children's dance show *Chic-A-Go-Go*, author of *TV-A-Go-Go: Rock Music on Television from American Bandstand to American Idol*, co-author of *Darkest America: Black Minstrelsy from Slavery to Hip Hop*, and editor of *A Friendly Game of Poker* and *Flying Saucers Rock n Roll*. He is a lefty catcher, but bats righty.

Jeff Boda grew up a Brewers fan, switched his loyalty to the Padres as a teen and ended up a Cubs fan as an adult. There is no truth to the rumor that being a Cubs season-ticket holder drove him to leave Chicago for Hong Kong in 2005, where he currently lives. When not editing for an international newspaper there, he spends his time running a company that imports America's other national pastime, (craft) beer, or watching Cubs night games live over the Internet while enjoying his morning coffee.

Matt Braun, born in San Rafael, Calif., on 9/4/73, Bats R, Throws R. Not known for his hitting, Matt holds both bachelors and masters degrees from the City University of New York and maintains that he once caused Pete Incaviglia to drop a fly ball simply by yelling at him. He makes his home in San Francisco, where he roots for the Oakland A's. An early '90s scouting report filed by the Seattle Mariners projected him to have little to no value at the major league level.

Sean Carswell is the author of five books (three novels and two short story collections). His latest, *Madhouse Fog*, was published by Manic D Press in the spring of 2013. He is the co-founder of the independent music magazine *Razorcake* and the independent book publisher Gorsky Press. He is an assistant professor of writing and literature at California State University Channel Islands.

Kevin Chanel is based in Lazytown, USA. A sometime writer of relative regard, Kevin responsible for such household-name periodicals as *Punk Rock Confidential* and *ChinMusic! Magazine*. Beginning his quest for publishing obscurity in the wastelands of San Diego, he quickly rose to the heights of anonymity and hovers the Skid Row Smith-Coronas awaiting the impetus to work. Currently he can occasionally be found at sites like bugsandcranks.com, thehallofverygood.com and his own dadtome.com ... sometimes.

Brian Cogan is a lifelong Mets fan, which is code for "he understands just how painful life really is." He is also a professor and writer and as his most famous book, *The Punk Encyclopedia*, will likely go out of print soon, he compares his Mets fandom to his professional career. As you read this, he is probably shaking his head and gnashing his teeth over some boneheaded move by the Wilpon family.

Ken Derr lives in the Bay Area and is failing really hard to be a gracious winner after two Giants World Series victories in three years.

Dan Dunford is a writer and teacher born in the Bronx, New York. At press time, he has been to over 19 major league baseball stadiums, as well as spring training and minor league games at every level. He resides in Manhattan with his wife, Marisa, who provides him constant inspiration and joy. He maintains that the only reason the Red Sox ever won World Series titles is because of their embrace of Yankees-style business practices and East German-level steroid usage.

Frank D'Urso is a member of SABR, and a Redsox fan since the Impossible Dream of 1967. He learned that all good things are tainted with bad UNTIL the Redsox won TWO World Series and now does not see why they cannot win every year. Frank and his brothers on Team G.A.L.CO still travel to Cooperstown for the induction every year.

Mike Faloon is the co-founder of *Zisk*. He is also the author of *The Hanging Gardens of Split Rock* (Gorsky Press) and the cofounder of *Go Metric* zine. He is a contributing writer to *Razorcake* and *Roctober*. He writes the online music column "Are You Receiving Me?" (gometric.typepad.com) and is currently working on the *Hypergood* trilogy with Brian Cogan. He lives with his family in Patterson, New York.

Dr. Nancy Golden grew up in New York, where she was raised a Yankees fan by her three older siblings and occasionally attended Mets games out of sheer convenience. As a wildlife toxicologist, her previous publications have appeared primarily in stodgy scientific journals and have afforded little opportunity for commentary on the finer aspects of baseball fandom. She currently lives in Washington, D.C., where as a Nationals fan she has witnessed the return of baseball, the debut of Strasburg, the end of Teddy's 525-game losing streak, and one glorious round of post-season baseball. So far.

Mark Hughson resides in Liverpool, New York, and roots for the Oakland A's. For some reason, his television picks up a station from Chicago, so most seasons are spent watching the Cubs. As an avid hunter of nostalgic moments, he can usually be found spinning an old record in his living room while reading a baseball paperback from the '80s. His writing has occasionally been found in the digital and printed pages of *Beat The Indie Drum*, *Go Metric*, *Now Wave*, and, of course, *Zisk*.

Bob Mason lives in New England where he's still mourning the breakup of one of the great comedy pairings of all time, Bobby Valentine and the Boston Red Sox.

Rev. Norb invented *Sick Teen* fanzine and sang for Suburban Mutilation and Depo-Provera in the '80s, wrote for *Maximum Rocknroll* and sang for Boris the Spinkler in the '90s, wrote for *Razorcake* and sang for Nob Dylan & His Nobsoletes in the '00s, and now sings for The Onions and is the author of *The Annotated Boris: Deconstructing the Lyrical Majesty of Boris The Sprinkler (And Other Tales As the Need Arises)*. He's currently the pressbox announcer for the Green Bay Bullfrogs of the Northwoods League and likes the Brewers and the 1976 Reds.

Steve Reynolds is the co-editor for *Zisk*. He's published an annual look at music and culture, *The Reynolds Top 20*, for the past 23 years. He's interviewed over a thousand musicians in almost two decades as a writer/reporter for Premiere Radio Networks. He's the frontman for the world's greatest live karaoke band, Bunnie England & the New Originals. He also dabbles as a DJ for hire ('90s nostalgia is a specialty). He's a proud resident of the Kensington section of Brooklyn and dreams of a day when the Wilpon family doesn't own the Mets.

John Shiffert has been a sportswriter for over 40 years and a baseball fan ever since his dad took him to Connie Mack Stadium in 1959 to see the Phillies lose to the Redlegs (you weren't allowed to say "reds" in those days). He is currently in his eleventh season of writing the *19 to 21* ezine, which looks at current events and people in baseball in comparison to historic events and people. Shiffert has written four baseball history books, including the acclaimed *Base Ball in Philadelphia* (McFarland).

Todd Taylor is the co-founder and executive director of *Razorcake* and Gorsky Press Inc., a non-profit punk rock fanzine and book publisher. He has been hit in the nuts very hard with a baseball and relishes any explosion involving the destruction of disco records.

Charlie Vascellaro, a Baltimore-based freelance writer, is a former Arizona resident and vagabond baseball traveler who returns to Arizona just after the pitchers and catchers each spring training season. His baseball-related travel stories have recently appeared in the *Los Angeles Times, The Washington Post, Chicago Sun Times* and *Cowboys and Indians* magazine. He also writes annually on the Cactus League for *U.S. Airways, Key Magazine*, and numerous Cactus League teams' spring training programs.

Ari Voukydis is a Brooklyn-based comedian and writer. He is raising his two sons as Red Sox fans, but other than that is a responsible dad. He has contributed to *Saturday Night Live*'s "Weekend Update" and has written for *GQ, Grantland, SPY, Esquire, Entertainment Weekly*, and many other magazines. You can follow him on Twitter, if you're into that sort of thing, at @AriVoukydis.

John Weber has been a lifelong Phillies fan since the days it wasn't cool to be a Phillies fan. Working in radio in 1980, he was able to slip into the Phillies' locker room the night they won their first series in—ever! In 1990, he became executive producer of Phillies baseball, an incredible six years of his life that ranged from meaningless September games against the Expos in a half-empty Vet to witnessing a walk-off World Series-winning homer by Joe Carter in a domed stadium in Toronto. Weber left to work for radio network MJI in New York in '96 (later acquired by Premiere Networks), where he is today a VP of programming. He still lives in the Philadelphia suburbs and is on the board of the Philadelphia Sports Writers Association as their second vice-president. And he plays way too much APBA baseball.

Kip Yates is a licensed massage therapist living in Brooklyn with his family. He is an Astros fan by choice, a Red Sox fan by necessity, and a Rangers fan by childhood geography. He is perplexed who to cheer for in the National League now that the 'Stros have moved to the junior circuit. Though the 'Stros and Sox are cellar dwellers, he wears both hats with pride. Besides, living in Brooklyn, he has his hands full keeping his kids from becoming Yankees or Mets fans.

Acknowledgements

This book wouldn't exist without the great roster of writers who have contributed to *Zisk*. More than 60 people have shared their thoughts about baseball and more with us over the past 14 years. We thank all of them for their efforts.

Thanks to David LaBounty (and his son, Gabe) at Blue Cubicle Press for seeing the potential for something great in the massive pile of text that we assembled years ago.

Thanks to Josh Wilker for taking time from his own book project to pen a foreword for ours.

Thanks to Jason Willis for the fantastic cover and art work.

Thanks to the folks at Quimbys, *Razorcake*, and Atomic Books for distributing our zine to the masses over the years.

This book was made possible by the generosity of 85 backers on Kickstarter. We'd like to send shoutouts to the following folks for believing in this project and helping us hit our goal:

Aaron Rennie / Jay Wade Edwards / Elizabeth Polhemus / Patrick Faloon / Dave Palmer / Abigail Gullo / Joe Evans, III

And very special thanks to Richie Zisk, who was aware of our existence at one time.

Mike thanks Jeff Wescott and Bob Mason for showing time and time again how well the worlds of baseball and humor fit together; Matt Braun and Evan Cohen for connecting baseball to the world of zines; all of the *Zisk* contributors past and present; Mike White for the design advice; Richard Nash and David Shields for pushing this project into motion; Rich, Steve, Pat, and Casey Faloon for the baseball conversations over the years; co-editor Steve for keeping the S.S. *Zisk* afloat; and Allie, Maggie, and Sean for cracking me up daily.

Steve would like to thank all the friends (too many to mention here) that over the years have said, "You really ought to compile some of your writings into a book." It never would have happened without that occasional inspiration. Special thanks to co-editor Mike for inviting me to contribute to *Zisk* before he even thought of the name. It's been a great excuse to get together, listen to music, and talk about baseball for 14 years. And all the love in the world to Tink, Aurora, Annie, and Heather.

CPSIA information can be obtained at www.ICGtesting.com
Printed in the USA
LVOW061110040613

336848LV00003B/9/P